TUCSON

American Historical Press
Sun Valley, California

TUCSON
Portrait Of A Desert Pueblo

John Bret-Harte

Previous Page
Wagon trains of the Tucson firm of Tully & Ochoa
were attacked four times between 1867 and 1870 by
raiding Apaches. This painting, showing one of these
attacks, was done by Edward Zinns, who may have
been one of the participants in the Camp Grant
Massacre of 1871. He also was an eye witness to the
events his painting depicts.

Library of Congress Catalogue Card Number: 2001096022
ISBN: 1-892724-25-1

CONTENTS

To Margaret

Without whose help, love, and
constant support this book could
not have been written.

San Xavier del Bac in 1854, (above) from John G. Parke, *Reports of Explorations and Surveys to Ascertain the Most Practicable and Economical Route for a Railroad from the Mississippi River to the Pacific Ocean.* 12 vols., Washington: Government Printing Office, 1853-1856. (Opposite) Papago Indians, from William H. Emory, *Report of the U.S. and Mexican Boundary Survey made under the Direction of the Secretary of the Interior.* 2 Vols., Washington: Government Printing Office, 1857.

The vibrant colors of the Sonoran desert in spring bloom.

A battle between Apache raiders and Spanish presidial soldiers. From an original painting by Cal Peters, owned by Sidney B. Brinckerhoff.

Tucson in 1852, from John Russell Bartlett, *Personal Narrative of Explorations and Incidents in Texas, New Mexico, California, Sonora, and Chihuahua in 1850, '51, '52, and '53*. 2 Vols., New York: D. Appleton & Co., 1854.

INTRODUCTION

In the days before photography, the portrait artist had two some-times-conflicting responsibilities. He had to create a painting that bore at least sufficient likeness to its subject that one would be identifiable as the inspiration for the other. At the same time, the work had to be flattering enough that the painter's patron would pay the fee. In both directions—toward too much flattery and toward too little—lay peril. The artist had to walk a fine line in his relation with truth.

The same problem confronts the author of a book designed as a verbal portrait of the community in which he lives. He must describe his town with enough of the inevitable warts showing that the most critical outsider can recognize it; but he also must tell the story in such a way that those who, like himself, make their homes there may find in his narrative at least a suggestion of the qualities that stir their civic pride and make them glad to be known as citizens of the place.

The task is not easy. Inevitably, as the narrative moves forward into a time within the memory of living citizens, events that some find laudable others will deplore. A vexing question also exists as to whom to include in discussing the movers and shakers of the community, and what names must be omitted reluctantly because there simply is too little space to mention everyone.

And there are other problems. Why mention one series of events to illustrate a point, rather than another that might do as well? Why emphasize business development at the expense of politics, or social development as opposed to statistical data on demographics?

In the long run, the answers to these questions come down to a matter of judgment. Some readers will agree with the author. Others will disagree, perhaps strongly but —it is to be hoped—not violently.

And, if the author is too far from the mark, room always is there for another book.

This brings up another point that needs to be made here. It is a truism among historians that every generation rewrites history in line with its own perceptions. And while, as a practical matter, this means that the history of great events is revised every 20 or 25 years, it also ought to mean that local subjects deserve periodic re-examination.

As the community that for many years was the most important in Arizona and still remains the state's cultural hub and second metropolis, Tucson receives obligatory mention in every general history of Arizona and the Southwest. Yet, apart from two works by Francis C. Lockwood and one by Bernice Cosulich, the last published in 1953, no full-dress study of the community has appeared. Applying the historian's

rule, then, it's time for another.

As a non-Indian community, Tucson has a history that extends back slightly more than 200 years. Only four months after colonial militiamen launched the American Revolution at Lexington, Massachusetts (or, as they believed, had it launched upon them by stiff-necked red-coats), a Spanish army colonel designated a spot in what now is downtown Tucson as the site for a royal presidio, or fort, the farthest north in what is now Arizona. It remained a garrison town for more than 70 years. Some of the first homes built by Anglo-Americans after the Gadsden Purchase made Tucson part of the United States incorporated sections of the presidial wall in their construction.

The Gadsden Purchase, signed in the last days of 1853 and ratified by the U.S. Senate six months later, was a decisive event in Tucson's history. By this treaty, Mexico—the heir to Spain's northern empire— ceded 29,670 square miles of territory, most of it desert, to the United States, which wanted it in order to secure an all-weather route for a transcontinental railroad. The purchase price was $10 million. It was the last territorial cession by Mexico to a foreign power, and it established the permanent boundary west of El Paso and east of California, between the two republics. Within present-day Arizona, the

Gadsden Purchase included all the land south of the Gila River. Tucson thus ceased to be an outpost on Mexico's northern frontier and became one in the largely unexplored American Southwest. Although the heritages of Mexico and Spain remain major influences on Tucson to this day, the Gadsden Purchase determined the direction of the community's entire development.

Yet the real watershed in Tucson's history occurred more than a quarter century after the Gadsden Purchase, when the first train of the Southern Pacific Railroad rolled into town. The date was March 20, 1880, just a century ago.

That momentous event ended the isolation that had plagued the community for more than a century. Although the telegraph already had made possible nearly instantaneous communication with the rest of the nation, the railroad did something more important still. It conquered the forbidding barriers of desert and mountain, opening this remote corner of the Southwest to a flood of people, goods, and ideas it never had known before.

Part of the change was physical; an army officer stationed in Tucson in 1875 who returned a decade later would have found the town wearing a very different look. Always scarce in pre-railroad days, wood now abounded, and domestic architecture, liberated from the constraints of low, thick walls and flat roofs that the native adobe imposed upon it, exploded in extravagant gables and high-Victorian gingerbread worthy of New York itself. Ladies dressed in silks of the most fashionable shades and carrying Parisian parasols now adorned Tucson's tree-lined streets. Books became part of a professional man's home, which now was designed to provide space for a library. Heavy steamboat-Gothic furniture, like what ornamented the White House of Presidents Grant and Hayes, found its way into prosperous Tucson homes, where it took its place beside chaste Greek statuettes and heavily beaded lampshades.

All these things—wood, silks, books, massive furniture, and bric-a-brac—had been available on the frontier before the coming of the railroad, of course, but only to those who could afford to pay freight rates of five cents a pound for every 100 miles to have them transported by mule train from San Diego; Wilmington, California; or Trinidad, Colorado. The great thing about the railroad, apart from its speed, was the astonishingly cheap rate for which freight could be carried. Suddenly, the imitated elegance of world capitals became accessible to Tucsonians, and the town turned its back on native traditions to court high fashion.

People, as well as goods, streamed into Arizona from the East and the Pacific Slope. Our army officer might have shared his coach with an Eastern financier or politician whose investments in Southern Arizona drew him to Tucson, or with one of the several Indian Service inspectors detailed to report on the conduct of affairs at the large and still-turbulent San Carlos Apache reservation. He might have enjoyed the society of a Methodist missionary lady determined to start a school among the Indians, of a gambler making his way to Tombstone, or of William Tecumseh Sherman, commanding general of the U.S. Army, who traveled through Arizona early in 1882, less than two years after he declared he would not run for president if nominated, and if elected would not serve.

And, of course, there was the blue-coated infantryman or cavalryman, whose commanders found the railroad a superb way of moving large numbers of men quickly to trouble spots on the frontier. Thus, General Irvin McDowell, commander of the Military Division of the Pacific, could flood Southern Arizona with troops in the wake of Indian disturbances at Fort Apache in the late summer of 1881. That the military concentration, and the unwise conduct of panicky commanders, offered Geronimo and his warriors the pretext for their first out-

break was no fault of the railroad.

In all these ways, and in others beyond counting, the railroad exerted a profound influence on the development of Tucson. It established a connection between the desert pueblo and the rest of the world that has continued to grow ever since.

Devotees of Wild West fiction and films conceive of a West stretching from Dodge City to San Francisco where lawlessness of every kind was endemic, and where civilization's fragile advance depended entirely on the marshal's ability to outgun the outlaw. It hardly needs to be said that this myth, a modern morality play, is grotesquely inaccurate. Nevertheless, in the boom camps of the West—towns like Tombstone, Virginia City, Ellsworth, and scores of others—law and order was a tenuous thing. These camps produced great wealth quite suddenly, and therefore attracted more than their share of undesirables.

Tucson, important from the beginning of the Anglo-American period as a center of business and banking, never drew the lawless elements that made life hazardous in Tombstone, less than 100 miles to the southeast. This is not to say that Tucson was without crime or lawlessness during the last four decades of the nineteenth century. But the disruptions of crime were precisely that—aberrations, not part of the fabric of normal life. No Earps, Clantons, and McLowerys battled it out on Tucson's streets, and law-abiding people of all occupations were grateful.

What follows here is a narrative of about 200 years in Tucson's life. It makes no claim to be definitive, nor is it specifically a book for scholars. Instead, it is written for the reader interested in finding out something of the history, color, and flavor of a city that today looks back to a proud past and forward to an exciting future.

If the book succeeds in this modest purpose, it will have justified the effort that has gone into it.

This map, drawn about 1700 by Father Kino, shows the Jesuit missions and *visitas* and the settlements of peaceful Indians in the Pineria Alta. Neither Kino nor any of his contemporaries explored or missionized north of the Gila River, which appears near the top of this map.

THE FOUNDING OF TUCSON

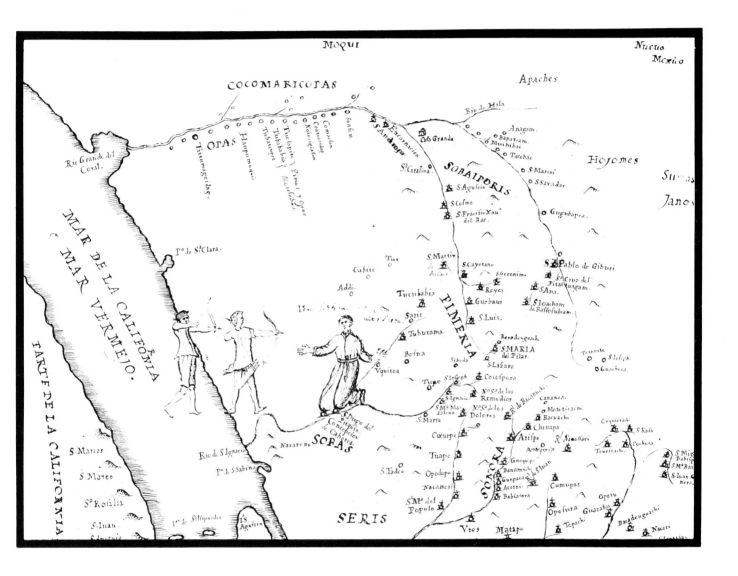

It may fairly be said that a blue-coated Spanish army officer and a Franciscan priest robed in brown presided over the birth of Tucson one hot August day in 1775. For the officer, Colonel Don Hugo Oconor, the act of founding this new community was only a small part of the great task of reorganizing the defenses on the ragged northern edge of the greatest empire on earth. For the priest, Father Francisco Tomás Hermenegildo Garcés, it was the culmination of seven years of work, politics, and prayer.

The community Oconor and Garcés launched that day had its roots in another founded 1500 years before by the ancestors of the Pima Indians who farmed the land in 1775, and whom the new settlement was designed to protect. Even the name the Spaniards gave to the town that would rise by the Santa Cruz River was a corruption of its Piman name: Schookson, the place at the foot of the black mountain. Spaniards transliterated the word poorly, added a saint's name (as was customary throughout all of Spanish America), and named it San Agustín del Tucson.

In August 1775, Oconor was tired. A huge, red-haired Irishman, his vigor, resource, and audacity long before had singled him out for leadership on the frontier, but for nearly four years he had been continually on duty, traveling, surveying, campaigning against hostile Indians, doing a job that should have been done years earlier and realizing that even his efforts would be defeated with false economy by a penurious crown across the sea.

Two decades earlier, Oconor had fought on the wrong side of a revolution in his native Dublin, and—the climate being inhospitable to losers—had fled to Spain, where he offered his talents in the service of the royal army. He was 31 years old, already a major of infantry and Knight of the Order of Calatrava, when he reached Mexico City in 1765 as part of a commission to reorganize the army of New Spain. But staff duty was not for him, and as soon as he was able he secured a presidial command on the frontier.

The presidio to which Oconor was assigned was one of 17 spread out along a line 2000 miles long that spanned the present-day states of Texas, Chihuahua, New Mexico, Arizona, Sonora, and California. Soldiers at these remote outposts had two desperately important responsibilities. First, they were to repel hostile Indians—Comanches, Navajos, and the dreaded Apaches—who raided as far as 1000 miles into Mexico, stealing horses and livestock, burning towns and putting their inhabitants to the sword. Second, by continuous campaigning, they were to drive those Indians ever farther northward, depriving them where possible of subsistence, killing or capturing their warriors in battle and, finally, reducing them to surrender.

In the Spanish imperial design, which sought always to advance the frontier northward in order to protect the wealthy cities, haciendas, and mines of the interior, the presidios had another purpose as well. They were to serve as nuclei of new settlements. Released from the army, soldiers and their families would become civilian settlers, joined, it was hoped, by adventurous young men from the south who would be drawn by the challenge and opportunity of the frontier.

Like many another well-conceived plan, the great presidial design worked less effectively in action than in theory. The garrisons always were small and often were below authorized strength; they lacked the force to deliver the pre-emptive strike or punish the raiders convincingly, and they did not have the numbers or the equipment for the continual patrolling that strategists of the era believed was necessary to prevent incursions below the line. And even the lure of free land could succeed only partly in making such a dangerous environment attractive to civilian settlement.

By the mid-1760s, it had become clear that the northern defenses were not functioning as they should, and a royal commission was dispatched from Mexico City to recommend how the line should be tightened. The survey, which took two years, advised numerous changes and the relocation of several presidios. In the summer of 1771, a council sitting in Mexico City approved the findings of the report and forwarded it to Madrid. In the same month, Hugo Oconor was promoted to a full colonelcy and placed in charge of the entire frontier as commandant inspector, with orders to implement the commission's recommendations. Oconor took up the task in January of the next year.

By the time he reached the Pima settlements on the Santa Cruz River in what is now Southern Arizona, more than three and a half years had passed and his job was nearly done. The years had been hard, and they had told on him. At 41, he was ready to stop.

Not so Father Garcés, the priest whom Oconor met at the little mission church the Pimas had built near the settlement they called Bac. For Garcés, indefatigable champion of the Pimas and inveterate strategist for their protection, Oconor's arrival represented an opportunity too long delayed.

Garcés had come to take charge of the little mission of San Xavier del Bac seven years before, the first Franciscan to do so. But the mission itself, and the Spanish presence in the Pimería Alta—the land of the northern Pimas—went back much further in time. Father Eusebio Francisco Kino, the great Jesuit missionary and explorer, first visited the Pimas at Bac in 1694, and before the end of that century established a church and the beginning of a permanent mission settlement there.

To Father Kino, as to every other missionary on the advancing frontier of New Spain, the mission was an institution with multiple purposes, the nucleus alike of a Christian fellowship, a civil community, and a self-contained economic unit capable of supporting its inhabitants at the same

Franciscan friars took over the missionary work in the Pimería Alta after the expulsion of the Jesuits in 1767. Father Francisco Garcés, a Franciscan, became the priest at San Xavier the next year.

time that it taught them the habits of industry.

From the point of view of the Church, needless to say, the most important role of the mission was to win to God the souls of the Indians for whom it existed. This meant teaching, catechism, marriage, and ultimately the sacraments. Often, missionary priests discovered that Christian doctrine was accepted most readily when it could be expanded to encompass— or at least not to deny—some vestiges of the native rites it was to replace. Mission art and architecture showed evidence of a fusion of cultures and faiths that wove a strong tapestry acceptable at once to Europeans and to their Indian converts.

Economically, the mission became the center of a new, permanent community for the Indians, many of whom were semi-nomadic. To achieve this, missionaries on the frontier fostered agriculture, teaching the Indians improved methods of planting, cultivation, and harvesting. They tried with varying success to introduce new crops. More significantly, they brought herds of cattle to the missions. Livestock expanded the Indian economy, furnishing beasts of burden for the first time. In turn, the animals tied the Indians more firmly to the mission community, where there were pasture and water, and where the cattle could be corralled and kept from wandering.

Inevitably, then, the mission, like the presidio, became an instrument for advancing the frontier. But while the job of the presidial soldier was to subdue the hostile Indian by force, the task of the missionary was to acculturate the peaceful Indian, bringing him within the scope of Spanish law and civilization.

Theoretically, each mission was to retain its mission status only 10 years, at which time it was to become a self-sustaining parish and community. Then the missionaries, moving as always in twos, were to push farther to the north in quest of more souls and a greater imperial authority.

The reality was different. The very success of the missions in drawing peaceful Indians together in communities and making them prosperous made the settlements prime targets for raids by Apaches, in whose economy plunder played an important role. Raiding increased traditional intertribal hatreds, and mission Indians continually were ready to take to the warpath against the hostile ones. As this understandable belligerence threatened to erode the mission community, the priests often sought to check it, even as the military, welcoming the prospect of native auxiliaries, tried to foster it.

Perhaps the greatest effect of Indian raids was the creation of a need for military protection available to the missions. It was a need that priests might deplore because of the moral danger they saw in the association of their mission charges with soldiers, but it could not be denied.

At Bac and the other Pima *rancherías* (or settlements) spreading north and south along the marshy Santa Cruz, military protection was much needed during the 1770s. The area was quite thickly settled; between Bac and the Santa Catalina Mountains to the north, there were no fewer than six Pima settlements, all relatively stable, all relatively prosperous, all subject to frequent Apache forays.

At Tubac, some 40 miles south of the mission, a presidio had been built in 1752, not—ironically—to ward off Apaches but to maintain harmony among the Pimas, who the year before had been shaken by an unprecedented nativist revolt that had destroyed the equilibrium of the frontier. The causes of the disturbance were many, among them Piman resentment of Jesuit heavy-handedness and the desire to be free of the yoke of Spanish domination. The revolt brought the death of more than 100 settlers who had left the relative safety of the interior to follow the lure of gold in the north. Several priests also lost their lives, and a number of missions were sacked. The uprising ended in a kind of negotiated settlement that restored the status quo in return for the removal of the most obnoxious priests. The presidio at Tubac established the Spanish military presence in the heart of the land of the northern Pimas, as a deterrent to further disturbances.

When the decision was made to locate the new presidio at Tubac, two Jesuit priests, Fathers Jacobo Sedelmayr and Philip Segesser, urged the governor of Sonora to consider placing a second fort either at the *ranchería* of Tucson or that of Santa Catalina. Both sites had distinct advantages, the priests reported. They had abundant water and adequate pasturage for the cattle and horses the soldiers would need. Beyond these considerations, a presidio located north of Bac could dominate the Pimas living below the Gila River, keep the Papagos to the west in line, and close off the raiding paths used by the Apaches roving north of the Gila.

But if any consideration was given in 1752 to the recommendations of Fathers Sedelmayr and Segesser, nothing came of it. The little garrison at Tubac was relatively successful in protecting the missions at Tumacacori and Guevavi, and the miners at Arivaca, but to Bac and other settlements on the lower Santa Cruz, the soldiers could offer no effective aid against the Apaches. A call for help took at least two days to answer. As a result, the raiders nearly always escaped unpunished.

Although Apache raids were a constant threat to the peaceful Piman settlements along the Santa Cruz in the years after 1752, other events also upset the frontier equilibrium. In 1767 the Spanish king, Charles III, abruptly ordered the Jesuits expelled from all parts of his empire. The peaceful Indians could not know that the order reflected global, not local, considerations, nor did the Jesuit fathers themselves understand the reasoning behind it. Their forced withdrawal could not help but demoralize the Indians among whom they had worked for more than three quarters of a century, and discipline suffered accordingly.

This model for a statue shows Father Eusebio Francisco Kino in a characteristic pose — exploring the Pimería Alta with a young convert at his side. The model was done by Mahonri Young, a grandson of Brigham Young. The statue, commissioned by the Kino Memorial Committee in 1927, was never built, but the design forms part of a Kino Memorial plaque that stands west of City Hall.

Spanish army captain Juan Bautista de Anza, who opened a land road from Tubac to San Francisco, was a good friend of Father Garcés. Anza was in titular command of the presidio at Tubac when the garrison was moved to Tucson.

Into this vacuum the next summer stepped Father Garcés, a native Spaniard 30 years old, ordained a priest in the Franciscan order just four years earlier. In the 13 years between his arrival in San Xavier del Bac in 1768 and his martyrdom at the hands of Indians on the Colorado River in 1781, he became one of the great missionaries in the history of the Spanish borderlands.

Even before he arrived at San Xavier from the Franciscan college at Querétaro, Garcés had struck up a friendship with Captain Juan Bautista de Anza, commander at Tubac, veteran Indian fighter and a third-generation frontiersman. The two shared a number of interests, chief among them a consuming passion for exploration. Together they opened the land route between present-day Arizona and California. From Tubac, Anza recruited and led the party that founded San Francisco in 1776. Garcés was one of the early pioneers in the Navajo and Hopi country of northern Arizona.

From the beginning, Garcés got along splendidly with the Pimas. Lonely for European companionship, he plunged himself into his job, adapting himself so well that a fellow missionary later wrote that he "appears but an Indian himself. . . . He sits with them in a circle, or at night around the fire, with his legs crossed. . . talking with much serenity and deliberation." For their part, the Pimas affectionately referred to Garcés as "the old man."

Although assigned by his religious order to San Xavier, Garcés had to divide his time between Bac and Tucson. There was reason for this. In the years since the 1751 revolt, there had been a great influx into Tucson by Pimas from pueblos farther south, until the settlement rivaled Bac in size. The migration was expanded still more by Sobaípuri Indians, famed Apache fighters, whom the Spaniards removed from their homes on the San Pedro River 50 miles to the east to help defend the Santa Cruz. It was a strategic blunder; the Sobaípuris were unhappy and threatened continually to leave, while their absence from the San Pedro opened up a raiding path they previously had closed.

Garcés joyfully wrote to Anza in 1768 that Pimas at Tucson had built him "a tiny brush hut in among their own" and that they had "made it known they want no father but me." But he was well aware of the danger the settlement faced. Apaches, attracted by the cattle and other livestock belonging to the mission at San Xavier, would swoop down in lightning raids, taking whatever animals they could, then retreating north along the river. Tucson was in their path both going and coming, and its inhabitants suffered from the raiders and their pursuers.

Both Garcés and Anza, who visited Tucson in 1770, realized its strategic importance. Anza ordered the construction of "an extensive earthen breastwork or corral, replete with gunports" at the center of the village for defense. The Pimas told him the only way to guarantee the continuity of the settlement was to build a church. Garcés approved, and remitted the Indians' tithe of grain to enable the community to build it uninterrupted.

By early 1771, the earthen fort was built, as was a permanent mission residence with rounded lookout towers at the corners. On February 1 of that year, the Tucson Pimas succeeded in repelling an Apache attack on their fortifications. The church, a larger structure than the residence, was under construction by the next year.

Thus, when Oconor arrived in the Santa Cruz valley in the summer of 1775, Tucson already was a permanent, fortified community, strategically located and capable of some self-defense. Yet Garcés and Anza both knew more was needed. If Bac and other settlements to the south were to be protected adequately, Tucson must become a major defensive center. This required locating a presidio there—and, given the penury of the Spanish military establishment on the frontier, that meant closing the presidio at Tubac and moving the soldiers north. The army could not afford two presidios in the valley in 1752. It was no more able to do so in 1775.

In a way, then, the outcome of Oconor's visit to Garcés at San Xavier was prefigured before it ever took place. Early on the morning of August 20, when the air was still cool, the two men, together with Oconor's aide and a few Indians, rode north out of the mission along the slow-running river, passing by irrigated fields where beans, maize, squash, melons, and wheat, all staples of the Piman diet, grew in abundance. The land was rich, Oconor noted. There were water, wood, and pasturage aplenty, and an open plain for defense.

The little party followed Garcés to a place on the east bank of the river. Priest and soldier dismounted, then walked off the lines where in time the presidial walls would rise, measuring the space they enclosed against the image of soldiers, horses, storerooms, houses, and a chapel that would occupy it.

After an hour or two, satisfied that the place was right, the two mounted again and rode off upriver toward the mission. There, that evening, Oconor wrote out the order that established Tucson:

"I selected and marked out in the presence of Father Francisco Garcés and Lieutenant Juan de Carmona a place known as San Agustín del Tucson as the new site of the presidio (now located at San Ignacio de Tubac). It is situated at a distance of eighteen leagues from Tubac, fulfills the requirements of water, pasture and wood, and effectively closes the Apache frontier. The designation of the new presidio becomes official with the signatures of myself, Father Francisco Garcés and Lieutenant Juan de Carmona, at this Mission of San Xavier del Bac, on this Twentieth Day of August of the year 1775."

And the three men signed it.

Leather-armored cavalrymen—the famous *Soldados de Cuera*—garrisoned the royal presidio of San Agustín del Tucson. Leather was as good a material for armor as was steel, and it was in much more abundant supply in New Spain.

SPANISH TUCSON

I t was one thing to decree the establishment of a presidio, but quite another to establish it. At the time Oconor chose the site of San Agustín del Tucson, Anza was at Horcasitas, just north of present-day Hermosillo, recruiting colonists for the expedition that would found the city of San Francisco early the next year. His deputy at Tubac, Lieutenant Juan de Oliva, was in no hurry to move; he had been attached to the Tubac garrison since its founding 23 years before, and the prospect of relocating doubtless seemed like leaving home. Besides, he was 60 years old, and ready to retire from the army.

So Apache war continued to howl around San Xavier and the Pima pueblo of Tucson, while the troops assigned to defend mission and settlement remained 40 miles to the south, inaccessible on less than a day's notice.

Oliva could not write, so no record exists to tell when the first troops from Tubac occupied the site of the new presidio. Although some soldiers may have moved north as early as the spring of 1776, Anza's continued absence, first in California, then in Mexico City, delayed the closing of the old post. Probably it was late summer or early autumn before the garrison finally packed up its weapons and supplies, said good-bye to civilian settlers who remained uneasily behind, and started north along the river toward the village called Tucson.

It was a small enough group of men to whom the viceroy, 1500 miles to the south, entrusted the defense of the great Spanish empire's northernmost frontier. Three companies of men—one each of heavy and light cavalry and a detachment of native auxiliaries—totaled only 73 soldiers. Five officers, including a chaplain, completed the garrison. Small though the force was, as a general rule it also was under strength. As a result, when the Apaches attacked, the job of defending the presidio and pursuing the attackers usually fell to a handful of men.

The soldiers who served under the Spanish colors when Tucson was born represented nearly as wide an ethnic mixture as the inhabitants of the metropolis two centuries later. Although the highest ranks usually were filled by Spaniards born in Spain or of peninsular ancestry, the troopers were of mixed racial stock. Some were *mulattos,* of Spanish and black parentage. Others were *moriscos,* the offspring of *mulatto* and Spanish parents. Still others the Spaniards called *coyotes;* their ancestry was three quarters Indian and one quarter Spanish. Finally, some of the lower-ranking leatherjacketed frontier cavalrymen were of pure European stock.

To racially conscious Spaniards, this frontier melting pot was not always a pleasing environment. They tended to look down on the nativeborn soldiers, who in turned scorned them. "Presidio soldiers," a Spanish observer wrote some years later, "are generally from this northern frontier and more accustomed to the rigors of Indian warfare than the Europeans, who seem overly preoccupied with the trappings of military life. The Europeans believe that americanos lack the esprit de corps and discipline for military life. Americanos take no care or interest in the maintenance of their weapons, asserting that in the past they have already proven their ability; and if this be so, it is because they are not lacking in spirit and are inured to war. These are men born and raised amidst conflict...."

In the very early days, Tucson was a presidio in name only. For more than six months after the last of the Tubac garrison moved north, there were no fortifications at all. Soldiers and their families lived on the open plain, in brush and adobe huts that offered little shelter and less protection.

Tucson's luck changed in June of 1777, when Captain Don Pedro de Allande y Saavedra arrived to take command—although the troops may have considered his advent a mixed blessing. Allande was a martinet, with a prickly sense of honor and a determination to run things his own way. His position gave full scope to his propensities, for, like all presidial commanders, he wielded sole authority—civil, military, and judicial—over the post and the settlement surrounding it.

Allande also was a rich man, and a strategist who appreciated the defenselessness of his command. Soon after reaching Tucson, he ordered a log palisade built to enclose the guardhouse, the armory, and a few of the buildings housing soldiers and civilians. Since no government funds were available, Allande paid for the fortifications out of his own pocket. Later, he paid for the presidio's first church as well.

A bridge connected the little fort with the Pima village, which was completely surrounded by the Santa Cruz River. South of the presidio and the village, the Indians farmed irrigated fields on both sides of the river. The crop was critical: it kept both the village and the presidio alive. Many Spaniards also farmed, but only part-time, and their military duties took precedence. Civilian settlers were obliged under Spanish law to serve as militiamen, at their own expense, when the need arose; unless they did so, they could not hold title to lands within five miles of any presidio.

Civilians found themselves on military duty in Tucson often enough. Within weeks after the presidio was established, Apaches began regular raids on the post livestock—horses and mules as well as cattle and sheep. The semi-nomadic Apaches depended on the plunder from their raids for a major part of their livelihood, and raiding for them was as clearly an economic function as farming was for the Pimas. Nevertheless, Spanish horse soldiers who saw their mounts vanishing in a cloud of dust could not be expected to view the theft except as an act of war. So they gave chase and, when they caught the raiders, punished them severely, killing the men and taking women and children prisoner. Such retaliation, natural to one side, seemed unjustified to the other, and what began as raiding for food in time became warfare aimed at driving the invader out. The Pimas, who joined the Spaniards as auxiliaries and scouts, likewise became enemies in Apache eyes.

So Allande's fort soon proved its usefulness. In November of 1779, a force of Apaches that Allande estimated at 350 attacked the presidio. The captain led out 15 soldiers—all those who were on duty—and after a long, running battle, the Apaches withdrew. Among the Indian casualties was a chief, whose head Allande cut off and mounted on a lance, terrifying the attackers. This head, with others severed in other battles, was displayed atop the stockade, a gesture of defiance to those who would disturb the peace further.

Tucson's greatest battle occurred about two and a half years later, on May Day of 1782. Since it was a Sunday morning, the Spaniards were even less prepared than they had been before, and the attacking party was larger—perhaps as many as 600. The onslaught began at mid-morning, the hostile force dividing, one wing to assault the bridge to the Pima village, the other to rush for the open presidial gate. For the first time, the attackers clearly intended to take the fort.

Two ensigns held the bridge, peppering the enemy with musket fire, which must have made up in fear what it lacked in accuracy. East of the river, a lieutenant pinned down some of the invaders by shooting from the roof of his house, which was concealed by a parapet. But the glory that day went to Allande, who, though severely wounded, held the gate into the stockade throughout the siege, even though toward the end he was so weak that another soldier had to hold him upright.

At least one good result came from this great battle. Convinced anew of Tucson's vulnerability, Allande at last pushed the permanent presidial wall to completion.

Three feet wide at the base and 10 to 12 feet high, the wall enclosed a square of land 750 feet on each side. The west wall paralleled *El Camino Real,* the royal road that ran south all the way to Mexico City; present-day Main Avenue, the first great street of Anglo-American Tucson, follows the line of this road. From the point where Pennington Street and Main once intersected, the wall ran north to a little beyond Washington Street, then turned east, going nearly to Church Street. From here it ran south to the southeastern corner of the old Pima County courthouse, then west again to Main. Probably there was a tower, or bastion, at the northeast corner, with gunports placed to cover the main route of Apache attack.

At first there was only a single gate into the presidio, a massive mesquite door that opened about where Alameda Street now interrupts Main. Great iron bolts secured this gate at night and during times of danger. On a platform above it, a soldier stood guard, protected by the rampart of

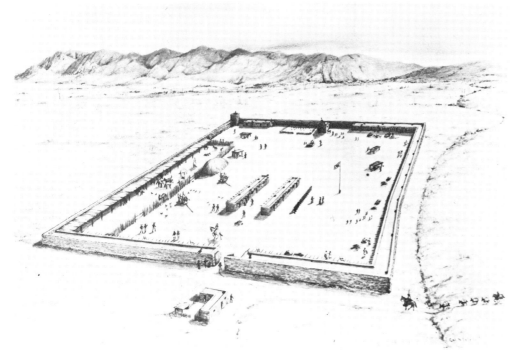

Above
Tucson's original presidial chapel, built with funds donated by Captain Allande. This sketch was made in 1860, and was published in John Warner Barber's *The Loyal West*.

Left
An artist's conception of the Royal Presidio of San Agustín del Tucson about 1795, after the wall and the chapel were completed. The gate, at the spot where modern-day Main Avenue intersects with Alameda Street, is open to permit the supply train coming up from the south to enter.

the wall. Across the valley, another sentry, this one an Indian, watched for Apaches from atop Sentinel Peak.

The wall enclosed 10 acres of ground, enough for the essential functions of the post and civilian settlement. Military headquarters were there, of course, together with the armory, powder magazines, and a smithy. Clustered along the west wall were two barracks, one for Tucson soldiers, the other for troops on campaign from other presidios. The commandant's house, with a brass cannon in front, stood where the art museum now stands. Stables lined most of the north wall. Near the center of the east wall stood the little church Allande built, with a cemetery on one side and a little plaza in front. Houses for officers, settlers, and soldiers backed up against most of the rest of the wall—small, windowless adobes with a single door that looked out into the presidio. These houses had an incidental defensive purpose, for occupants could stand on their roofs and fire over the wall. Near the center of the presidio there was a communal well, two stores—one civilian, the other military—and the jail.

From first to last, military activity dominated the little community. Tucson was not merely the farthest outpost on the Sonoran frontier but also a critical link in land communication with California. As long as Anza's road remained open, a prime mission for Tucson's soldiers was to keep it safe from Apache attack. In the summer of 1781, however, Yuma Indians at the

Colorado crossing did what Apaches had been unable to do. They rose up and slaughtered most of the settlers in the two missions that had been planted near the river to secure the road. Among the victims was Father Garcés, the guiding light behind the settlements. The Yuma massacre closed the land bridge to California. It remained closed until after the end of the Spanish period.

Spartan though life was in eighteenth-century Tucson, it had its diversions. The high point of the year was the feast of San Agustín, the patron saint, on August 28. In good times and bad, it always was the occasion for a fiesta, with music, dancing, plenty of mescal, and all sorts of merriment. The feast of San Juan Bautista on June 24 was another important day, for by tradition it marked the beginning of the life-giving summer rains. And there were other recreations: horse and foot races between Spaniards and Indians; hunting along the banks of the river and up into the hills; and, for the children, the same games children have played since the beginning of time.

Sometimes the broad world beyond the frontier opened up, if only vicariously. One such occasion came early in 1781, when word reached the north country that the Spanish king, Charles III, was appealing for voluntary contributions to assist Spain's efforts in behalf of the 13 American colonies then fighting for their independence from Great Britain. Though there was no coercion, Tucson's civilians and soldiers gave a total of 459 pesos, a substantial sum for a new settlement and more than twice the amount contributed by residents of the wealthy Sonoran capital at Arizpe. Just how great Tucson's gift was can be measured by the fact that the whole community probably had fewer than 500 souls, and that a Spanish peso was equivalent to an American dollar of the period—which bought perhaps 20 times what its contemporary descendant does.

The completion of Tucson's presidial wall signaled a change in tactics: troopers moved from the defense to a vigorous offensive that saw them taking long scouts deep into Apache country several times each year. This activity mirrored a new, two-sided policy established for all the frontier by Don Bernardo de Gálvez, viceroy of Mexico, in 1786.

On the one hand, the army should step up its scouting in Apache country, threatening the hostiles with extermination and convincing them they could find no security from reprisal as long as they remained at war. On the other hand, once the Apaches, defeated and hungry, finally sued for peace, they should be received at the presidios and permanently settled where they could farm and live at peace. In these *establecimientos de paz,* the Indians would be rationed at the public expense, receiving beef, sugar, and liquor—this last to keep them submissive and dependent upon the Spaniards for supply. For the same reason, the policy called for providing the Apaches with antiquated firearms; the Indians would have to rely on Spanish

As late as 1915, portions of Tucson's presidial wall were still standing and serving a useful purpose.

armorers for repairs and ammunition.

This Spanish reservation policy, so like the American one 80 years later, proved successful beyond the wildest hopes of its authors. A group of Chiricahua Apaches settled peacefully at Bacoachi, north of Arizpe, the same year the policy was launched. That also was the year Allande retired, but vigorous campaigning by his successors brought results. In January of 1793, a band of 92 Arivaipa Apaches came in to make peace. The presidial commander, Lieutenant José Ignacio Moraga, established their reservation north of the Pima village and west of the river; traditional animosities between Pimas and Apaches made the distance prudent.

Soon the Apaches were serving the army as auxiliaries. They also adapted well, and quickly, to farming life, raising orchards of pomegranate and quince. Under Spanish direction, they built a large, two-story adobe building that served first as a religious center and industrial school for them and later as a granary. As late as 1900 the ruins of this structure still were visible, but Tucsonians of that day, having no idea who had built it or why, referred to the building as the *convento,* and spun legends about an ancient Spanish mission it was supposed to have housed.

The peaceful Apache colony near the Tucson presidio had a long life. The original Arivaipa settlers were joined by a large band of more than 200 Pinals, a related subtribe, in 1819. The colony lasted until the 1850s, when it finally was absorbed into the hybrid Spanish, Mexican, Indian, and Anglo population of Tucson.

The Gálvez policy brought peace all across the northern frontier. Although soldiers from Tucson and other presidios continued scouting after raiders, civilian Spanish settlement flourished as never before. Mining camps sprang up as prospectors eagerly followed tales of gold and silver strikes. Great ranches started on vast tracts of land granted by the Spanish crown to persons to whom the king owed debts of money or of gratitude. Relatively safe from Apache attack for the first time, the cattle herds on unfenced ranges grew so fast that by 1820 they clogged the royal road, making it difficult for packtrains to get through.

The years of peace also saw completion of the mission of San Xavier del Bac, perhaps the finest example of Spanish mission architecture in the present-day United States. Planning for the church began soon after Father Juan Bautista Velderrain reached Bac in 1776. He laid the cornerstone seven years later. His successor, Father Juan Bautista Llorens, presided over the mission's completion in 1797.

No documents survive about the construction of San Xavier, but if it followed the same pattern as that of other frontier mission churches, it was designed according to specifications of the resident priest and built by private contractors working for the royal government. The government

The so-called *Convento*, built by Tucson's peaceable Apaches as a religious center and industrial school in the 1790s, remained a substantial ruin a century later, when this photograph was made.

stipulated the materials to be used, the thickness of the walls, the height of ceilings, and all other structural details. The royal treasury paid the bills—which in the case of San Xavier amounted probably to 40,000 pesos. Although the architect and contractors probably were Spanish, Indians did the actual labor, including most of the high-relief ornamentation and statuary on the inside.

San Xavier del Bac, the farthest north of any Spanish church in present-day Arizona, also was the largest. "Other missions here in the north should really be called chapels," reported José de Zúñiga, presidial captain at Tucson, in 1804, "but San Xavier is truly a church." Why had the government seen fit to build so large a church in such a remote place? Zúñiga thought it was not only to gather and minister to the Pimas living nearby, but also "to attract by its loveliness the unconverted Papagos and Gila Pimas beyond the frontier."

In the same report, directed to the Sonoran governor at Arizpe, Zúñiga gave an excellent description of Tucson in the late Spanish period. The whole settlement, including the Pima pueblo, covered less than two square miles; the population, including soldiers, settlers, and Indians, a-mounted to 1015 persons. Civilian militia service entitled the settlement to exemption from all personal taxes to the government and church, and from all sales taxes except on tobacco. The presidial paymaster collected this levy, which in 1804 yielded 2,210 pesos, indicating the popularity of the noxious weed even then.

Like many another border outpost, Tucson had no public works except the mission. The royal road was the only one worthy of the name, though there were other trails "which we use . . . for stockraising and chasing Apaches," Zúñiga reported. Mail went up and down the royal road by packtrain or courier, and goods came north, for although Tucson produced the staple foods it needed, commodities from silver to chocolate and from wax to woolen cloth had to be brought from the interior of Mexico. The total commerce at the presidio's two stores came to 7500 pesos a year.

Tucson's main industry was stockraising. The whole settlement had about 3500 head of cattle, 2600 sheep, 1200 horses, about 100 mules, and 30 burros. Cattle on the hoof sold for three pesos each; sheep, for a peso and a half. These prices doubled when the animal had been butchered and dressed. About 300 beeves and 200 sheep were slaughtered for food every year, nearly half the cattle going to feed the peaceful Apaches. Beef hides and tallow were sold to the south.

Although irrigation water was plentiful, agricultural production lagged. Zúñiga reported that the entire community produce came to less than 4000 bushels a year. The largest crop—more than two thirds of the total—was wheat, some of which was grown as far away as Tres Alamos, north of present-day Benson on the San Pedro River. Probably the meager produce reflected disputes between Spanish settlers and Indians over water rights. This perennial tension began soon after the presidio was founded, and lasted as long as Tucson remained a farming community. Today's disputes between Papagos and the City of Tucson over groundwater usage are merely the latest chapter in a long saga.

In 1804, about a fifth of Tucson's population was involved full-time in farming and stockraising. Another 20 men worked at various industrial trades serving military needs. Four men in the settlement operated pack-trains. Of the rest, most probably were involved directly or indirectly with the presidial garrison.

There was little other chance for employment. Tucson had no mines nearby, and, as Zúñiga pointed out with some disgust, most of the small household industries had not taken root, probably for want of teachers to start them. There was no shoemaker and no tanner, though the cavalry-men's armor was made of leather. Tucson had no hat-maker nor even—surprisingly—a saddlemaker. Although the Pimas grew cotton, neither they nor the Europeans wove the fiber, and the roughest wool and cotton cloth had to be brought from New Mexico or from the interior. Thus Tucson had a serious imbalance of trade, and although the paymaster paid the troops in good silver coin, much of it went elsewhere for the many goods that had to be imported.

Within a few years after Zúñiga wrote, the war that changed the life of the frontier forever began in the interior of Mexico. In September 1810, Father Miguel Hidalgo y Costilla proclaimed the "grito" of revolt against Spain in the little town of Dolores. Although Hidalgo was captured by Spanish forces and executed less than a year later, the war he began spread throughout Mexico and Latin America. By the time it ended in 1821, Mexico had won its independence, just three centuries after Hernán Cortez had established New Spain on the ruins of Aztec civilization.

In the far north, Tucson felt the reverberation of war. Scores of presidial soldiers from Sonora were sent south to fight—on the royalist side. Among the officers who served was Miguel Ignacio de Arvizu, Tucson's last regularly assigned Spanish commander. Alas, he was a better soldier than administrator, and Tucson suffered accordingly; many settlers abandoned the presidio.

Arvizu left Tucson late in 1818 and was succeeded early the next year by Captain José Romero, who became acting commander. It was Romero who gathered the officers and men of the Tucson garrison together one hot summer evening in 1821 and made them swear allegiance on their swords to the Plan of Iguala, which proclaimed Mexico's independence.

An era had ended.

Apache hostility continued to threaten the very existence of Tucson during the Mexican period, even as it had when the presidio was an outpost of the far-flung Spanish empire. This photograph of an Apache warrior, obviously posed in a studio, dates from the 1870s.

TUCSON UNDER MEXICO

Just as the founding of Spanish Tucson had been overshadowed by Anza's epochal expedition to California, so the birth of Mexican Tucson was obscured by another in the same direction. In June of 1823, Captain Romero and a handful of Tucson soldiers set off to reopen Anza's road. They succeeded. Regular mail service was established between upper Sonora and California for the first time, and for a few years there was some overland trade. Romero's accomplishment received wide notice as far south as Mexico City before he returned to Tucson early in 1826, a lieutenant colonel ready for retirement after 37 years of military service.

The attention paid to the Romero expedition in its own time, and its continuing fame, are among history's ironies. For the overland road was closed again within a decade, a casualty of renewed Indian warfare. California, always remote, sank from Tucson's consciousness altogether, until settlers forgot it even existed. For Tucsonians, the vital road remained the one leading south toward Mexico City. Tucson could live without contact with California; it could not survive without its economic lifeline.

Even more ironic than the brevity of Romero's achievement was the fact that his expedition masked a development less dramatic but of far greater consequence. The passing of Spanish rule ended, once and for all, the unchecked supremacy of the army in the frontier settlements. What emerged for the first time was civil government run by elected officials, and a society dominated by frontier civilians.

The Hispanic frontiersman had a remarkable resemblance to his Anglo-American counterpart, who was just then starting to penetrate the old Spanish borderlands. He was self-reliant, resourceful—particularly in dealing with Indians—and passionately proud of his citizenship. Confident he was the equal of any man alive, he yielded only reluctantly to authority imposed from above, preferring to work out his destiny as a free man. The order and structure that had characterized society everywhere in imperial Spain melted in democracy's fierce sun.

Independent Mexico ruled Southern Arizona for 32 years. For Tucson, it was a time of rapid change, much of it unwelcome. Political chaos, endemic in northern Mexico, increased frontier isolation, making it harder to get the goods the town needed in order to live and, more important, depriving its citizens of the military assistance they urgently needed. Professional soldiers who continued to garrison Tucson all too often were detailed south to fight, first for one side, then for the other. Tucson, meanwhile, was left defenseless as Indian warfare howled around it.

Despair crested in Tucson late in 1828 and found a poignant expression: the entire civilian population decided to abandon the settlement and seek safety elsewhere. A report from Manuel Escalante y Arvizu, military commander of the Arizpe district (which included Tucson), left no doubt their grievances were genuine.

Despite constant vigilance, Escalante wrote, settlers could not protect their property from Apache raids. Not a single Tucsonian could claim a herd as large as 25 head of cattle. Bulls and work oxen they guarded only by bringing them inside the presidial walls at night. The only reason any horses remained was that, when the garrison was in Tucson, soldiers guarded the entire herd 24 hours a day.

Not only was Tucson's cattle industry disseminated, but there were difficulties with the Pimas over water. According to treaty, three quarters of the irrigation water was reserved for the Pima village and only one quarter for the settlers on the east bank of the river. Although the Pima settlement had lost population, the arrangement did not change, and civilian agriculture suffered accordingly. Furthermore, the exodus of civilians during Arvizu's time had ended the farming at Tres Alamos. As a result, grain had to be imported from the San Ignacio Valley, more than 100 miles to the south, to feed soldiers and settlers.

Finally, Escalante noted, the Mexican government had failed to pay the Tucson troops in money and with provisions. The resulting poverty in the military economy devastated the civilian economy that depended upon it.

Escalante offered a number of suggestions for turning the situation around. A better water law was needed. The state military commander should be ordered to provide settlers with the ammunition they needed for self-defense. The central government should make every effort to keep the Tucson garrison up to strength, and the military should be ordered to buy provisions whenever possible from Tucson civilians, rather than seeking better prices elsewhere. Finally, Tucson needed "a local military commander who would rather sleep with his gun than with his wife, but who has at the same time enough political sense to work with the civilians, supply their needs and understand their way of life."

No more eloquent evidence of the importance of civilians in Mexican Tucson exists than Escalante's report, but the record is not clear whether it did any good. State authorities may have acted on some of its recommendations, or Tucson's settlers may simply have gained hope from the fact the commander knew about their plight. In any case, they stayed—so Escalante perhaps was responsible for the continued existence of Tucson. But things did not get much better, and discontent continued, particularly about the presidio's woefully inadequate defenses.

Mexican dominion brought another profound change in frontier life. Like other revolutionary countries, Mexico divorced church from state. Thus, by a single act, the mission system that had civilized the frontier lost its

Top
With a handful of soldiers from Tucson, Captain José Romero set off on June 8, 1823, to reopen Anza's road to California. He succeeded, and for a few years in the early Mexican period, Arizona and California again were connected by overland road. This photograph is of a diorama by Cal Peters depicting the departure of the Romero party. It is located at the Arizona Historical Society.

Above
Pima Indian cowboys such as this one tended the mission herd at San Xavier during the period when the Spanish flag flew over the presidio of San Agustín del Tucson.

Right
From time immemorial, Pima Indians lived in brush-and-mud huts like this one, photographed in the 1890s.

main source of funds. But Mexican officials went further in their determination to bring the church to heel. Chronically short of revenue, they cast greedy eyes at the wealth of the missions—and decided to put it to the service of the state. The vehicle was a federal decree late in 1827 that banned from the mission field all priests born in Spain; thereafter, the missions were to be administered by civil commissioners whose positions mission wealth would support.

On the northern frontier the decree was applied with a vengeance, since state authorities chose to circulate a rumor that the Franciscan missionaries had incited Indians under their charge to rebellion. Faced with certain persecution if they remained, most of the priests withdrew, leaving only a handful to continue the work in the Pimas' country. The effect was immediate. Civil authorities literally plundered the missions until, less than two years later, all eight missions in present-day Sonora and Arizona did not have enough wealth to support one commissioner.

Worse still than the wholesale robbery of mission property was the effect on the Indians of the missionaries' expulsion. The Pimas, one observer reported in 1830, were "in a state of shock." Missionaries had provided the oxen, tools, and seeds they needed for a stable agricultural life, but the state gave them nothing. As a result, many began leaving their villages and straying into the desert, where they joined disaffected Papagos. The fields went untended, weakening Tucson's economy still more. Even the village of San Xavier started disintegrating; there were no elected native leaders, and whatever local administration there was rested with the Pimas from the village outside the presidio. To all intents and purposes, the mission had ceased to function.

The beginning of the year 1830 may have marked the low point in the history of San Xavier and the other missions, for the Franciscans were allowed to return thereafter. But this was nearly the only bright spot in an otherwise dismal scene. Long before the end of the first decade of Mexican independence, the frontier was again aflame with Indian hostility. War began with the Yaquis in 1825, the conflict reaching as far north as Cananea, just below the present international boundary. Tucson troops, together with others from other presidios, were ordered into battle against the hostiles, to the dismay of settlers who had counted on their protection. The next decade saw war with the Yumas and Papagos in the western deserts. But, by this time, Tucson's attention was fully occupied once more with Apache hostilities.

Chronic fiscal chaos on the frontier and in Mexico City was responsible for fracturing the 30-year peace that Gálvez's policy had brought. As early as the mid-1820s, the Mexican government found itself unable to provide the rations that fed the peaceful Apaches. At the same time, the "broncos"—Apaches who had resisted the lure of peace—began to see the weakness and disorganization of Mexico's frontier army. Raiding began, directed indiscriminately against the property of presidio, mission, peaceful Indian, and civilian. Before the end of the decade, these raids had escalated to the level of full-scale warfare—and in the process revealed the total inadequacy of the presidial garrisons and volunteers to deal with it.

Beset with dangers, Tucson's civilians clung together, trying to mount a common defense against the enemy. One such occasion came in February of 1827. The presidial troops all had been called south to fight hostile Yaquis when rumors began that the Yaquis intended to attack Tucson. Once there, it was believed, they would join with Apaches, Yumas, and Papagos to lay waste the entire settlement.

Faced with this threat, Mayor Juan Romero called an emergency meeting at his home inside the presidio. Tucson's defenses were in a shambles, he told the assembled citizens; even the presidial wall was falling down, the victim of too many summer rains and too little maintenance. Now, if they wanted to survive, they must turn to and defend themselves.

They turned to. "In a spirit of unity and with admirable patriotism," Romero reported to the acting governor of the state, "all agreed to begin at once making adobes and securing timbers to restore our military wall to its original strength....They willingly abandon their work in the fields at a moment's notice to chase the raiding Apache."

Tucson was spared the threatened Yaqui attack, and doubtless the community's defenses profited from the citizens' public-spiritedness. But worse was to come. In 1832 the peaceful Apaches at Janos, in Chihuahua, revolted against presidial authorities and went onto the warpath, launching a chain reaction of rebellion that swept up most of the reservation Apaches on the frontier.

Tucson was spared this final indignity at least. Although a few of its warriors left, the presidio's colony of peaceful Apaches, under a chief named Atuna, remained peaceful and cooperated with civilian and military efforts against the raiders. Atuna's loyalty was all the more notable for the fact that, several months earlier, the Janos Apaches had made secret contact to urge that he and his people join the revolt. Atuna refused, instead sending out a party to make peace with some of the raiders. The mission failed, blood was shed, and Tucson was subjected to a frightening display of Apache wrath when 50 warriors rode at full speed around the presidio and settlement, uttering savage war cries. The incident must have been all the more alarming as the warriors were Pinals, members of the same subtribe as most of Atuna's people.

Spreading chaos on the frontier at last galvanized civilian settlers to effective action. In May of 1832, a civilian force of more than 200 men took to the field. Most of the volunteers were from settlements along the San Ignacio and San Miguel valleys far to the south, but Tucson contributed a detachment of troops. The next month, the whole force engaged a large party of Apaches in Arivaipa Canyon, northeast of Tucson. If official reports are to be believed, they won a handsome victory. Seventy-one Apaches were killed, 13 children captured, and 216 stolen horses recovered. One Mexican was killed and 12 were wounded.

Two years later, the Sonoran legislature at last was able to afford a major offensive against the Apaches. Headed by General Escalante, now governor of the state, it was not only the first large-scale expedition in five years but also the largest ever fielded against Apaches before the Anglo era. The force consisted of nearly 450 militiamen and volunteers, plus another 100 men guarding a remount herd of more than 3000 animals. Tucson Apaches served the force as scouts. Escalante's army remained in the field several months, striking into western New Mexico, where rebel Apaches were being supplied with arms.

As Escalante's army moved east, a far smaller detachment of volunteers—27 civilians, with 10 Pima allies and 20 Apache scouts—moved out of Tucson headed north. Pausing at the Gila to pick up a large contingent of friendly Indians, the party advanced far into Apache country along the lower Verde River. Like the earlier strike into Arivaipa Canyon, this expedition succeeded brilliantly. The Pinals, completely surprised, lost heavily; the Tucson contingent, not at all.

Although Escalante had authorized the organization of the Tucson detachment and coordinated it with his own strategy, the expedition was mounted by civilians and undertaken on civilian initiative. It had the marks of a volunteer effort—it moved fast, penetrated more deeply into Apache territory than any non-Apaches had gone before, and must have helped convince the raiders there was no sanctuary, even in mountain fastnesses, for marauders and their plunder. Above all, like the more famous Camp Grant Massacre 37 years later, the Tucson expedition of 1834 was a barometer of civilian frustration. It offered terrible evidence of what frontiersmen would do if pushed too far.

The offensives of 1834 brought significant results, though they did not appear immediately. Not until March of 1836, more than a year after the campaigns ended, did the Pinal Apaches come to Tucson to seek peace. Then, however, it was the largest peace parley the presidio had ever seen, with war chiefs and warriors representing all the hostile Pinals. Still shocked by their defeats, the Indians wanted a firm treaty with the Mexicans. The treaty they got allied them with Mexican forces against "all aggressors"— including their nearest Indian neighbors; forbade them to make peace with any other group without Mexican permission; dictated where they should live; and placed restrictions on their movements. In return, the Mexicans guaranteed nothing except that they would not attack as long as the Pinals remained at peace.

Even this agreement proved temporary. It neutralized the Pinals for a few years but did nothing to end raiding by other Apaches. Citizens and soldiers continued to resist where and when they could, but the triumphs of the early 1830s were not repeated. Before the end of the decade, the northern Sonoran frontier was so demoralized that citizens openly talked of secession from Sonora and even from Mexico.

It was no wonder. As the 1840s opened, a fair observer in Tucson or any other border settlement would have had to admit that 20 years of Mexican rule had brought little but catastrophe. Although citizens now governed themselves and had a say, at least, in Sonoran affairs, they were more isolated and defenseless than at any time since the earliest days of Spanish settlement. Constantly in danger from Indian attack, they also suffered frequent privation, lacking not merely the bright blankets, cloth, and metal goods that streamed over the Santa Fe Trail into neighboring New Mexico, but even the basic necessities: guns that worked and shot to fire.

The borderlands hung by a slender thread, ripe for the plucking.

Captain Philip St. George Cooke led the Mormon Battalion through Tucson on its way to California in December of 1846. Like other Anglos in the late 1840s, he was not impressed by the town.

THE COMING OF THE ANGLO

Tucson met its first Anglo-Americans on the last day of December, 1826. We do not know their names—only that there were three of them and that, in accordance with orders of Manuel de Leon, the presidial commander, they "appeared to present their passports" but ventured no farther west.

These Anglos were fur trappers, lured to the wilds of what is now central Arizona by the Sonoran beaver, which abounded in the Gila River. Beaver peltry had drawn trappers westward—from Quebec, from New York, from St. Louis—for more than a decade before they began penetrating the inhospitable Southwest. The trade in beaver pelts was responsible for the exploration of the Rocky Mountain West, and the "mountain men" who trapped its streams and rivers charted the first overland paths from the Mississippi Valley to Mexican California.

By the late 1820s, California itself had become a lure drawing men westward. Los Angeles, a collection of adobes clustered around Mission San Gabriel, offered a promising market to merchants enterprising enough to cultivate it. Boundless grazing lands pledged a life of plenty to anyone willing to take them up and domesticate their wild cattle. The challenge brought the men. One was Jonathan Warner, a member of an 11-man overland party that passed through Tucson westbound in October of 1831—the first large Anglo contingent to do so. Of all the 11, only Warner wrote about the trip, and as he was unimpressed by Tucson, his note was cryptic: "A military post and small town." Nothing more.

From the first, however, the Anglo presence created suspicion on the Mexican frontier—and with good reason. Typical frontiersmen, Anglo trappers and travelers showed little respect for the niceties of diplomatic protocol when they stood in the way of convenience or profit. Since their business in the wilds often brought them into contact with Indians, the Anglos made their own accommodations with the tribesmen. Frequently these arrangements involved contraband; Indians traded stolen horses and mules to the Anglos, who in turn supplied them with guns. Although aware of this nefarious trade, Mexican authorities were unable to police or stop it.

And there was more. Under virtually continual siege by warring Apaches, authorities in Chihuahua and Sonora had turned to the desperate expedient of offering cash bounties for the scalps of hostile Indians. Anglo frontiersmen became the entrepreneurs in this loathsome trade, but sometimes they did not confine their slaying to Apaches. The sale of scalps from friendly Indians, and even from Mexican citizens, did nothing to create confidence in bountymen on the part of their employers.

The final entry in Mexico's catalogue of Anglo perfidy was manifest destiny, the creed of the United States at mid-century, which, freely translated, meant land hunger and greed with a thin overgloss of idealism.

The Mexicans first experienced it in their frontier province of Texas, where Anglos, invited to colonize if they converted to Catholicism and became Mexican citizens, refused to abide by the rules. With considerable American help, they fought a successful revolution and transformed Texas into an independent republic. That was 1836.

Nine years later, the United States annexed this sovereign state, at the same time accepting a Texan claim of an international boundary at the Rio Grande, 150 miles south of the Nueces River, which had bounded Texas to the south since the earliest Spanish settlement. That boundary dispute became the pretext for the Mexican War that erupted in 1846, but both President James Knox Polk, the dour, ambitious Scot in the White House, and officialdom in Mexico City were under no delusions: America's objective was California, where a quarter century had proved the weakness of Mexican rule, even as it had demonstrated the value of the great harbors along the coast. Since American strategy was plotted to secure California, Arizona and the rest of the borderlands could not be unaffected.

The American thrust westward from the Mississippi Valley was led by General Stephen W. Kearny. Hastily organizing an army at Fort Leavenworth in May of 1846, he struck southwest to Santa Fe, which surrendered to him in August without the firing of a single shot. Kearny then divided his force, striking westward fast but leaving a wing under the command of Captain Philip St. George Cooke to break a wagon road from the New Mexican capital to California. To Cooke's force—a battalion of 397 Mormon men and five women—fell the honor of conquering the Southwest for the United States.

Cooke left Santa Fe late in October, heavily encumbered with wagons and beset with the complaints of soldiers certain that their religion gave them a monopoly on righteousness and truth. Progress was slow. The expedition crossed the Continental Divide near Guadalupe Pass only with the greatest difficulty, then had to fight its only engagement of the entire war near present-day Benson—against a herd of wild bulls. That obstacle overcome, the Mormon Battalion headed west toward the Santa Cruz Valley and the presidio of Tucson.

Cooke had heard along the way that a Mexican military force was gathered at Tucson, and he decided in advance to avoid conflict if he could. But initial contacts failed to secure a surrender agreement from presidial commandant Antonio Comadurán, so the Mormon Battalion approached prepared for battle—only to learn upon arrival that the entire Mexican garrison of 153 men, as well as many of Tucson's civilians, had withdrawn south. So the Americans entered Tucson, took temporary possession, and raised the American flag in the military plaza in front of the commandant's house. It was December 17, 1846.

Samuel E. Chamberlain, traveling with the same military party as Lt. Cave J. Couts, sketched this scene of San Xavier del Bac in October of 1848.

Despite the significance of Cooke's bloodless conquest, neither Tucson nor its capitulation impressed the Anglo commander very much. "Like Santa Fe, Tucson is not seen until very close by," he noted. "Of course, its adobe houses are the same in appearance, but inferior. There is a wall with abutments and battlements in bad repair, which surrounds the barracks; it is on the highest ground...It is a more populous village than I had supposed, containing about five hundred [persons]."

If Tucson failed to charm Cooke, those of its inhabitants who

remained made an impression on the Mormon soldiers. "We were kindly treated by the people of Tucson," one wrote, noting that they "brought Flour, Meal, Tobacco, Quinces to the camp for sale, and many of them giving such things to the Soldiers." In view of the reputation that had preceded the American force, these courtesies may have been in the character of peace offerings, but they were welcome nevertheless.

The Mormon Battalion remained only two nights in Tucson, then struck camp, marching north along the Santa Cruz and out of the town's history. The episode was virtually Tucson's only exposure to the Mexican War. Moreover, when the war ended in February 1848, the town remained what it had been—a northern outpost of Sonora. Although the Treaty of Guadalupe Hidalgo ceded about one million square miles of territory to the United States, the boundary crossed Arizona at the Gila River. The settled part of the present-day state stayed with Mexico.

The fact that Tucson six years later became an American town was the result of an accident: the discovery of gold in California and the tremendous rush of people westward from the settled parts of the country to seek their fortunes there. The rapid settlement of this fabulous *el dorado* brought statehood to California in 1850, even as it dramatically illustrated the need to build a rapid, reliable transportation system linking the Atlantic and Pacific coasts. Tucson was in the middle of the last piece of foreign territory the United States needed for an all-weather transcontinental railroad route. There could be no clearer sign of its destiny, though the railroad—a technological undertaking as daring in its day as manned moon landings in ours—was not built for another generation.

Meanwhile, about 50,000 argonauts—about a fifth of all who went to California—came along the southern immigrant route, following Cooke's road. This assortment of mid-century adventurers, Tucson's first major contact with the world beyond the frontier of hostile Apachería, for the most part were unimpressed with what they saw.

"Ft. de Tucson," observed Army Lieutenant Cave Johnson Couts in October 1848 was "no *great deal*," though its people were "much in advance" of some his column had met on its march from the Gulf Coast, and "think Americans are *everything*." Their technology, however, left much to be desired: "Every house...is furnished with a Buro *flour mill* [an arrastre] and are kept grinding incessantly, probably grinding a half bushel of wheat in 24 hours."

Hostile observations increased with the migrant flow. The saguaro cacti on Sentinel Peak and the May heat were more impressive to New Orleans newsman John E. Durivage the next year than was Tucson, "a miserable old place" whose peaceful Indian population was "cowardly and imbecile...unequivocally a miserable, degraded set." A. B. Clarke, passing through Tucson late in 1849, thought the Mexican presidials so worthless that the three bushels of grain he heard they were given for a year's service were more than they deserved.

Despite racist presuppositions, which existed on both sides, the meeting between the two cultures was generally harmonious. From the beginning, Tucsonians welcomed Anglo travelers as a source of goods they could get nowhere else. Every sort of merchandise was in short supply, and one enterprising Anglo who anticipated the demand sold $400 worth of goods in two hours. Obviously, the economic starvation that began with the founding of Tucson continued still.

Yet matters were not so desperate as Anglo accounts made them appear. When John Russell Bartlett, the Rhode Island bibliophile who served as the United States commissioner to survey the 1848 boundary, reached Tucson in 1852, he reported that Apache warfare made life in the Santa Cruz Valley virtually impossible. The population of Tucson barely subsisted, he noted, and would be lost without the Mexican troops. "The houses of Tucson are all of adobe, and the majority are in a state of ruin. No attention seems to be given to repair; but as soon as a dwelling becomes uninhabitable, it is deserted, the miserable tenants creeping to some other hovel where they may eke out their existence."

It is true that when Bartlett was in Tucson, Apache raiding was severe, as it had been for years and as it continued to be for a decade more. Yet the view he painted of life in Tucson was far from the experience of people living in the town. Hilario Gallego, born in Tucson in 1850, remembered a row of houses inside the presidial wall—humble enough dwellings, but not subject to systematic desertion as they literally dissolved under the elements. There were, Gallego remembered, a store and a bar inside the presidio. Outside there were three stores. Food came from the hills around, or from the Pima and Maricopa Indians on the Gila. About every six months, the town government sent to Hermosillo for cloth, and probably other necessities. Residents of Mexican Tucson doubtless lived close to the bone, but only someone foreign to the style of frontier life could characterize their existence as Bartlett did.

The Gadsden Purchase, negotiated at the end of 1853 and ratified six months later, did nothing immediately to change that life-style. Although Tucson was included in the 29,670 square miles of territory the United States bought from Mexico for $10 million, the immediate beneficiary of annexation was not Tucson but Tubac. There Arizona's first Anglo mining industry took root late in 1856, thanks largely to the explorations of Charles D. Poston, a sometime customs-house clerk in San Francisco, and the backing of the Wrightson brothers of Cincinnati. During the second half of the decade of the '50s, Tubac was—in Poston's phrase—the Athens of the West, a cosmopolitan, hospitable community whose dinner tables at any single time were graced by speakers of six or eight European languages. Over this arcadian idyll Poston claimed to have reigned as benevolent despot as well as host, judging legal cases, marrying couples, issuing paper money, and baptizing children, as the Sonora Exploring and Mining Company and its subsidiary, the Santa Rita Mining Company, dug rich silver from the ground and sent it east. Such a metropolis was Tubac that it even gave birth to *The Weekly Arizonian,* Arizona's first newspaper, which made its appearance early in 1859.

If conditions in Tubac were never as gracious and prosperous as Poston remembered them in his less fortunate days—and they were not—Tubac at least had the lion's share of American settlers and American prosperity in the Gadsden Purchase before 1860. But Tucson also got its share, and its newcomers turned out to have more staying power.

In 1855 came Mark A. Aldrich, a native of New York who followed the frontier to Illinois, then California, before reaching Tucson. He became the town's first Anglo merchant, its first postmaster (a job that demanded little of its incumbent in the days before regular mail service), and later its first criminal judge. This last position he angrily resigned late in 1860 because, as he told his fellow citizens in an open letter, "With the exception of a few cases of stealing (and the accused were Mexicans) where public whipping was inflicted, not a single case has ever been made [since the adoption of a new criminal code several months before] for the arrest and punishment of persons who do not hesitate, for any offense (either supposed or real) to violate and set at defiance the laws, by shooting at each other in the streets and saloons, endangering the lives of other citizens in their immediate vicinity."

Aldrich was one of Tucson's most important Anglo citizens in the 1850s, but he was by no means the only one. The decade gained Tucson a flock of pioneers whose names became great in the history of the town and the Territory of Arizona: German-born Charles H. Meyer, Tucson's first druggist and most famous justice of the peace; Samuel Hughes, Welsh-born merchant, cattleman, and civic leader; Hiram Stevens, his brother-in-law; Solomon Warner, another early merchant and later proprietor of one of Tucson's first water-powered flour mills; the Oury brothers, William and Granville, the one a cattleman, the other a lawyer, and politicians both; John Davis, a blacksmith; John B. Allen, merchant and post trader, known as Pie Allen because he got his start selling pies to soldiers and civilians in Tucson. By the end of the decade, the Anglo presence in Tucson was large enough to make itself felt, and, because it did so, Anglos began to assume leadership in the community.

Meanwhile, the pace of change accelerated. The last Mexican troops left Tucson March 10, 1856, nearly 21 months after the Gadsden Purchase had been ratified; there had been no Anglo force to take their place, and there was none when the last 29 presidials departed for Sonora. The absence of military protection did not dampen spirits that day; indeed, nine Anglos pieced together ocotillo canes to make a flagpole and ran up Old Glory in what is now El Presidio Park. But Tucsonians increasingly felt their isolation. There was an army garrison at Fort Yuma on the Colorado River, 250 miles to the west, and another at Fort Fillmore on the Rio Grande at Mesilla, about

the same distance to the east. Between, it seemed, there were only hostile Indians, who were becoming increasingly so as Anglo cattle herds attracted intensified raiding. Anguished, Tucsonians appealed to the military Department of New Mexico for protection, and that headquarters in July ordered Major Enoch Steen to take four companies of the First Dragoons and establish a post at Tucson.

Steen and his command reached Tucson in mid-November of 1856. But Steen promptly concluded that the town was an unsuitable site for a post. After stopping briefly at San Xavier, he explored southward and eventually chose a site near Calabasas, just above the international boundary. Rebuked for his disobedience, he moved his post to a spot along Sonoita Creek, east of present-day Patagonia, where his men built Fort Buchanan. Tucson remained without effective military protection.

The army, however, already had launched another venture whose effect on Tucson ultimately was more important than any amount of Indian fighting. Beginning soon after the end of the Mexican War, the military undertook a series of surveys for railroad and wagon routes across the newly acquired Southwest. Even before the Gadsden Purchase was ratified, a party headed by Lieutenants John G. Parke and George Stoneman made its way from the Gila down Cooke's road to Tucson, and thence to the Rio Grande. It was the beginning of the opening of Southern Arizona to the rest of the United States.

In the summer of 1857, less than a year after Steen refused to establish a post at Tucson, came a sight never before seen in the desert town—a stagecoach, with lettering on the door proclaiming it the "San Antonio and San Diego Mail Line," which appeared one scorching August day, the first fruit of the military surveys. As a means of transportation, the coach had distinct disadvantages, primary among them the fact that the road over which it traveled in many places was unfit for heavy vehicles. Because passengers on the mail coaches had to get out and ride muleback over the roughest spots, the line acquired the rather unfriendly nickname of "the Jackass Mail." Nevertheless, it provided mail from both east and west and, perhaps even more important, regular transportation in both directions.

Late the next year, the Jackass Mail was supplanted by the Butterfield Overland Mail, a far more ambitious operation. With an annual government subsidy of $600,000 (an astronomical sum in 1858), John Butterfield undertook to run regular mail service from St. Louis to San Francisco in 25 days or less. Since the route was 2400 miles, the schedule meant nearly 100 miles of travel a day, a backbreaking trip when the average distance an army dragoon could travel on horseback between sunup and sundown was 40 miles. Butterfield's coaches stopped only to change teams every 10 miles and drivers less frequently. Passengers on its run were strictly extra, and paid through the nose for their 25 miserable days: the one-way fare from the Mississippi Valley to the Pacific was $200.

But with all its misery, the Butterfield line offered the fastest transportation that had ever existed across the West. It was a marvel of its time, and when the first coach passed through Tucson westbound on October 2, 1858, the town gained an irradicable place on America's map.

Despite all advances, Tucson's residents faced a perennial, intractable problem. Justice—apart from the purely local variety—courts of record, the services of the U.S. marshal, the land office, the surveyor-general or any other federal officer—indeed, every service of government except the military was 300 miles distant, at Santa Fe. In 1850, Arizona north of the Gila had been attached to the newly created Territory of New Mexico; four years later, the Gadsden Purchase became Doña Ana County, New Mexico.

It was a bad mismatch. For one thing, the entire Gadsden Purchase was separated from Santa Fe by a dangerous stretch of desert; for another, it was essentially a unit. Men realized this as they groped for a name for the area, calling it first "The Purchase," then, gradually, "Arizona"—a term defining the country south of the Gila between the Rio Grande and the Colorado.

Since this "Arizona" had no logical tie to New Mexico, it soon became obvious to most thinking men that the area should be a separate federal territory. Fifteen bills were presented in Congress between 1857 and 1862 to create one; none passed. Five times, citizens of the Gadsden Purchase elected a delegate to Congress; five times he was refused a seat.

In the late 1850s, the United States was embarked on a course that led inevitably to civil war. Concerns about the expansion or geographical limitation of slavery dominated the day, drowning out the cries of a far-off people struggling to survive amid almost incessant Indian warfare, and to have a government close enough to perform the routine functions that only government could perform. A northern Siberia of the Spanish empire and the Mexican republic for 75 years, Arizona remained a Siberia still.

So it was that a meeting assembled at Tucson in April 1860 to form a separate territorial government. One Dr. Lewis Owens of Mesilla was chosen governor; local elections the next month produced a crop of officials solidly pro-Southern in their views. Men knew the nation stood at the point of dividing; to Arizonans, any alternative was preferable to the Northern-dominated Washington government. The reason had nothing to do with national issues. Rather, the federal government had ignored the vital interests of the Gadsden Purchase—it had not subdued the Indians. Arizonans were ready to throw in their hands with any power that promised to do so.

Brigadier General James Henry Carleton led the Union advance that reconquered Arizona from the Confederacy in 1862. He also taxed Tucsonians heavily for the security his troops provided them.

TUCSON, ARIZONA TERRITORY

Connecticut-born Charles Trumbull Hayden was a merchant in Tucson for more than a decade before moving to the Salt River Valley in 1871 to start the Hayden Flouring Mill there. His settlement on the Salt River, first called Hayden's Ferry, later became known as Tempe. His son, Carl, represented Arizona in the U.S. House and Senate for more than half a century.

In January of 1861, Apaches raiding near Fort Buchanan seized a 12-year-old boy named Feliz Martinez and carried him off, together with a herd of cattle. The lad's stepfather, John Ward, hurried to the post with the news, and a company of 54 infantrymen under command of Second Lieutenant George N. Bascom was dispatched to pursue the boy. The expedition brought about the so-called Bascom affair, the most famous incident in preterritorial Arizona history.

Bascom and the Chiricahua chief Cochise confronted each other in February at Apache Pass, near the present-day New Mexico state line, in a botched diplomatic encounter that resulted in several deaths on both sides. Two months later the Butterfield Overland Mail, several of whose employees were casualties in the incident, closed its operations in the Southwest. Three months after that, in July, the United States closed Forts Buchanan and Breckinridge, the only two military posts within what is now Arizona, and the Apaches had the satisfaction of seeing the blue-coated soldiers march down Butterfield's road toward the Rio Grande. The conclusion that the troubles at Apache Pass had been responsible for both events must have been irresistible.

It was, of course, erroneous. The United States began breaking apart in December of 1860; the secession of Texas, the last of the states of the Deep South to join the Confederacy, on February 1 made it necessary to reroute the Butterfield line through the central territories, which remained loyal to the Union. The troops at Buchanan and Breckinridge were withdrawn to fight in New Mexico and farther east.

The withdrawal of the Butterfield line deprived Tucsonians of their link with the outside world, while the troops' departure left them again unprotected. Before autumn, the desolation Commissioner Bartlett thought he had seen nine years earlier became actual. The mines around Tubac closed, their owners and workers fleeing for their lives. Ranchers abandoned their property, retreating for protection to Tucson. Commerce dried up, municipal life took on the aspect of life under siege, confidence evaporated.

Meanwhile, citizens of the Gadsden Purchase had cast their lot with the Confederacy. Early in February, a meeting convened in Tucson to consider the region's loyalties. Although its leading lights were sympathizers with the Southern cause, the Mesilla newspaper—whose editor was a secessionist—had to acknowledge that "Adherence to the 'Star Spangled Banner' seemed to be the sentiment uppermost in the crowd." On March 23, Mark Aldrich presided over a gathering in Tucson that declared: "That under any and all circumstances our sympathies are with the Southern Confederacy, and in the event that it shall be composed of a majority of the Southern States, we earnestly desire that she [sic] will extend to us the protection necessary to the proper development and advancement of the

Territory."

The key was protection. Although some citizens were dedicated to the Southern cause, most of the enthusiasm for the Confederacy was rooted in the hope that the new government would offer the effective aid against Indian hostility that the old one never had given.

That summer, Confederates from Texas seized control of Mesilla and proclaimed the Confederate Territory of Arizona, an area defined by its governor, John R. Baylor, as embracing all of present-day Arizona and New Mexico and a bit of Nevada. No sooner was the territory organized than Tucsonians held another mass meeting and elected Granville Oury as delegate to the Richmond Congress.

Once ensconced in New Mexico, Confederates turned naturally toward California, whose gold, food supplies, coastline, and Confederate sympathizers were an irresistible lure. As a first step in the conquest, General Henry H. Sibley dispatched Captain Sherod Hunter from Mesilla with 65 volunteers to occupy Tucson and secure the road farther west against any enemy advance eastward.

Hunter's force reached Tucson February 28, 1862, after a march through some of the worst winter weather ever recorded in Arizona. Once there, he lost no time determining loyalties: either townspeople took an oath of allegiance to the Confederacy or they were invited to leave town. Dangerous as this alternative was, most of the prominent pioneers took it. Sam Hughes went to California, to return later the same year with Union soldiers. Peter R. Brady, a surveyor and mining entrepreneur who first opened the mines at Ajo, went to Mexico. So did Solomon Warner. Charles T. Hayden, another pioneer merchant of the 1850s (and father of the late U.S. Senator Carl Hayden), already had left Tucson by the time Hunter arrived, but returned to resume his business after Hunter left. To Estevan Ochoa, a native of Chihuahua who already had established himself as a successful businessman when he reached Tucson in 1860, Hunter offered the same choice that he did to the Anglos. Ochoa hesitated not a minute. Gathering a few personal belongings, he set out, alone, across the Apache-infested desert on horseback toward the Rio Grande. No one expected him to survive. He did, and, when he returned to Tucson after the Confederate departure, he became one of the town's great businessmen and philanthropists.

Tucson's Confederate interlude ended almost as soon as it began. Even as Hunter occupied Tucson, a Union force many times larger was gathering under command of Colonel James H. Carleton in California, preparing to advance east and dislodge Sibley from New Mexico—and, incidentally, any Confederates from Arizona. The advance guard of this California Column encountered a scouting party of Hunter's at Stanwix

Texan John Robert Baylor led Confederate troops into New Mexico in the summer of 1861, and established the Confederate Territory of Arizona, of which he named himself Governor. Tucsonians, weary of neglect by the federal government in Washington, eagerly supported him.

Station near Yuma. Small contingents from both forces met and fought a brief skirmish at Picacho Peak, 40 miles northwest of Tucson, in mid-April. This engagement, locally famous as the westernmost battle of the Civil War, delayed the Californians' eastward push only slightly. Carleton's advance guard reached Tucson late in May. Realizing the hopelessness of resistance, Hunter already had withdrawn. He had been of no assistance to Tucsonians in their struggle against the Apaches, and some probably felt justified in a bitter laugh when they learned that Apaches had attacked his force on its way to the Rio Grande.

Carleton's task in Tucson was nothing less than resurrecting civil society. The town was virtually deserted when he arrived early in June; Confederate sympathizers had left with Hunter, and many of the Mexicans also had sought safer climes. Beyond the depopulation—a condition that righted itself as the weeks passed—there was neither government nor law. Remaining Southern sympathizers went unpunished, notable among them Sylvester Mowry, a former army officer, owner of the Mowry mine near the Mexican border and in the '50s a perennial delegate to Congress from the phantom Territory of Arizona.

In the absence of law, Carleton set up military courts before which Mowry, Palatine Robinson, and others were tried, convicted, and sent to prison at Yuma. Civil government remained in abeyance, though Carleton—by now a general—established a Union Territory of Arizona, with himself as governor, whose eastern boundary extended as far as the Californians happened to be at the time. This new political creation had greater staying power than the Confederate version, but it was not Arizona's final territorial organization. That came, by act of Congress, early in 1863 and lasted 49 years.

Amid his other concerns, Carleton took steps to assure that Tucsonians paid for the security his forces had brought them. He laid a tax of $5 per month on every local business except those selling food and clothing; if the monthly yield came to less than $500, businessmen learned, the levy would go up. To regulate saloons he taxed them $100 each a month, while gambling dens paid at the rate of $100 per gaming table. The social effects of these measures are undocumented, but Tucson remained neither better nor worse in its manners and morals than other frontier towns.

Carleton left Tucson with the last 1400 troops on July 20, but behind him he left a permanent military presence, and Camp Lowell, a permanent post located where the Santa Rita Hotel now stands downtown. It was a supply depot, but it was garrisoned. For the next three decades, Tucson did not lack military protection.

When Carleton left for the Rio Grande, he divided his Territory of Arizona, assigning command of its western district—from Apache Pass to the Colorado—to Major David Fergusson, his commissary officer. Before the year was out, Fergusson saw to it that two services Tucsonians badly needed were performed for them.

The first was an inventory of real property and its ownership, a task made necessary by the fact that Mexican troops, when they withdrew in 1856, had taken all the presidial records with them. (Atanacia Santa Cruz de Hughes, Sam's wife, who watched them depart, later reported that the soldiers disposed of Tucson's archives by using them as cigarette papers.) As a result, occupancy was the only proof of ownership. Fergusson assigned William S. Oury to compile a list of properties and their owners.

To clarify the location of the properties Oury listed, Fergusson also ordered John B. Mills, a surveyor, to prepare a map of Tucson and its surrounding fields. Like the Oury inventory, the so-called Fergusson map is one of the basic documents of Tucson's history.

Outside Tucson, other events in 1862 presaged even greater changes for Arizona than the war had caused. Two gold strikes occurred during the fall, first on the Colorado River, then on the Hassayampa, near present-day Prescott. Small-scale gold rushes followed, and inevitably more gold was discovered. Suddenly, Arizona seemed to promise a fabulous future. Such dreams of wealth played a significant part in the politics that created the federal Territory of Arizona on February 24, 1863.

Territorial government, like colonial rule, was imposed largely from above; except for an elective territorial legislature and some local officials, its leaders were appointed by the administration in power in Washington. In 1863, the nation had a Republican administration and Congress, so Arizona's first governor, secretary, justices, marshal, and Indian superintendent all were Republicans. This was one of two reasons that Tucson, the only substantial town in the territory, was bypassed when Governor John Noble Goodwin and the government party chose a site for the capital; the town was still tarred with the brush of Democratic sympathy and secessionism. The other reason was even more direct: gold had been located on the Hassayampa, not the Santa Cruz, and territorial leaders wanted to be close to the diggings. Prescott, sheltered by Fort Whipple, which Carleton ordered built to protect the miners, became the territorial capital.

With all the momentous events of the early 1860s, the most significant change, from Tucson's point of view, was the permanent presence of the army in Arizona. By the time the Civil War ended, California volunteers serving in the territory had established at least five posts critically positioned so troops could strike into the heart of the mountainous country where hostile Apaches had been safe from reprisals from the beginning of time. From these camps and others—Arizona at the height of the Indian wars had 14 permanent army posts—soldiers could punish raiders and at the same

time cut off their traditional means of livelihood. The result was that, as early as 1864, groups of Apaches began appearing at army posts seeking peace in exchange for rations.

To Tucson, the significance in all this lay not only in improved (though still far from perfect) security but also in the prosperity it brought the community. The army and the Indians were major consumers of all sorts of goods—from beef and flour to shovels and from vegetable seeds and blankets to work animals. All these the federal government obtained from civilian suppliers. Most purchases were by contract negotiated after national bidding, although federal law allowed purchases on the open market if circumstances demanded them. In the early years of Arizona Territory, successful bidders for the big military and Indian Service contracts tended to be large Eastern mercantile houses, but even then there was something in it for Tucson, since contractors often found it cheaper to subcontract with local suppliers for perishable commodities than to freight them from distant points. Thus, a good share of the federal bounty routinely ended up in local pockets.

The ripple effect of federal money, coupled with the wealth made and spent by miners and ranchers for whom Tucson was a natural market, plus

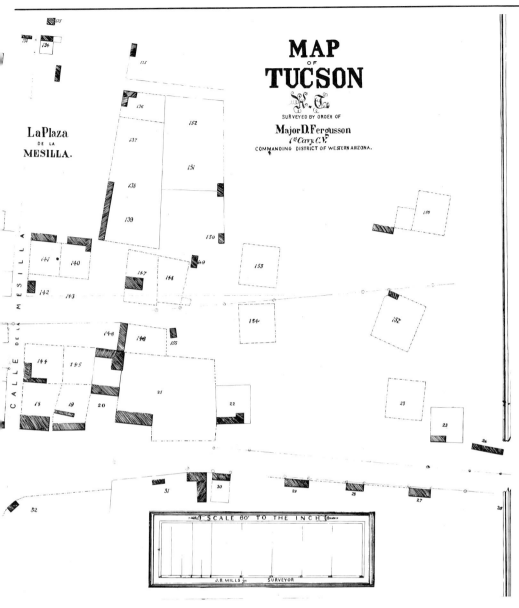

MAP
OF
TUCSON

SURVEYED BY ORDER OF

Major D. Fergusson
1st Cavy. C.V.
COMMANDING DISTRICT OF WESTERN ARIZONA.

La Plaza
DE LA
MESILLA.

SCALE 60' TO THE INCH

J.B. MILLS Jr   SURVEYOR

The 1862 Fergusson map, drawn by surveyor John B. Mills, is a basic document of Tucson's history.

the trade that came because the town sat athwart Arizona's main east-west road, made Tucson prosperous. It also drew population like a magnet. Tucson's first Anglo census, taken in 1860, recorded 620 people, all but a handful Mexicans—but among that handful, interestingly, eight blacks. The troubles of the Civil War probably reduced that population by half, but once order returned, so did people, and migration resumed. A special census taken in 1864 to apportion seats for the first territorial legislature showed Tucson with 1,568 people, more than twice the prewar total. Six years later, the decennial census revealed that the population again had more than doubled, the count standing at 3,224 residents.

In this climate, business flourished. By the early 1870s, Tucson had a half-dozen major merchants, all of whom diversified their interests and investments. Everyone was involved in ranching, mining—or at least mining speculation—merchandising, and freighting. Some also were pioneer bankers, following an occupation that began as the simple storing of valuables and the issuance of credit. Business giants of that day included such men as Edward Nye Fish; the Jacobs brothers, Lionel and Barron; Charles T. Hayden (who migrated to the Salt River Valley in 1871 and became the father of Tempe); and the Zeckendorfs, William and Louis, who in 1869 opened a

Edward Nye Fish, territorial merchant and owner of the city's first steam-powered flour mill, came to Tucson in 1865. A widower, he married Maria Wakefield, one of Tucson's first two female school teachers, in 1874. The house where they lived, at the corner of Main Avenue and Alameda Street, still stands.

branch of a business that already had been very successful in Santa Fe. In time they split up, forming two general-merchandise companies. These brothers had a nephew named Albert Steinfeld, who followed his uncles to Arizona Territory. Around the turn of the century, he bought out Louis Zeckendorf (William's business had failed long before) and renamed the store for himself. Steinfeld's survives today.

But two businesses in Tucson exceeded all others in importance in the years before the coming of the railroad. One was the firm of Tully & Ochoa, a partnership begun before 1860 between the enterprising and patriotic Estevan Ochoa and Pinckney R. Tully, a native Southerner who had been all over the West and had participated in all kinds of business before reaching Arizona. Tully & Ochoa (later Tully, Ochoa and DeLong, after Sidney R. DeLong became a partner in 1870) was into everything on a grand scale, from Indian Service contracting to post traderships. But if any single activity made the firm famous, it was freighting—an expensive, dangerous occupation. Four times between 1867 and 1870, Tully & Ochoa lost wagon trains to Apache attack.

The only firm to rival Tully & Ochoa in importance was Lord & Williams, another big, diversified business. Its partners were Dr. Charles Lord, a physician who had come to Arizona after the Civil War as an army contract surgeon, and Wheeler W. Williams, Tucson's postmaster in the late 1860s—a position Lord held in the next decade. Lord & Williams, Tully & Ochoa, and William and Louis Zeckendorf were among the first Arizona merchants to become prime government contractors, and by the late 1870s Lord & Williams was the biggest of the lot.

Lord & Williams' failure in 1881 was due in part to the United States government. The story revealed the dangers of doing business with Uncle Sam. Contract purchases, secured by annual appropriations, were paid promptly, but a merchant who sold to an Indian agent or an army quarter-master on the open market could wait for decades for his payment. The government in Washington suspected that all exigency purchases cloaked fraud, yet it forced its agents into this kind of arrangement by chronically shorting them of food and every other necessary commodity. Merchants who regularly contracted to supply goods often were called on at the end of their contracts to supply that little bit more that kept the Indians peaceful or the soldiers fed. But, grateful as the government's agents were for these sources of provender, the government nearly always seized on technicalities to forestall payment. The Bureau of Indian Affairs in the late 1880s still had unpaid Arizona accounts dating from the early 1870s.

The government's tardiness in settling its accounts, the peculiarities of its inspection system, and the dangers of doing business across wide stretches of Apache-infested country should give the lie once and for all to

Top Left & Center
Coming from California, brothers (a) Lionel and (b) Barron Jacobs established themselves as leading merchants in Tucson in the early 1870s. They also were among the city's first bankers. The house they built on Alameda Street, which was just east of Main Avenue, was a two-story Victorian adobe.

Top Right & Center Left
Territorial merchants (a) William and (b) Louis Zeckendorf opened a branch of their already successful New Mexico business in Tucson in 1869. They soon divided the firm into two businesses. William Zeckendorf failed in 1883, a casualty of competition fostered by cheap railroad freight rates. Louis Zeckendorf sold out to his nephew, Albert Steinfeld, around the turn of the century. The business continues today.

Center & Right Center
Two merchant princes of prerailroad Tucson: (a) Estevan Ochoa (b) Pinckney R. Tully. Founded before 1860, their business throve in adversity until railroad competition forced it to close in the 1880s.

Bottom
Business giant Edward N. Fish built his home at 141 N. Main Avenue in 1868. When this photograph was taken two years later, Main — the old Camino Real — still marked the western edge of Tucson. Beyond that were irrigated farm lands. The Fish home adjoined that of Hiram and Petra Stevens, whose doorway appears just to the right of the tree. Both homes still stand.

Above
The dapper Dr. Charles H. Lord, who
came to Arizona as a contract surgeon
for the U.S. Army after the Civil War,
became a partner in Lord & Williams,
Arizona's largest business house in the
1870s.

Top Left
Wheeler W. Williams was a partner,
with Dr. Charles H. Lord, in Arizona's
largest mercantile house before the
coming of the railroad in 1880. A
combination of railroad competition
with Lord & Williams' freighting business and U.S. government slowness in
paying its accounts caused the firm to
fail in 1881.

Top Right
Frontiersman, cattleman, businessman
and politician, William S. Oury was
one of Arizona's most important
pioneers of the 1850s. In 1871, he
helped organize and lead the Camp
Grant Massacre, an event he later de-
fended as indispensable to the establishment of Anglo supremacy in
Arizona.

the myth of a "ring" that bought preferential consideration by cutting politicians in on the proceeds of their contracts, and then prospered by cheating on their obligations. Yet suspicions were rife that such a ring existed. Men referred to it variously as the Indian ring, the Tucson ring, the government ring, and the federal ring. It was supposed to be so obsessed by the desire for lucrative army contracts that it literally drove the Indians out onto the warpath by bilking them of the food they needed to live. Thus, the army would be sure to remain. No one paused to consider that the first people to suffer from Indian uprisings were the purveyors of goods to the reservations and army posts. Nor did anyone in the 1870s or a century later look for evidence to confirm the suspicions. Had anyone done so, he would have discovered that the rumors began with the merchants who had bid on contracts unsuccessfully, and that they circulated mainly among other would-be contractors and army officers who were convinced, as an article of faith, that all civilian suppliers could be bought, and that most were.

Even as business expanded in Tucson after the Civil War's disruptions, the town itself began to mature. In May of 1864, Governor Goodwin visited Tucson and designated it an incorporated municipality and the seat of one of the territory's three judicial districts. That autumn, the first territorial legislature created Arizona's four original counties and made Tucson the seat of Pima County, an area embracing nearly one quarter of the present-day state.

For reasons that doubtless were political, Goodwin, a Northerner and Republican, named William S. Oury, a Southern Democrat and former secessionist, as Tucson's first Anglo mayor; among the councilmen were Hiram Stevens, Mark Aldrich, and Juan Elias, a prominent Mexican-American. These men represented Tucson's power structure, and it behooved territorial officials—most of whom had broader political ambitions—not to offend anyone with a constituency.

Late in 1867, the second territorial legislature moved the territorial capital to Tucson, amid the howls of Prescott's disappointed citizens. Logic supported the move. With its population approaching 3000, Tucson was 10 times the size of any other Arizona town; and since, capital or not, its citizens were a political force to be reckoned with, it made sense to move the center of government to them. Actually, Tucson got little more than honor out of being the capital. The governor—by then Richard C. McCormick, a consummate politician—moved there, as did most other territorial officers. *The Weekly Arizonian,* then published in Tucson, got the lion's share of government advertising. But since territorial government was unencumbered with bureaucracy, and even the legislature met only every second year, neither Tucson's population nor its economy felt much effect from the move. Nor did the removal of the capital back to Prescott 10 years later create more

Left

The Wasp, a San Francisco magazine, published this cartoon of the supposed Tucson Ring in the 1880s. A tiger, whose legs and tail are labeled with the names of the alleged profiteers, nudges former governor and delegate Richard C. McCormick toward the capitol, where the contracts he is carrying will be approved. As McCormick wonders how much he will make on the deal, Delegate Granville H. Oury, a Democrat, contemplates busting "that little game."

Above

Petra Stevens, Hiram's wife, posed with her dog in front of the house at 165 N. Main Avenue where she and her husband lived. The home adjoined that of E.N. Fish and his wife, Maria.

General George Stoneman, commander of the military Department of Arizona in 1871, told a Tucson delegation seeking additional military protection that Tucson was large enough to take care of itself. The result was the infamous Camp Grant Massacre that April.

than a stir of resentment.

In that decade, Tucson did a good deal of maturing. In 1871, largely to make property titles secure, the town formally incorporated as a village. Two years later, with the government still heavily in debt to the surveyor who had done the village plat, the mayor and council imposed the first property tax— $1 per $100 of assessed valuation of personal and real property. The burden was cushioned, however, by the governing body's agreement to issue a town lot, gratis, to any citizen paying $4 in taxes. The property tax yielded nearly $3800 before the end of the year and got the village out of debt. In 1877, in debt again, Tucson incorporated as a city.

Perhaps the most famous incident involving Tucson in the 1870s did the town no credit. This was the Camp Grant Massacre, a terrifying example of the frontier mentality at work.

Apache raiding had continued despite the presence of the army. Alone of Southern Arizona settlements Tucson was secure, and that only because of its size. Once again, Apaches despoiled ranches in the Santa Cruz Valley, raided wagon trains—even those carrying food for the Indians to military posts where they were rationed—and closed down mining. The spring of 1871 brought no relief. In desperation, Tucsonians dispatched a delegation headed by William S. Oury to Florence to meet with General George Stoneman, the departmental military commander. Stoneman rebuffed them. Tucson was large enough to take care of itself, he told Oury, while there were too few people in the Santa Cruz Valley to justify additional troops there. Further complaints, Stoneman warned, might well "have the effect to withdraw the troops entirely." Clearly, if Tucsonians wanted further security, they would have to look to themselves for it.

Suspicion in Tucson focused on a band of Arivaipa Apaches who had come in to Camp Grant, 55 miles away by wagon road, to live at peace and be fed. Frontiersmen generally mistrusted such arrangements. Rumors spread around Tucson that the Camp Grant Apaches were responsible for a particularly sanguinary raid in the Santa Cruz Valley. Papagos from San Xavier reportedly had tracked hostiles who had stolen some cattle, and found the track led directly to Camp Grant. It did not matter that the post commander was convinced his charges were blameless; Tucsonians had decided they were guilty.

Late in April, amid great excitement, Oury and Jesús María Elias, a rancher, formulated plans for a raid against the Camp Grant Apaches. Early on the morning of April 28, 148 men—six Anglos, 48 Mexican-Americans and 94 Papagos—assembled at Pantano Wash, far east of the village. There, by prearrangement, they met Sam Hughes, the territorial adjutant general, who issued them a wagonload of government rifles and ammunition. Thus armed, the raiders started north.

They reached the Apache settlement five miles from Camp Grant just before dawn on April 30. Ironically, most of the Apache men were away hunting; only women, children, and a few old men were still asleep in their wickiups. Upon these unfortunates the raiders fell with fury, raping, shooting, stoning, and mutilating their victims. The attack soon ended. Eighty-five Apaches lay dead, all but eight of them women and children. The raiders then set fire to the camp and left, taking with them 28 children whom, by time-honored custom, the Papagos would sell as slaves. Vengeance was complete.

The national furor that erupted when news of the massacre reached the East produced the only benefit connected with the grisly incident, for it prompted the Interior Department to establish regular reservations for Arizona's Apaches. Tucsonians, however, remained defiantly unrepentant. When the attackers went on trial for murder in December 1871, it took a local jury only 19 minutes of deliberation to find them innocent of all charges.

The Camp Grant Massacre was an aberration in an era that otherwise saw much progress toward peace and order. The telegraph reached Tucson late in 1871, further eroding the community's isolation. As the decade progressed, transportation improved, with regular stages to Prescott, the settlements on the Gila, the new farming towns in the Salt River Valley, and, in the late 1870s, to Tombstone. Military campaigning against hostile Indians off the new reservations made Arizona safer than it ever had been before, and settlement thrived. Tucson's population also grew steadily, standing in 1880 at 7,007, once again more than double what it had been 10 years earlier.

The year 1880 was epochal in Tucson's history, for the long-awaited railroad, building east from California, reached the little city that March 20. Ever since the Southern Pacific had crossed the Colorado River into Yuma late in 1877, Tucsonians had been living in a frenzy of expectation; the railroad was a technological marvel that promised to revolutionize the community's life. For the first time, the world would be at Tucson's doorstep, and Tucsonians confidently expected a flood of people from all parts of the globe. The railroad would make it possible to travel almost unimaginably fast—only a day to Los Angeles, for example, and two to San Francisco—and to ship goods at unbelievably low prices: a half cent a pound per 100 miles, as compared to the five to five and a half cents it cost to ship by stage. So most articles would be cheaper, and at the same time there would be a far greater variety of goods than ever before.

Naturally, Tucsonians planned grand festivities for the great day when the first passenger train rolled into the city. Important dignitaries would be aboard—Charles Crocker, one of the Big Four who had built the

Above
Pima County's first courthouse, built in 1868, was a single-story adobe structure whose only concessions to Anglo taste were shutters on some windows and a modest false gable. This 1871 photograph shows the defendants in the Camp Grant Massacre murder trial, with Judge John Titus (center foreground, standing). The raiders were found not guilty after the jury deliberated just 19 minutes.

Opposite
Tucson's first railroad depot was not finished when the Southern Pacific reached the city in March of 1880. Once finished, later that year, it remained in use until 1907.

Left
During the time Levi H. Manning was mayor, he prevailed on the SP to build a new depot, of stuccoed brick with a tiled roof, which was more resistant to fire than the old wooden structure. The second depot still stands.

Central Pacific and now controlled the Southern Pacific; and his son, another Charles, who was president of the Southern Pacific of Arizona. Tucsonians hung bunting in patriotic red, white, and blue across their dirt streets, especially along newly built Toole Avenue, which fronted the tracks. The city's two hotels, the Palace and the Cosmopolitan, were full of would-be revelers.

The train, due at noon, arrived an hour early, so most people who had planned to be present to greet the iron horse missed the show. Mayor Bob Leatherwood, members of the Council, and dignitaries on the reception committee were assembled quickly, however, and toured the train's sumptuous cars. Outside, the 6th Cavalry band blared away in the warm sun, drawing an excited crowd. Various legislators made grandiloquent speeches of welcome. The senior Crocker was presented with a ceremonial silver spike made from the first ore taken out of the fabulous Tough Nut mine in Tombstone and inscribed by Dr. T. S. Hitchcock, a surgeon who doubled as an engraver.

When the festivities finally ended, the dignitaries—and everyone else—adjourned to Levin's Park, Tucson's favorite watering place, where the leading citizens feasted, then, with all their fellow townsmen, spent the rest of the day and most of the night congratulating one another and Tucson on what seemed the most momentous event in the city's history.

Three days before, on March 17, Mayor Leatherwood had dispatched telegrams to dignitaries far and wide, announcing that Tucson was about to be joined by rail to the outside world. In his exuberance, he decided to inform the Pope in Rome and ask his benediction. Probably the message never left the telegraph office, but clerks there, doubtless feeling no pain after the great day's festivities, determined to have a little fun with the city's dignity. Which was why, late in the evening, a telegram was delivered to the mayor at Levin's Park. He opened it and read:

"His Holiness the Pope acknowledges with appreciation receipt of your telegram informing him that the ancient city of Tucson at last has been connected with the outside world and sends his benediction but for his own satisfaction would ask, where in hell is Tucson?"

That was one side of it. The other could be found in the reaction of an 11-year-old Papago girl. "When word came that the iron wagon had come and that it made a screaming sound as it went, I wanted to see it very much," she remembered years later. "So I came with a group of people to see it. They told me that it came early in the morning and that it made a whistling sound. The next morning I watched and saw it come. It brought material of all kinds such as coffee, beans, sugar, dress goods and many other things that the wagon trains usually brought. . . ."

A new era had dawned.

Above
A 4-4-0 locomotive with a diamond stack, such as this one, pulled the first passenger train over the newly laid Southern Pacific tracks into Tucson on March 20, 1880.

Left
The brewery and beer garden at Levin's Park made it Tucson's favorite watering place in the 1880s. Here the entire city came to celebrate the arrival of the railroad.

Post-railroad elegance: John Black's Jewelry Store sold jewelry, clocks, and silverware. The poster in the window advertised a coming performance of the Calhoun Opera Company at Levin's Park. John Black, the proprietor, is second from the left. The Indian at the far right undoubtedly was not a customer.

CIVILIZATION ON THE SANTA CRUZ

Polish-born Philip Drachman came to Arizona in 1863 and established a general merchandise store at the corner of Main Avenue and Congress Street. Later, his son Mose recalled, "he met with business misfortunes — lost everything he had." However, he was successful in begetting children, as he left ten behind him when he died at the age of 58. His descendants still flourish in Tucson.

T he most wonderful scatteration of human habitations [the] eye ever beheld—a city of mud-boxes, dingy and dilapidated; cracked and baked into a composite of dust and filth; littered about with broken corrals, sheds, bake-ovens, carcasses of dead animals, and broken pottery; barren of verdure, parched, naked, and grimly desolate in the glare of a southern sun. Adobe walls without whitewash inside or out, hard earth-floors, baked and dried Mexicans, sore-backed burros, coyote dogs, and terra-cotta children; soldiers, teamsters and honest miners lounging about the mescal-shops, soaked with the fiery poison; a noisy band of Sonoranian buffoons, dressed in theatrical costume, cutting their antics in the public places to the most diabolical din of fiddles and guitars ever heard; a long train of Government wagons preparing to start for Fort Yuma or the Rio Grande— these are what the traveller sees, and a great many things more, but in vain he looks for a hotel or lodging house. The best accommodations he can possibly expect are the dried mud walls of some unoccupied outhouse, with a mud floor for his bed; his own food to eat, and his own cook to prepare it; and lucky is he to possess such luxuries as these."

Thus J. Ross Browne, sailor, civil servant, and inveterate traveler, described Tucson as he saw it in 1864. The "metropolis of Arizona," as he called it with gentle irony, had no appeal for him. He liked best the town's "rear view," seen from the road to Fort Yuma.

Mina Oury, Granville's wife, had no more enthusiasm for the town that was to be her home when she reached it, after a five-month trip, the next year.

"At last we have drifted into port," she confided to her diary, "but alas! I look around with sinking heart and wonder if this can be the goal we have been striving so hard to reach. Excepting the wretched, squalid town of Janos, in Mexico. . .I do not remember ever having seen a less inviting, less promising prospect for a home. Tucson certainly is the most forlorn, dreary, desolate, God-forsaken spot on earth."

Army Lieutenant John Gregory Bourke, who first saw Tucson about 1870, found other curiosities to remark upon. One was the filthy condition of the streets, which gave rise to "a weird system of topographical designation," he noted. " 'You want to find the Governor's? Wa'al, podner, jest keep right down this yere street past the Palace s'loon, till yer gets ter the second manure-pile on yer right; then keep on yer left past the post-office, 'n' yer'll see a dead burro in th' middle of th' road, 'n' a mesquite tree 'n yer lef', near a Mexican *tendajon* [small store], 'n' jes' beyond that's the Gov.'s outfit. Can't miss it. Look out fur th' dawg down ter Muñoz's corral; he's a salviated son ov a gun." Tucsonians, Bourke also noticed, did not date occurrences according to the calendar, but from notable—and bloody—events: "Jes' about th' time Pete Kitchen's ranch was jumped," or "Th' night after Duffield

Left
Five years after Philip Drachman arrived in Tucson, he returned to the East Coast to marry Rosa Katzenstein, whom he brought back to Arizona with him. The couple had ten children, among them Harry, Mose, and Emanuel. Samuel Katzenstein, Rosa's brother, married Albert Steinfeld's sister, Freda. Philip's brother, also named Samuel, was a successful merchant and longtime Tucson civic leader.

Above
Born in Tucson in 1869, Harry Arizona Drachman was the oldest son of Philip and Rosa Drachman and, according to legend, the first white child born in Arizona Territory. This portrait shows him, elegant and serious, at the age of 21.

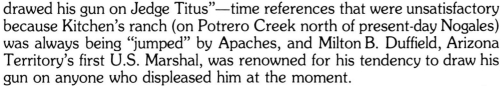

drawed his gun on Jedge Titus"—time references that were unsatisfactory because Kitchen's ranch (on Potrero Creek north of present-day Nogales) was always being "jumped" by Apaches, and Milton B. Duffield, Arizona Territory's first U.S. Marshal, was renowned for his tendency to draw his gun on anyone who displeased him at the moment.

Early in 1869, Harry Arizona Drachman was born in Tucson, the eldest of 10 children of Philip Drachman, a native of Poland who had arrived in the town six years earlier. Late in his life, Harry Drachman recalled the Tucson of his childhood. His parents' home, like all others, had a dirt roof and floor, a ceiling of unbleached muslin (which caught some of the dust), and thick adobe walls that kept out the heat and made Tucson summers bearable in the era before cooling and air conditioning. When it rained, the roof leaked and mud dripped down through the muslin ceiling onto the carpets and furniture below. Drachman remembered the hard work of taking up the carpets, retamping the dirt, beating the rugs, then laying fresh newspapers on the earth so the carpets would not get any dirtier than was necessary.

Most houses had wells behind them. Some householders, like Sam Hughes, had windmills to pump the water; others drew it by bucket. In an era before any municipal sewer system—sewage routinely ended up in the

Above
Mose Drachman, son of Philip and brother of Harry and Emanuel, was one of Tucson's movers and shakers — and also one of its best early historians.

Opposite:
Top Left
Pioneer merchant Albert Steinfeld was a major force in Tucson's economy for nearly half a century. With his wife, Bettina, he also helped establish a new standard of elegance for life in the city.

Top Right
Determined to create a civilized environment for herself and her family in Tucson, Bettina Steinfeld had the city's first bathtub with running water installed in her home, and sent her children to dancing school. "Our mother was determined to have us raised very formally," her daughter recalled.

Center
Sam Hughes had a windmill behind his house on Main Avenue to pump water. Some other Tucsonians had to draw it by bucket or buy it from watermen Joe Phy and Adam Sanders. In this photograph, Hughes is the fourth man from the left. His brother-in-law, Hiram Stevens is to the right of him.

Bottom
Harry Arizona Drachman grew up to found a shoe store. This 1899 photograph shows him in front of his business. A couple of Indians found Drachman's corner a good place to sit and converse.

streets, where it dried if the weather was fine and washed away if it rained—some question existed as to the healthfulness of water out of the wells in town. Two enterprising men, Adam Sanders and Joe Phy, had an artesian well west of El Tiradito and made a good business selling water for five cents a bucket. If their customers had no money available, the watermen would tally up the charge on the door frame. Anyone could have cheated by changing the marks, but no one did. "Everyone had confidence in one another," Drachman remembered. "Doors were never locked and I never carried a gun, never was stopped or held up at night, although the streets were not lighted until the gas was put in." That event occurred in 1882, when Drachman was 13 years old.

The Tucson of Harry Drachman's youth was a small town. It extended really no farther than Stone Avenue on the east, although there were a few houses on Congress Street beyond Stone and growth tended in that direction. To the north, Alameda marked the edge of town, though Sam Hughes, Hiram Stevens, and E. N. Fish lived north of it along Main Avenue. Main also was the western boundary, while Kennedy Street was the southern edge. Most of the business centered on Congress west of Church Street, but Meyer and Mesilla streets claimed their share of the town's commerce.

Tucson's recreations in the 1870s were much as they had been for a century. Periodically, Mexican circuses (Browne's "Sonoranian buffoons") came to town. If it was summer, admission to the sunny side cost a quarter, while it took 50 cents to look on from the shade. In winter, the situation was reversed. Every summer there were two fiestas—one on San Juan's Day (June 24), when the whole town got drunk; the other beginning on San Agustín's Day (August 28) and lasting about two weeks. At other times, there were cockfights and horse races and *bailes,* to which respectable girls invariably came chaperoned by mothers or maiden aunts. Officers at Fort Lowell, seven miles from town, held dances for the young ladies of Tucson; the young ladies reciprocated, much to the envy of their would-be swains in town. There also were saloons, where men repaired to drink and gamble at faro and monte, but women did not. Establishments that sold both liquor and food had family entrances separate from those used by the drinkers and gamblers.

When Harry Drachman was 14, Albert Steinfeld—then 28—brought his formally educated bride, Bettina, to Tucson, and shortly after began raising a family. Tucson had no conveniences such as the new Mrs. Steinfeld was used to, but she undertook to create a civilized environment for herself and her family. It included the town's first bathtub with running water, and dancing school for her children. "Our mother was determined to have us raised very formally," recalled Bettina Steinfeld's daughter, Irene Pizzini.

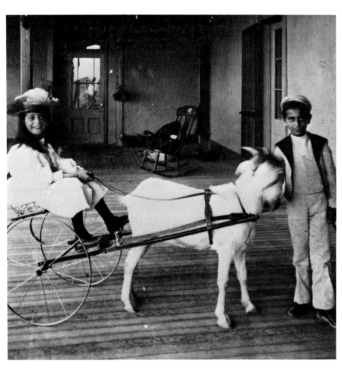

Left
Harold Steinfeld and his sister Irene (later Mrs. Andrew Pizzini) with goat and cart. "Our only problem was to keep the goat from eating the decor."

Right
This unindentified Tucson hotel doubtless offered Spartan accommodations in the days before the railroad connected the city with the rest of the nation and brought an influx of tourists and settlers to Southern Arizona.

She carried her dancing slippers to classes in a velvet bag, wore white gloves, and learned to curtsy to the dancing master.

For such sheltered children, summers must have dragged monotonously. But even they discovered that one could keep cool—at least less warm—by walking down Congress Street and stopping at the entrance of one of the saloons, for the swinging doors stirred the air and created an illusion of freshness, even as the "twinkling music" of the player piano within contrasted with the braying of burros on the street.

Fourth of July parades were high points in the life of the Steinfeld household. The children had a little goat cart that they decorated and drove at the end of the column. "Our only problem," Mrs. Pizzini recalled, "was to keep the goat from eating the decor."

Dancing school and goat carts—Tucson was growing up. The prime instrument of change was the railroad, whose arrival in 1880 truly marked the watershed in Tucson's history. But there were other institutions, both technological and cultural, that also charted the evolution.

Much of the change the railroad wrought was physical. The rails brought people of all backgrounds and races who had come from every part of the world. Most were decent, law-abiding folk who came for legitimate reasons of business, health, and sometimes recreation, but others migrated for less honorable motives. These were the shysters, the crooked gamblers,

and the outlaws. Most of them went to Tombstone, which until the mid-1880s remained wide open, but enough of them stayed in Tucson to trouble the city's peace quite considerably throughout the decade.

Even more than people, the railroad brought a wild profusion of things—bolts of silk, sewing machines, beaded lampshades, Grecian statuettes, rifles, porcelain ewers, ladies' high-button shoes and gentlemen's boots, saddles, canned oysters, steamboat-Gothic furniture, Persian rugs, books. And bricks and wood, which now traveled at freight rates low enough that men could afford to build with them—could ornament the houses that already stood, putting fashionable pitched roofs onto the broad, low adobes, and could build new ones that soared two or three stories high, to be adorned with broad verandas and the endless gingerbread of which the late nineteenth century was so fond.

So the city's face changed. The farther north one went along Main Avenue, the city's choicest residential thoroughfare, the more ornate and elegant the structures became. No more flat facades flush with the street, but houses set back, separated from the concourse of people and animals by green lawns, another novelty. Meanwhile, an entirely new neighborhood grew up in the two decades after the railroad's arrival, its growth a direct outcome of the Southern Pacific's presence. This was Armory Park, situated south of the tracks—the right side, there being nothing substantial except

Left
The railroad brought Tucson a wild profusion of things, of which the most important was wood. This 1891 photograph of the Tucson Lumber Co. yard suggests, by the amount of wood on hand, how popular the material had become.

Right
After the railroad's arrival made it possible to import all goods more cheaply than before, George Martin Sr. (at left) opened a drugstore in 1883. By 1891 the store had moved to 28 West Congress Street, where this photograph was taken.

the fledgling University of Arizona on the other. Some of the neighborhood stood on the land used by Camp Lowell before its move to the Rillito River in 1873. Armory Park to this day reveals the variety of styles and materials that builders and owners found beautiful and utilitarian before the turn of the century.

For some Tucsonians, however, the coming of the railroad proved a misfortune rather than a blessing. Instead of benefiting from the availability of cheap freight to obtain low-cost goods, most of Tucson's largest merchants suffered because they could not dispose profitably of their expensive inventories in the face of new competition.

Particularly hard hit were the great freighting firms. There was a savage irony in the fact that Estevan Ochoa was chosen by his fellow citizens to present the silver spike to Charles Crocker the day the first train reached Tucson, for Ochoa's firm failed because of railroad competition. So did Lord & Williams, which crashed down in 1881—partly because of dilatory government payments but primarily because no wagon freighter could compete with railroad rates. Safford, Hudson & Co., one of Tucson's first banks, failed in 1884; William Zeckendorf had gone under a year earlier. Solomon Warner closed his mill in 1881, about the same time that Hiram Stevens began having the business difficulties that eventually drove him to suicide. The railroad decimated Tucson's business community even as it benefited the mass of the city's citizens.

Some changes antedated the railroad. By 1880, for example, Tucson had three newspapers. Not quite 10 years before, in October of 1870, the weekly Arizona Citizen made its debut under the proprietorship of John Wasson, one of territorial Arizona's most distinguished journalists. Its initial cause was the candidacy of Richard C. McCormick for another term as delegate to Congress, but once that battle was won, it branched out into the broader concerns of the town and territory. When a bitter editorial feud resulted in the demise of The Weekly Arizonian the next spring, the Citizen commenced a monopoly of Tucson's news market that was broken only in 1877, when Louis C. Hughes, a lawyer and brother of Sam's, had a hand in founding the Daily Bulletin. Within a month the sheet, by then a triweekly, had been renamed the Star. That summer, it became weekly and, early in 1879, daily. A month later, the Citizen, then under the ownership of former Indian agent John P. Clum, followed suit.

Meanwhile, in 1877, Carlos H. Tully, son of Pinckney R. and partner with Hughes in the Star, had founded Las Dos Republicas, Tucson's first Spanish-language newspaper and reportedly the one with the largest circulation within two American territories and three Mexican states. Its popularity did not give it long life, however; it went out of business in 1879. Its demise probably resulted from the founding, the previous year, of El Fronterizo, a

Top
The first Grace Episcopal Church, built at the corner of Camp Street (now Broadway) and Stone Avenue in 1889, did not reflect Southern Arizona's architectural heritage. This church stood for more than twenty years.

Above
Begun in 1862 and finished in 1870, the Roman Catholic cathedral church of San Agustín was the earliest permanent Christian church in American Tucson. This photograph was made in 1880. Seventeen years later, the diocese of Tucson built a new cathedral and sold this one, which was converted into a hotel.

weekly, also in Spanish. Carlos I. Velasco, its originator, published it continuously until 1914.

Throughout the West, newspapers were an ambitious pledge of a town's permanence and maturity. So were churches and schools. Tucson saw the beginnings of both in the decades before the coming of the railroad.

Among the denominations, the first to take hold in American Tucson was the Roman Catholic, a fact related more to working ecclesiastical organization than to the religious traditions of the community. Indeed, in the last years of Mexican dominion, the Church had been more conspicuous for its absence than for its presence. After the Gadsden Purchase, however, the Holy See assigned Tucson to the Diocese of Santa Fe, whose energetic prelate, Bishop Jean Baptiste Lamy, determined that the town, overwhelmingly Catholic, should have a ministry appropriate to its needs. In 1859, Lamy sent Father Joseph Machebeuf, another Frenchman, to survey church matters in Arizona. Machebeuf found no church building within or near Tucson that was in good enough repair to hold a Mass. A two-room house was offered, then extended by the addition of a porch. At that point, unfortunately, Lamy recalled Machebeuf to Santa Fe.

The next priest to arrive in Tucson, Father Donato Rogieri, came probably in 1862, and it was he who began construction of the first San Agustín church west of present-day Church Street between Broadway and

Congress. Father Donato would celebrate Mass, then ask his congregation to wait until he changed out of his vestments. Then the entire flock, led by the priest, would troop down about a half mile to the site where the adobes were made. Each would pick up a brick, return to the church, and add it to the growing walls.

Father Donato left Tucson after only a year, leaving behind an unfinished church and a congregation hungry for further ministry. Yet it was early in 1866 before Lamy could send another priest to Tucson. That priest was Jean Baptiste Salpointe. He remained in Tucson 19 years, became the first vicar apostolic (with the rank of bishop) when the vicariate was established in 1868, built the church up from scratch, and introduced parochial education into Tucson. As a spiritual force he was formidable; as a man, much beloved.

Although occasional Protestant clergymen—and in 1874 even an Episcopal bishop—visited Tucson to preach and see to the needs of the town's non-Catholic Christians, no Protestant denomination established itself permanently until a Presbyterian congregation was organized in 1876. Three years later, its parishioners built a large adobe church where city hall now stands. In 1879, a Baptist church was founded, and so was a Methodist Episcopal congregation, which built a church at the corner of Pennington Street and Stone Avenue. Late in 1881, 21 men and women met to form

Two views of post-railroad Tucson. (a) Sunset Park (the Plaza de las Armas of presidial days and El Presidio Park today), with the Presbyterian Church behind and, on the other side of Alameda Street, the Jacobs home, a two-story Victorian adobe. (b) Alameda Street, with Sunset Park and the church on the left, and the Jacobs house on the right.

Grace Episcopal Church. The group included some of Tucson's most prosperous citizens: Mayor John S. Carr, banker Charles Hudson, and U.S. Attorney Everett Pomeroy. They evidently had no difficulty pledging the munificent sum of $1,250 to get the enterprise going. About seven and a half years later, on April 30, 1889, Bishop John Mills Kendrick laid the cornerstone for the first Grace Church building at the southwest corner of Camp Street (now Broadway) and Stone Avenue.

Other Christian denominations established themselves in Tucson as time went by, including the city's first African Methodist Episcopal Church, the Prince Chapel, soon after 1900. But the Jews, already an influential if not a numerous minority by the time the railroad came through Tucson, did not. Some among their number felt the lack of regular opportunities for worship.

Isadore Gotthelf, who came to Tucson early in 1880, remembered that, when the High Holy Days came that year, "I got a list of all the Jewish citizens of Tucson, and with my brothers, Jake and Dave, appealed to them to help us form a congregation. We then went to Alex Levin, who agreed to lend us the Hall at Levin's Park. I held the Services and gave the sermon, aided by Sam Drachman. Then, for quite a few years, services for the holidays were held at the home of Julius Wittelshoefer, where Joe Goldtree Bar Mitzvahed his son, Morris. By that time (about 1892) we had a Torah."

Early in 1904, a group of Jewish women met in Tucson to form an aid society. A year later, under the aegis of Clara Ferrin, a campaign began to raise funds for a synagogue. The structure, built on South Stone Avenue at a cost of slightly more than $4700, opened for worship on Rosh Hashana Eve, October 3, 1910. It was Temple Emanu-El, the first synagogue in Arizona Territory.

In territorial Tucson, the needs of philanthropy often exceeded the ability of a particular group to raise funds. At such times, a real community cohesiveness asserted itself. Jacob S. Mansfeld, who reached Tucson in the early months of 1870, recalled that the Anglo population then numbered about 200. "They were a good Set of People and No Lines were drawn in Society; Society in fact did not Exist. To the Credit of the Pioneers of this Town it should for Ever be remembered, that they were a generous People; if a Church or a School was to be established the Pioneer whether Catholic, Protestant, Jew or Infidel gave freely to help others not asking any Questions about Religion, or Nationality. . . Unity and good feelings among the Citizens of this Town made Tucson in Early Days as good a Place as could be found any weres on this Coast."

Formal education, like the churches, began in Tucson in the years before the railroad came. As early as the fall of 1867, the Pima County Board of Supervisors created Tucson School District 1 (now Tucson Unified School District) to encompass all the land "within one mile each way from

the Plaza de la Mesilla" in what then was the center of the town. The first school, probably located near Levin's Park at the foot of Pennington Street, opened the following January with Augustus Brichta its sole teacher. Fifty-five Mexican boys were enrolled, but Brichta, educated in Cuba, was bilingual and took the class in stride. What he could not overcome, however, was a shortage of funds that closed the school in six months, leaving him unpaid for the last two.

In the late 1860s, pressures mounted for something more than a nominal educational system. In 1867, Salpointe began planning a convent school to adjoin the church he was building; indeed, the walls of both structures went up simultaneously. The fact that he counted on popular enthusiasm for the school to supply the energy for roofing both buildings said a good deal about the impatience of Tucsonians for some institution of formal learning. So did the grand reception—with fireworks, torches, and a cast exuberantly estimated at 3000—that greeted the Sisters of St. Joseph of Carondelet when they reached Tucson on May 17, 1870, after a harrowing

Opposite:
Top
Tucson's first permanent public school was built at the corner of Congress Street and Sixth Avenue in 1875. Estevan Ochoa gave the land on which it stood to the school district, and contributed more than $5,000 out of his own pocket to complete the building. It remained the only public school until 1884, when the Plaza School (later renamed for Governor Safford) was opened.

Bottom
This imposing late territorial building in the Armory Park neighborhood was the second home of St. Joseph's Academy. From there, the school moved out to the Villa Carondelet east of present-day St. Joseph's Hospital.

trip from Omaha via San Francisco, San Diego, and Yuma, to take up their duties as teachers in the desert. Their school, variously known as the Convent School, St. Joseph's, and the Villa Carondelet, educated young women in Tucson for 99 years.

Under the prodding of Governor Anson P. K. Safford and Estevan Ochoa, public education in Tucson soon revived. Safford rammed a school bill—and tax—through the territorial legislature in 1871, over the opposition of lawmakers who held that the dangers of Apache raiding were so great as to make schools unnecessary. Ochoa introduced the bill and later gave—or sold for a nominal sum—the land at the corner of Congress Street and Sixth Avenue where Tucson's first permanent school stood. He followed this generosity by contributing more than $5000 out of his own pocket to complete the building, which opened in the fall of 1875.

Even before this, there had been another school, located at McCormick and Meyer streets, at which Swiss-born John Spring educated about 100 boys ranging in age from six to 21, in Spanish, English, math, drawing, hygiene, penmanship, and punctuality. Discipline was strict under the former soldier and brewmaster, and thrashings frequent. The boys learned.

Early in 1873, after a year of being the school's only teacher, Spring went to the school board to request either an assistant to teach the lower grades or an increase in salary from $125 to $150 a month, so he could hire one out of his own pocket. The board turned him down on both counts, the members saying they could hire two women for the salary they paid him. Spring then resigned, and the board proceeded to hire its schoolmarms: Maria Wakefield and Harriet Bolton, both unattached and attractive. They reached Tucson that November. By the middle of the next year, E. N. Fish, a widower, had taken Miss Wakefield as his second wife, while editor Wasson had married Miss Bolton. Both ladies then retired from the academic arena.

During Spring's tenure as schoolmaster, Josephine B. Hughes, a formidable crusader and wife of the *Star's* editor, opened a girls' school in the old Pioneer Brewing building at Levin's Park. To an ardent temperance advocate, the location doubtless seemed unfortunate, though probably it did not lead to the illness that forced Mrs. Hughes to close the school permanently in May of 1873, after only five months of operation. But her school, though short-lived, opened the way for various other experiments in private education. In 1874, a parochial school for boys, San Agustín's, opened at the corner of Stone Avenue and Ochoa Street. Thereafter, a lively and not always pleasant competition began between the church and the public school for male students. By 1881, two other private schools had come into

existence, the Modern School of Carrillo's Gardens and Leceo Mario on Cushing Street. Both were coeducational and had primarily Mexican-American youngsters. Neither lasted long.

Meanwhile, by the mid-'70s, public education had become permanent. It had its vicissitudes in the early days, such as the time late in the

Above
Pima County legislator C.C. Stephens made his constituents so angry by getting only the University of Arizona, rather than some more lucrative prize, for them that he was threatened with physical violence when he got home. As a result, he "had a large Negro named Garcia go about with him when he appeared on the streets."

Opposite:
Top
Architect Henry Trost, who designed the Carnegie Free Library building on South Sixth Avenue, also designed the first Drachman School, which stood at 17th Street and Convent Avenue. This photograph was taken before 1910.

Center
Members of the Tucson High School band, directed by Arthur W. Sewell, posed aboard their rented truck in front of the Santa Rita Hotel.

Bottom
The original Holladay School, begun in 1901 and completed the next year, was one of the first schools built north of the railroad tracks. It stood on the site now occupied by Tucson High School, and was demolished in 1923 to make way for that institution, which opened the next year.

decade when 75 percent of the students were withdrawn by their parents because the principal of the Congress Street School decided to educate boys and girls in the same classrooms. The boycott ended after a week, and education resumed. By 1881, the school, still the only public institution in the city, had four teachers. Nine years later, School District 1 could boast three schools, including the one built in 1884 and known as the Plaza School, which in 1910 was renamed for Governor Safford. Although the area was growing, there had been some objection to building a school so far east of town; citizens feared that roving Apaches might attack the children.

Teachers of the primary grades were paid $70 a month, while those teaching the more advanced grammar grades received $75. Top pay on this not very lavish pay schedule subsequently was increased to $80 a month, when it was discovered that janitors in the system received $70.

The decade of the '90s saw two other Tucson school districts established—Amphitheater and Fort Lowell—while the next decade, the first of the new century, found District 1 starting to build north of the railroad tracks, at Roskruge and the site now occupied by Tucson High School.

Ironically, Tucsonians neither sought the University of Arizona, its greatest educational institution, nor welcomed its prospect when the territorial legislature offered it in 1885. The legislature was in a dispensing mood, handing out such plums as a territorial insane asylum, prison, and normal school as well as a university. Tucson, meanwhile, still resented the loss of the capital to Prescott eight years before, and influential citizens armed businessman Fred Maish with $5000 to lobby for its return. Maish reached Prescott when the session was well under way. Not only did he fail to get the capital back; he also arrived too late to secure any of the legislature's choicest gifts. Phoenix, the upstart town on the Salt River, not even 20 years old, would get the coveted insane asylum; Yuma would get the prison; the normal school would go to Tempe. The university—the crumbs of patronage—was allotted to Tucson. Worse still, it developed, Tucson's two legislators, C. C. Stephens in the upper house and Selim M. Franklin in the lower, actually had proposed the legislation that perpetrated this outrage on the city.

Tucsonians were furious. They felt cheated. Without a high school anywhere in the territory, it surpassed imagination how a university could convey any economic benefit on the city. A bartender in one of the saloons summed up the community's anguish: "What do we want with a university? What good will it do us? Who in hell ever heard of a university professor buying a drink?"

Stephens caught the brunt of his fellow citizens' wrath when he returned to Tucson. According to Mose Drachman, Harry's brother, the legislator was threatened with bodily injury and, as a result, "had a large

Negro named Garcia go about with him when he appeared on the streets. He called a meeting at the Opera House to explain why he had favored the university—why it was greater than anything else in the state [sic]. In that meeting, rotten eggs were freely hurled at him. He told them sadly that the day would come when Tucson would thank him for his work."

The *Citizen* did not think so. A series of editorials in March of 1885 excoriated the hapless Stephens as "a dirty bird that befouls its own nest" and "a shystering nincompoop." "The citizens of Tucson have no further use for you, Mr. Stephens," thundered editor Sam Manlove, "and we beg leave to inform you that we are not speaking for the *Arizona Citizen* but for the bona fide taxpayers and citizens of Tucson who look upon you with loathing and contempt, as a man who has betrayed his trust and is no longer worthy of their countenance or consideration." Speculating on the purpose for Stephens' existence, Manlove could find none, except "to make a horse thief feel respectable by comparison."

The legislature had appropriated $25,000 for the university, and bonds were to be sold by a certain date to raise the money. But Tucsonians, staggered by their ill fortune, did nothing. At length the bonds were marketed and the proceeds deposited with the territorial treasurer. Thereupon, a group of citizens began talking about using the money to find artesian wells for the city. Fortunately, Jacob Mansfeld, a member of the first board of regents, squelched the idea. Then another problem arose: Tucson's use of the $25,000 depended upon the city's securing—on its own—40 acres of land for the university. Needless to say, no one came forward to volunteer a donation, but once again Mansfeld came through, persuading gamblers E. B. Gifford and Ben Parker and saloonkeeper William S. Reid to give the territory the required acreage. The land, on a rise about three miles from the town, appeared completely useless, and Gifford, Parker, and Reid must have laughed at the impracticality of even thinking of building a university on it. Nevertheless, planning went forward and ground was broken for a building that would house all the classrooms and offices the institution would need.

Unfortunately, the plan turned out to be extravagant. That is, the cellar and two stories were built, together with verandas on all four sides. Then the money gave out, and Tucsonians had to go back to the legislature, hats in hand, for a supplemental appropriation to provide a roof. The lawmakers provided what was needed, and the university opened October 1, 1891, with a tiny class, most of whose 32 members were in the high-school division. The university continued to offer a high school as well as a college curriculum for 24 years.

It was a modest enough start for an institution that now boasts of being one of the best in the American Southwest.

The office of the Tucson Gas & Electric Light Power Company, formed in 1895, boasted an electric sign exhorting Tucsonians to be modern and cook with gas.

GROWING UP

The increase in Tucson's stability in the 1870s and 1880s resulted, at least in part, from the fact that the Apache menace at last had begun to recede. The government started a permanent reservation system in the early '70s, and though Tucsonians mistrusted it for years, Indian agents beginning with John P. Clum made it work. Arizona became safer for settlement after 1874 than it ever had been before, and Tucson, the center of the territory's population and trade, benefited accordingly. Even the resurgence of Apache troubles that began with Geronimo's outbreak from the San Carlos reservation in the fall of 1881 had little effect on the city. Apprehensions revived and a party of Tucsonians organized to stage another Camp Grant massacre. Fortunately, nothing came of their efforts. Mariano G. Samaniego, a prominent Tucson businessman, lost a wagon train carrying food and goods from Willcox to San Carlos; his brother Bartolo was killed in the Apache attack. This tragedy aside, Tucson did not suffer, although everyone breathed easier after Army Lieutenant Charles B. Gatewood flushed the last of the renegades out of the mountains of northern Mexico in the fall of 1886, and General Nelson A. Miles shipped them, and all of Arizona's other Chiricahua Apaches, off to prison in Florida.

Fourteen months later, on November 8, 1887, Tucson put on a great parade, reception, and ball to honor Miles, whom they also presented with a handsome, ceremonial dress sword. Miles, a man of monstrous ego and great meanness, arranged that Gatewood should not be present at the festivities nor receive any public acknowledgment of his role in Geronimo's surrender.

Despite a protracted business decline between 1884 and 1896 that actually resulted in a loss of population for the city, Tucson matured rapidly in the years after the railroad came. There were two hotels, the Palace and the Cosmopolitan, in 1880. Overcrowding in them convinced the Southern Pacific to build another; the San Xavier, a handsome, two-story structure with verandas clear around and a fashionable gabled roof, opened in 1881. Being next to the railroad station and built of wood, it was inevitable that the San Xavier eventually would catch a live spark from the stack of an SP locomotive and burn—and so it did in 1903. By that time, however, other hostelries had opened up, notable among them the Orndorff, at the corner of Pennington Street and Main Avenue, known as the best place in town to meet and eat and the leading bachelor residence; and the San Augustine, housed in what until 1897 had been the cathedral church of the Roman Catholid vicariate apostolic. When the present cathedral was opened in that year, Salpointe's successor, Bishop Peter Bourgade, sold the old one over the protests of most of Tucson's older residents, and it began a series of weird permutations that saw it become, in Harry Drachman's words, a "hotel, cheap hotel, cheaper hotel, whorehouse, taxi stand, garage, service

Levi H. Manning, Tucson's premier businessman in the 1890s and the first decades of the new century, completed the Santa Rita Hotel, was the first president of the Tucson Chamber of Commerce, owned the land on which Tucson's first airport was built, and participated in every civic endeavor. Because he was Surveyor General for Arizona during Grover Cleveland's second administration, he was thereafter known as "General Manning."

station, bootleg headquarters, fight arena, etc." At length, over heated objections, it was demolished in 1936, but Tucson newspaper executive and civic leader George W. Chambers preserved the splendid stone facade and rose window carved in the early 1880s by Jules Le Flein. They now form the facade of the Arizona Historical Society.

Meanwhile, in 1901, a bedbug bite in an unidentified hotel convinced Los Angeles businessman L. V. Raphael—who had commercial connections in Tucson and came often to the city—that it needed a new, modern hotel. Raphael discussed the idea with Levi H. Manning, Tucson's leading businessman, who secured the business community's support and the City Council's assent. After numerous setbacks and delays—caused by Raphael's going broke when the building was only half finished—Manning bought the project and pushed it to completion. The Santa Rita Hotel opened in February of 1904, with five stories and the city's first real dance floor. It was beyond question the most elegant establishment in the city's history. Two thousand people, one seventh of Tucson's entire population, attended its grand opening, and the *Citizen* devoted three front-page columns to the event.

Post-railroad Tucson for the first time found itself able to take enough time from duty to relax. Opportunities for recreation and relaxation developed to meet the demand. West of Main Avenue and south of Simpson, Leopoldo Carrillo had 13 acres with assorted attractions: flower gardens and shrubs; three willow-shaded ponds (which passed in the press of the 1880s for "lakes"), complete with rowboats; a dance pavilion, restaurant, and bar; and even a small zoo. Carrillo's Gardens soon overshadowed Levin's Park and became, by the '90s, Tucson's main amusement spot. In 1903, Emanuel Drachman—brother of Harry and Mose—bought the property and, with a fine classical touch, renamed it the Elysian Grove. It continued as a park until the city acquired the land and subdivided it in 1921. Only the Carrillo School, built in 1930 on what had been the eastern edge of the Gardens, perpetuates the original name.

Outside the city were other, more substantial lakes: a mile and a half to the south, Silver Lake, impounded by a dam built by Fred Maish and Thomas Driscoll, owners of the Palace Hotel; and to the west by Sentinel Peak, Warner's Lake, which spread behind a dyke that dated from Spanish times and whose waters drove Warner's mill. Silver Lake especially became a popular resort, and Maish and Driscoll improved its success by building bathhouses and a two-story hotel with dining room and bar below and rooms above. For some years, particularly after regular coach service from the city began, Silver Lake was the favorite place to take a Sunday picnic and, in the summer, to swim. In time, however, gentle folk took to picnicking at Sabino Canyon and swimming at the new natatorium in town, and Silver Lake

Top
An unidentified patriotic occasion gathered this group of rather purposeful-looking merrymakers at Seward Restaurant, on Congress Street just off Stone Avenue, in the early 1890s. Louis C. Hughes, editor of the *Arizona Star* and at this time governor of Arizona Territory, is at the far right.

Center Left
The Santa Rita Hotel represented a standard of luxury the city had never known before. The great lobby, with columns and balcony, was the hotel's showplace.

Above
Fred Maish and Thomas Driscoll dammed Silver Lake and built the two-story Silver Lake Hotel (right) in the 1880s. A favorite spot for Tucsonians for several years, it later became a place of rendezvous for the sporting element. When the hotel burned in the 1890s, it was not rebuilt.

Center Right
One of the main amusement spots in post-railroad Tucson was Carrillo's Gardens — thirteen acres of gardens, ponds and other attractions located where Carrillo School now stands. This 1887 photograph suggests that it must have been a very pleasant place to spend an afternoon in the late spring.

Top Left
Emanuel Drachman, son of Philip and brother of Harry and Mose, bought Carrillo Gardens in 1903 and renamed it the Elysian Grove. There he showed the first movies ever shown in Tucson, and also sponsored the city's first aviation show.

Right
Jacob S. Mansfeld came to Tucson in the early months of 1870, and founded the Pioneer News Depot, the town's first lending library.

Opposite
Top Left
This large crowd — including burros — gathered at the theater at Levin's Park at the western end of Pennington Street to attend a performance by the Calhoun Opera Company in the 1890s. Presumably, the burros were excluded from the theater.

Right
Jacob S. Mansfeld's Pioneer News Depot was Tucson's first lending library. Mansfeld (in the background, left) also sold newspapers, garlic, cigars and tools.

Center
Billy Reid's Opera Saloon and Felix Levy's Opera Bath House, which stood next to each other on Pennington Street in the 1890s, probably helped draw business to Reid's Opera House.

Bottom
Bishop Jean Baptiste Salpointe yielded to the urging of the Southern Pacific Railroad and directed the Sisters of St. Joseph of Carondelet to open a hospital. St. Mary's, Tucson's first civilian hospital, opened in April, 1880, with twelve beds. This photograph was made that same year.

became a place of rendezvous for the sporting element. When the hotel burned in the 1890s it was not rebuilt, and the dam itself washed out in the great flood of 1900. Contemporary Tucson's only reminder of the lake is Silverlake Road, a stretch of 29th Street that crosses the dry riverbed of the Santa Cruz, then loses its identity in Mission Road.

Theaters also made their appearance in Tucson around the time the railroad did, although with Victorian grandiloquence they generally were labeled opera houses. Alex Levin, genial host of Levin's Park, built one in 1878 that reportedly could accommodate 2000 patrons, though surely the number was exaggerated. By the mid-'90s, William Reid's Opera House, on Pennington and Meyer streets, was doing a healthy business, due perhaps partly to the fact that Reid's saloon and a public bathhouse adjoined it. After Emanuel Drachman took over the Elysian Grove, he too built a theater and for a time had a resident acting company.

The growth of popular culture in Tucson had a more serious side as well. In 1871, Jacob Mansfeld started the town's first lending library out of his Pioneer News Depot. For a long time it remained the principal source of reading matter for Tucsonians, although the Southern Pacific provided a reading room for its employees that adjoined their bunkhouse north of the railroad tracks, and, in the '80s, there was a tiny municipal library opposite Sunset Park. In time the city applied for a library endowment from Andrew Carnegie. He gave one and, in 1900, the handsome library building that still stands opposite Armory Park on South Sixth Avenue was built.

Along with increasing care for the enlightenment of its citizens, Tucson also began considering their physical well-being. Not strangely, the Southern Pacific took the lead in this, its officers doubtless realizing that not only railroad workers but passengers as well would need skilled medical attention from time to time. Even before the railroad reached Tucson, the company had gotten in touch with Bishop Salpointe and asked him to consider starting a hospital. Salpointe had had an Indian school in mind, but, good citizen that he was, he also understood the railroad's logic. St. Mary's Hospital, staffed by the Sisters of St. Joseph of Carondelet, opened its doors April 24, 1880, with 12 beds. The Indian school came along later—under the auspices of the Presbyterian Board of Home Missions.

In the years after the coming of the railroad, Tucson experienced an explosion of useful technology, each part of which citizens greeted with the enthusiasm reserved only for the great god progress. The year 1881 saw the creation of Tucson's first telephone exchange—just five years after Alexander Graham Bell had invented the instrument. From the exchange, located next to the post office, Tucsonians could call all over the city. The same year, the Tucson Land and Street Railway Co. was chartered by P. R. Tully, J. S. Wood, and James Buell.

Above Right
Participants in a popular sport of the 1890s, this crew of Tucson bicyclists seemed intent on proving that the "bicycle built for two" was not a vehicle for romance only.

Opposite:
Top
As late as 1909, Tucson's fire department still relied on horses to provide the mobility the force badly needed. The horses, for their part, look fairly enthusiastic about their work.

Right
Arizona Commandery No. 1 of the Knights Templar attracted the allegiance of many of Tucson's leading citizens, including Louis C. and Sam Hughes, Charles T. Etchells and surveyor general George J. Roskruge.

The arrival of the railroad had spurred various intracity public transport schemes, simply because the depot was three quarters of a mile from the business district, while other attractions such as Silver Lake were more distant still. The charterers of the Land and Street Railway firm were interested in providing transportation, but they also wanted to sell the land Buell had northeast of the city and north of the tracks. The best way to make this distant and inaccessible land attractive seemed to be to provide transportation to it. The company failed, however, and the street railway to Buell's addition remained a dream. Although various taxi and transit services took hold in town, no streetcars appeared until 1898.

The year 1881 also saw one Sylvester Watts of Albuquerque begin Tucson's first municipal water system. The water that started flowing through city mains a year later was drinkable; there also was enough of it to use for fire protection, and the city installed 35 hydrants. The same year, Tucsonians also organized a volunteer fire department. Two years later, a new city charter provided for a regular department. A hand-drawn hook-and-ladder truck appeared on the scene in 1886, along with a hose and two hose carts.

The coming of a municipal water system ushered in the era of indoor plumbing, and paved the way for Bettina Steinfeld's bathtub. Others followed where she led, and by the turn of the century bathing at home became almost a commonplace. This development marked the beginning of the end for Tucson's public bathhouses, the first of which had been founded by Samuel Bostwick, the town's earliest black businessman, in 1869.

On March 20, 1882, two years to the day after the arrival of the railroad, gas lights made their first appearance in Tucson. The *Star* proudly pointed out that its offices and Louis Zeckendorf's store were ablaze with this newest convenience. Other businesses hastened to follow suit. So did the city fathers, and Tucson's major streets soon had lights. Electricity also came in 1882, but it did not succeed immediately. Not until 1895 did Tucson have functioning, dependable electric service.

Paralleling these technological developments, Tucson society also developed, moving away from the arcadian age Jacob Mansfeld had described. By the early '80s, a host of fraternal organizations were springing up: a lodge of Masons, one of Odd Fellows, one of the Ancient Order of United Workingmen, a Turn Verein, a division of the Brotherhood of Locomotive Engineers. Knights of Pythias appeared; so did Knights of Columbus in plumed magnificence. Women stayed at home, venturing abroad—if at all—to the sewing circle or the ladies' aid society.

Organizations like the Masons, Odd Fellows, and Knights of Pythias had predominantly Anglo membership, a fact emblematic of a dawning ethnic consciousness in the post-railroad era. On their side, the city's

Mexican-Americans also began forming social and fraternal groups with the long-term purpose of preserving and perpetuating their Hispanic heritage. The first of these societies, the *Junta Patriotica Mexicana,* emerged as early as 1885, and was primarily social. Nine years after its founding, the *Alianza Hispano-Americana* was born in the print shop on West Cushing Street where Carlos Velasco published *El Fronterizo.*

The *Alianza,* the longest-lived and most influential of all Tucson's Mexican-American organizations, began—according to some accounts—as a political club. If so, it soon changed, becoming fraternal and protective. It also functioned as an insurance company, writing mainly life insurance for its members. From the first, the *Alianza* was successful; it began branching in 1895, the year after it was founded, and within 35 years had 240 lodges in six Western states and Mexico. At its apogee, its membership numbered about 20,000.

In the 86 years since the founding of the *Alianza,* Tucson has seen numerous Mexican-American organizations, spanning a range of activities from social friendship to political activism and from neighborhood rehabilitation to the promotion of intercultural understanding. Some have passed into history; others remain as vital forces in contemporary Tucson. Past and present, they have done a great deal to unify Tucson's Mexican-American community and to preserve the cultural diversity that is one of the city's greatest assets.

Some of the early Anglo organizations furnished aid more tangible than mere companionship to their members. One such was the group first called the Camp Street Mess and later known as the Owl's Club. Another, founded in 1907, was the Old Pueblo Club, "a gentlemen's club for social purposes." Both originally came into being to provide their members—all bachelors in the case of the Owl's Club—a place where they could live and eat in congenial company and at reasonable cost.

The Owls around the turn of the century built a splendid large house on the west side of Main Street. When matrimony or mortality reduced their number to three, they sold the property to Levi Manning, who in turn sold it to Albert Steinfeld. Manning went on to build the elegant mansion on the Paseo Redondo that now houses the Elks Club. Both it and the Steinfeld house became the apogee of elegance of which Bettina had dreamed. The Old Pueblo Club, on the other hand, began its life in the respectable but less elegant building on the southeast corner of Stone Avenue and Jackson Street—a structure brand new in 1907 and adjoining the hospital owned and run by Dr. Mark A. Rodgers, the club's first president.

In 1884, probably stunned by the rapidity of change that had transformed Tucson in a decade from a frontier town to something like a progressive metropolis, the territory's oldest pioneers gathered to form a society of their own. As might have been expected in a group of unreconstructed individualists, participants at the initial business meeting of the Society of Arizona Pioneers fell to wrangling over what the cutoff date for arrival in Arizona should be to qualify for membership. When a motion passed to make it January 1, 1870, many in attendance found themselves excluded, and Charles D. Poston, who had issued the invitations to the meeting, resigned in disgust. He later accepted honorary membership.

According to its articles of incorporation, the Society was to serve "historical and humanitarian purposes" and "perpetuate the memory of those whose sagacity, energy and enterprise induced them to settle in the wilderness and become the founders of a new state." Part of its purpose was benevolent; members established a fund for widows and orphans and another for victims of Apache depredations—the latter very necessary, given the notorious slowness of the federal government in settling those claims.

But perpetuating the memories of pioneer achievements remained the Society's central purpose. Members started a library, and held meetings monthly, at each of which one of their number delivered a personal historical reminiscence. They also urged everyone to write his Arizona experiences. In 1897, almost by default, the Society became the repository of federal and territorial records, which were added to the slim but growing collection of pioneer materials.

The institution fell on hard times as the pioneers died off, and for a while it appeared doomed. But in the 1920s, businessman Monte Mansfield —Jacob Mansfield's son—prevailed on Edith Stratton Kitt, a pioneer herself,

An unknown photographer captured William Zeckendorf, his family and his friends at a familiar and popular recreation in the late 1880s — the Sunday picnic. Zeckendorf is seated toward the rear of the group, in front of the man with the boater hat.

to take on the job of historical secretary. Her unflagging efforts not only saved the Society but also guided it toward the regional and national prominence its museum, library, and archives now enjoy.

The progress of Tucson's civic life did not mean the city lacked a seamier side. Although Tucson never had the sort of street violence and lawlessness that made Tombstone infamous, crime was not uncommon and citizen retaliation not unknown. In the summer of 1873, the murder of a Mexican-American pawnbroker named Vicente Hernández and his pregnant wife infuriated citizens, for Hernández, though not a longtime resident, had many friends. The killers—three Mexican men—were quickly apprehended and, caught with some of the goods stolen from Hernández' store, confessed. The next morning, a mob led by William Zeckendorf assembled to decide their fate, along with that of an Anglo man who already had been found guilty of another murder but was appealing the verdict. The crowd, impatient with the law's vagaries, demanded the felons' death without benefit of court or jury. The sole dissenting voice was that of Milton B. Duffield, the same man who, according to Bourke, was always drawing his pistol on someone. And Duffield's objection was only that, while it was permissible to lynch a Mexican, a black man, or a Jew, as he put it, one might not apply the same remedy to an American citizen. Although Duffield was a huge and powerful man, he had been drinking. The crowd decked him and proceeded with the hangings.

Tucson also had a red-light district located on two blocks of Maiden Lane, a short street north of Congress and separated from it by a triangular strip of land known as the wedge. For reasons of morality, traffic, and business, there was talk for years of removing the wedge; West Congress Street, only 25 feet below it, could not compete with the commerce being generated on East Congress. Finally, in 1907, the wedge was condemned and leveled, and its territory was made part of the street. The ladies of the night then moved their operations south to a little street called Gay Alley that ran a single block, from McCormick Street to Ochoa between Meyer and Convent.

Gambling remained a problem. Mose Drachman recalled that, in the early days, games of chance went on around the clock, and the saloons that accommodated their patrons never closed. This situation continued more or less unabated until 1903, when O'Brien Moore, co-owner of the *Citizen*, launched twin crusades against public gambling and against saloons doing business on Sundays.

It took time for the ideas to catch hold. Many Tucsonians assumed the city would lose both residents and revenue if gambling were curbed, let alone shut down. In 1905, however, local Democrats nominated Levi Manning for mayor on a generally reform plank. Since Manning was a close

friend of Moore's, the gamblers—who, according to Drachman, had controlled nearly every election Tucson had had—assumed that he was committed to running them out of town. They were mistaken, at least at first. Manning had no feelings one way or the other. Like most other Tucson businessmen, he went to the saloons, had his drink, and lost his money. But he was a fighter by nature, and when the gambling and saloon interests joined forces against him, he took up the gauntlet. "If I am elected mayor and can get the Council to support me," he declared, "I will close all the gambling places in Tucson at the first meeting of the City Council in January."

Despite heavy opposition from the electric-light company, the ice company, and most of the business community, to say nothing of the gamblers and saloon keepers, Manning won in what was perhaps the most bitter election Tucson had ever had, and made good his promise. Gambling was banished from Tucson, but to the surprise of the doomsayers, the city continued to flourish. The next year, the territorial legislature followed Tucson's example and banned public gambling from Arizona.

There is an interesting footnote to the story of Manning and the gamblers. Early in February 1906, one Homer M. Dubois, proprietor of the Legal Tender Saloon, sued the mayor in federal District Court, claiming he held a check of Manning's in the amount of $7500 that His Honor refused to make good. It was widely suspected that since Dubois was a gambler (who had just lost his license), the check represented payment of a gambling debt, and that Manning refused to honor it for the same reason he had closed down gambling in the first place—that he was a tool of Moore's, and Moore had a personal grudge against Dubois.

"Here is Manning's predicament," a newspaper story proclaimed. "Either he must pay the $7500, pungle up, come through, loosen. Or, he can set up the defense that the check was issued in payment of a gambling debt, and therefore null and void. If he does that, he must admit that he, the anti-gambling mayor, is a gambler himself and shock the highly moral among the voters. He also must admit that he is a man who does not pay his gambling debts, and thereby earn the contempt of every man in Tucson who

Opposite:

Top Left & Center
Members of Tucson's bi-ethnic ter-
ritorial aristocracy: (a) Atanacia and
Sam Hughes, with their daughter
Lizzie; (b) Petra and Hiram S.
Stevens. The two women were sisters.
Their husbands were best friends. The
families lived a few houses from one
another on North Main Avenue.

Top Right
Members of Tucson's Mexican-American aristocracy in the territorial
period: Estevan and Altagracia
Salazar de Ochoa. More than twenty
years younger than her husband, Mrs.
Ochoa was described as "a large and
beautiful woman with milk-white
skin."

Center
This elegant, early-day float, with its
driver and high-stepping horses, was
part of a Fourth of July parade in the
late 1890s. This photograph was
taken at the corner of Stone Avenue
and Congress Street.

Bottom Left
Thirteen young ladies (perhaps representing the thirteen original states?)
posed in patriotic garb one Fourth of
July in the 1890s.

Bottom Right
Life in Tucson's Mexican barrio in the
1890s showed little influence of the
railroad or the technological revolution that followed it. A.S. Jones posed
with his Mexican friends outside the
home of one of them.

has ever sat in a game of poker."

There is no record of the outcome of the case. Very likely it never came to trial. Manning served out his term and retired to tend to his many business endeavors. Gambling did not return to Tucson with his departure.

People like Levi Manning represented the new wave of Tucson pioneers, separated from the old—the generation of William S. Oury, "Pie" Allen, and Sam Hughes—by the railroad, the great divider of the city's history. The change had a lot to do with experience; Tucson in 1890 was a far safer place than it had been 20 years earlier. Manning and the men and women who established themselves in Tucson in the '80s and '90s never participated in a Camp Grant massacre or a lynch mob. But the change went deeper than experience, and one of its manifestations was a drawing apart of Tucson's two communities, the Anglo and the Mexican-American.

The first Anglo pioneers, the men of the 1850s, had married Mexican women. The step was quite natural, for Anglo women were few and nearly all already married. Cross-cultural marriages broke down the suspicions with which Anglos and Mexicans had viewed each other when they first had met. Furthermore, the fact that community leaders like Sam Hughes and Hiram Stevens had married Mexicans (their wives were sisters, Petra and Atanacia Santa Cruz) lent such unions a respectability they probably would not have had anywhere outside the Southwest, including in Mexico.

Even though there was little ethnic consciousness, Anglos were firmly in control of the city's power structure by 1880; of the hundred-odd leading citizens who served on committees preparing for the arrival that year of the first train only a handful had Mexican names. The railroad increased migration, and the new arrivals were mainly Anglos, a fact that contributed to the city's further Americanization. Even more significantly, the railroad brought women as well as men to Tucson. The new generation of arrivals permeated all phases of society, from the tenderloin and the saloons to the great houses on Main Street. But, significantly, interethnic marriages became rarer and cross-cultural understanding diminished, to be succeeded by an insidious kind of racism. By the end of the territorial period, the separation was nearly complete. Mexican-Americans, who many times were lower on the economic ladder than the Anglos, became the servants, gardeners, mechanics, and laborers, while Anglos monopolized the professions and business. In the Cathedral of San Agustín, the two groups sat on different sides of the aisle and did not associate. Even this arrangement provided too much proximity for some tastes, and in 1914 the Anglo contingent seceded and formed its own parish, All Saints, with its own Anglo priest.

In little more than a half century, Tucson society had gone full circle, from prejudice to understanding to prejudice again.

The New Mexico & Arizona Railroad and the Sonora Railroad met at the international border on October 25, 1882. The place was an isolated and unpopulated open range on the Los Nogales de Elias Ranch. The ranch gave its name to the two border communities of Nogales, one in Sonora, the other in Arizona.

TWO TUCSONS

Coming out of a long business recession in 1896, Tucson businessmen founded a Chamber of Commerce. Inevitably, they elected Levi H. Manning to head it. The Chamber's purpose, quite simply, was to promote Tucson. It published the first booster literature specifically about the city, spreading word of its assets—in opportunity and climate—to other, less favored regions of the nation. If the recession ended earlier than the normal cyclical movement of business would have dictated—and there is no evidence either way—the Chamber's efforts probably were responsible for the recovery.

The Chamber's formation signaled more than an attempt to end a business slowdown, however. For the first time, the city's merchants, bankers, and investors recognized the need to act in common to achieve the commercial destiny they foresaw for Tucson in the new century.

Those who dreamed of that destiny and planned for it were citizens of one Tucson—progressive, enterprising, relatively affluent, civic in spirit. Citizens of the other Tucson, separated by geography and circumstance from the more fortunate community, did not share the vision. They were the pariahs of the city, segregated from its development, its spirit, and, most of all, its optimism. They were the tubercular invalids, many of whom had come to Tucson with nothing more substantial than rags and a prayer, in search of recovery in the dry desert climate. Men and women of the other community called them lungers. They lived in a tent city north of the University of Arizona that they called Tentville, and in other, smaller colonies scattered around the fringes of the community.

Although Tucson and the rest of Southern Arizona had been a refuge for people with lung trouble since the beginning of the Anglo period, victims of tuberculosis began coming in force only in the 1880s and 1890s. The availability of quick, cheap transportation on the railroad, of course, brought the influx. Tentville grew up around the turn of the century and continued growing for two decades, by which time Tucson's tubercular population numbered about 7000—perhaps a third of the entire population of the city.

Those who suffered from tuberculosis lived apart from the rest of the community for two main reasons. First, the overwhelming majority were poor, and the fact that many could not work condemned them to lives of continued poverty. Even had Tucson welcomed them with open arms, they could not have afforded to live as most of their fellow citizens did. The other reason for their exclusion from the mainstream of city life certainly was more important. Tuberculosis was highly communicable, and healthy persons lived in dread of infection. The community probably would have tolerated no arrangement other than the segregation of these unfortunates.

Tentville spread about three quarters of a mile north of Speedway between First and Campbell avenues. Living conditions there were primitive

at best, bestial at worst. Most inhabitants did not own their tents, and many suffered the abuses of landlords who cared more about collecting rent than about the condition of the quarters they rented. Some tents lacked wooden sides to keep out the desert reptiles; a few even had no floors. None, of course, had indoor plumbing. The invalids hauled their own water from shallow wells their landlords had dug. Toilet facilities consisted of outhouses. Since no public transportation went as far north as the fringes of Tentville, those who needed to venture out had to walk a mile or so to the university's main gate to catch the streetcar. This could be difficult if tuberculosis already had claimed a lung. If they went downtown, the invalids had to face the implicit hostility of healthier Tucsonians, who, if they were not purposely unfriendly, nevertheless insisted on keeping their distance.

The fortunate few among the victims of tuberculosis who had money found health care available to them. From the time it opened in 1880, St. Mary's Hospital treated tubercular patients. The Whitwell Hospital—later the Southern Methodist Hospital and Sanatorium, still later the Villa Maria Geriatric Center—opened on North First Avenue in 1906. The Desert Sanatorium started up in 1926 far east of the city, north of present-day Grant Road and east of Swan, to care for the tuberculars, and there were other facilities as well. But most sufferers could not afford them, and lived out their lives in wretchedness.

The first relief for this squalor and misery came about 1910, when the Reverend Oliver E. Comstock, a sometime newspaperman, printer, and Baptist preacher, opened the Comstock Mission, later and better known as the Adams Street Mission. Comstock had come from Tennessee because one of his 10 children had contracted tuberculosis; he financed the start of his healing ministry with life insurance from another who died early. Comstock's whole later life was marked by a care and concern for the tubercular invalids that no one else in the community demonstrated.

From his mission—at first, three tents—he supplied food, blankets, clothing, soap, towels, hope, and encouragement. Since one of the tents had wooden sides and four beds for the desperately ill, the mission soon became Tucson's first charity hospital. Comstock drummed up support for it in the community, relying heavily on his ties to union labor and the connections he maintained—and upon which his brother Baptist clergy frowned—with fraternal organizations in the city. Comstock ministered in many ways. A familiar figure with a shining bald head and long gray sideburns, he was often seen riding his bicycle down the dusty paths of Tentville, a pot of soup hanging from his handlebars, bringing physical and spiritual sustenance to his flock.

Gradually, other individuals and groups came to assume some share of responsibility for Tentville's inhabitants. Ann-Eve Johnson, a grand-

Above
The Reverend Oliver E. Comstock, sometime newspaperman, printer and Baptist preacher, founded the Adams Street Mission, the first charity to work with impoverished tubercular residents of Tentville. His Mercy Emergency Hospital later became Comstock Children's Hospital.

Top Left & Right
A study in contrasts: (a) the residence of Francis Heney, a Tucson lawyer in the 1890s (b) a Mexican dwelling in the barrio around the same time.

 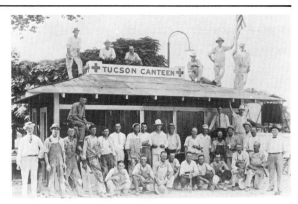

Above
Tent houses such as this one offered meager accommodations to the tubercular invalids who flocked to Tucson because of its dry climate, and generally lived in wretched poverty in "Tentville" north of the University of Arizona.

Right
The Red Cross set up this canteen near the Southern Pacific tracks in Tucson to provide meals for World War I servicemen coming through the city on the train. Fifteen years later, the same sort of facility, operating under the guidance of Tucson Organized Charities, provided free meals to vagrants before sending them on their way, east or west.

daughter of Jacob Mansfeld, recalled that her mother, Vivian Ainsworth Mansfeld, "always had something on the stove" to take to them, and doubtless this charitable impulse existed among many of Tucson's more fortunate residents. Concern also became institutionalized. Tucson Organized Charities, the ancestor of the Community Chest and the United Way, was founded in 1915, and the next year made Comstock's hospital its major project. Early in 1918, St. Luke's-in-the-Desert, an Episcopal sanatorium, opened its doors, after two years of vigorous work by Bishop Julius A. Atwood, head of the church's missionary district in Arizona. Atwood conceived the idea of founding a hospital after hearing of a poor invalid who had begged door to door for food, always unsuccessfully, until at last he had died of hunger and despair in the desert. Unlike Comstock's Mercy Emergency Hospital, care at St. Luke's was not free—but patients unable to pay the customary $9 a week were never evicted.

The Episcopal Church, under Atwood's prodding, also founded St. Luke's Home in Phoenix and St. Luke's-in-the-Mountains in Prescott, where the invalids from both the other facilities went during the hot summer months. Since the church, then as now, tended to have a fairly prosperous membership, funding for these institutions was never short. In Tucson, the Board of Lady Visitors of St. Luke's-in-the-Desert raised money with "silver teas" and through sponsoring the annual Baile de las Flores, the city's oldest and most successful charity ball.

After World War I, the federal government also became involved in the fight against tuberculosis, since it became apparent that many of the poorest sufferers were ex-servicemen who had come to the desert in a last, desperate search for health. The Chamber of Commerce, in the person of Orville McPherson, its energetic secretary, determined to do something about the plight of these invalids. McPherson got on a train to Washington, where he hammered on the desks of influential men until he came to the one belonging to then-Representative Carl T. Hayden. Hayden saw to it that the government furnished $25,000 to enlarge the Community Veterans' Hospital at Pastime Park, on the north side of the city. The facility, once an amusement park and beer garden, had been converted with a $4000 grant from the Red Cross and help from the city, the county medical association, and Tucson Organized Charities. News of the promise of federal largesse caused a citywide celebration, McPherson later recalled. Citizens donated labor, lumber, and supplies, and set to work building cottages that would accommodate 275 patients. To their amazement, they learned that 1000 additional veterans were clamoring for admission. With the need evident for more space, the government eventually built the present Veterans Administration Hospital on South Sixth Avenue, which opened in 1928. It cost the then-astronomical sum of $1,400,000.

Above
A victim of tuberculosis himself, novelist Harold Bell Wright helped put Tucson on the nation's map as a health center. He also worked tirelessly to raise money for poverty-stricken tubercular sufferers, and helped mightily raising relief funds during the Depression.

Left
St. Luke's-in-the-Desert, an Episcopal sanatorium, opened its doors early in 1918 as a treatment center for tubercular invalids. Although it was not free, no one ever was turned away who could not pay the $9 weekly fee.

Long before this, all Tucson tubercular invalids—and all the good people interested in helping them—found a boon in the arrival in the city of novelist Harold Bell Wright, a sufferer from tuberculosis himself. Wright, a native of New York State and a sometime minister before he turned to writing, came to Tucson in 1915 and set up a camp in the Catalina Mountains. With the arrival of winter, however, he caught a severe cold and spent Christmas in St. Mary's Hospital. The care he received there convinced him he should do something to make similar medical attention available to the poor.

As he recovered his health and resumed his writing career, this idea germinated. An article, "Why I did not die," published in *American Magazine* in 1924, attracted national attention to Tucson as a health resort and established Wright as the city's top publicity man. But his contributions to the cause of tubercular invalids were more direct and more munificent.

In 1920, Wright got the idea of presenting a dramatization of his immensely popular novel, *The Shepherd of the Hills,* in Tucson. The male lead would be played by the movie actor Harry Lonsdale, but all the other actors would be local, and all proceeds would go to charity. The plan worked like a charm. The performances—three of them—raised more than $3000 and drew congratulatory telegrams from some of the greatest personalities of show business: Tom Mix, William S. Hart, Douglas Fairbanks, and Sam Goldwyn. A year later, Wright repeated the success with a production of *Salt of the Earth,* a play he had written with a Tucson setting. For the production, he imported former Follies actress Emma Carus, who reportedly threw over a $10,000 role to star in it. The proceeds were earmarked for an addition to Comstock's hospital. The play was so successful that it went on tour in the East in the fall of 1921.

Many of Wright's charities attracted much less attention. In gratitude to the Sisters of St. Joseph, he furnished their convent at St. Mary's Hospital. He often paid the hospital bills of penniless invalids. From his 165-acre estate east of Wilmot Road and south of Speedway, he used his influence with Hollywood's growing movie industry—especially with Principal Pictures Corp., which had bought the rights to nine of his novels—to film them in Arizona and to hold their gala premiere in Tucson. The money, of course, went to charity. During the Depression, he worked tirelessly for the Emergency Relief Committee of Tucson Organized Charities. Before he left Tucson for southern California in 1936, an early victim of urbanization and automobile pollution, he had become one of the city's foremost citizens, and one of its most useful.

Eventually, medical facilities expanded to meet Tucson's needs, and medical science learned how to cope with tuberculosis. Tentville began to shrink soon after 1920, its space being given over to new housing develop-

ments to accommodate the city's mushrooming population. The Tucson of the lungers passed out of existence as the other city boomed.

The first great result of the business determination to increase Tucson's prosperity and importance came in 1910, when the Southern Pacific Railroad built down the Santa Cruz Valley to meet the railhead of the Southern Pacific de Mexico at Nogales. The rail connection between Tucson and the border was not new; Tucsonians had had indirect rail service to Mexico since 1882, when the Santa Fe Railroad had completed a line from Benson to Guaymas. When the Santa Fe 14 years later finished building a line into Phoenix from the north, it occurred to Epes Randolph, a Southern Pacific vice president who had come to Tucson for his health, that the rival railroad had only to lay 135 miles of track from Phoenix to Tucson and it could effectively destroy the SP monopoly in the southern part of the territory.

Randolph communicated his logic to his close friend Collis P. Huntington, president of the Southern Pacific, and Huntington persuaded the Santa Fe to sell its trackage between Benson and Guaymas. Thereafter, the SP routed passengers and freight coming north out of Mexico directly to Tucson without stopping at Benson, an arrangement obviously beneficial to Tucson's commerce. About 1908, however, the railroad reverted to the old plan of stopping and changing at the junction of the lines. Tucsonians, realizing that the change could cost them considerable business, were most upset. Fiery editorials denouncing the SP decision appeared in the newspapers, and businessmen stared gloomily at the prospect of another depression.

Not so Mose Drachman, who reasoned that the SP could save money by building track directly to Nogales. Not only had the territorial legislature recently passed an act giving all new railroads in Arizona a 10-year tax exemption, but the resulting road would be considerably shorter than the old route via Benson, and thus cheaper to operate. Best of all, it would put Tucson at the head of an international railroad.

Drachman took his plan to the Chamber of Commerce, but the majority of its members were skeptical, believing the SP would never undertake the project. Thereupon, Drachman and a few other progressive spirits went to Randolph and worked out a deal: Pima County would float a $150,000 bond issue, the money to go to the railroad as a bonus for building the new line. Randolph agreed, and so did the rest of the top SP management. Tucson voters approved the bonds, the track was laid, and the line was finished in May 1910. The timing was providential. That November, the Mexican revolution broke out, creating economic chaos and ending foreign investment. Had the railroad delayed even a little, the line from Tucson to Nogales probably would not have been built.

The SP, however, never got its bonus. Since Arizona was still a territory, Congress retained a veto over its bonding authority and that of its political subdivisions. Possibly the federal memory was long enough to remember the bonds Pima County had issued a generation before to build a narrow-gauge railroad north from Tucson to Globe. All the bond money had gone to build 10 miles of track, and local taxpayers had been stuck with an immense bill for a railroad that went nowhere and did no one any good. In any case, when a bill was introduced to approve the bonds the county had issued for the SP's benefit, it failed. For once in its long association with Tucson, the Southern Pacific came out on the short end of a deal.

Two years after the Tucson-Nogales line was built, Tucson landed another railroad—the El Paso & Southwestern, a line the Phelps-Dodge Corporation built because of its own disagreements with the SP. Originally, the mining company intended to build it from El Paso to San Diego; the Arizona segment would go from Bisbee through Benson, then along the San Pedro and Gila valleys to Phoenix. Tucson would be bypassed. Once again, the business community intervened. The Chamber of Commerce appointed a three-man committee to meet Walter Douglas, the Phelps-Dodge president, at Bisbee. Douglas expressed surprise that Tucson even wanted the El Paso line—"I thought you were wedded to the Southern Pacific and wouldn't care for any other railroad," he told them. They provided more than verbal assurances that he was wrong; on the spur of the moment, they offered depot sites and a right-of-way through the city at no cost to the railroad. The offer won Douglas over. It cost Tucson businessmen $75,000, but Phelps-Dodge returned their investment in the form of a new YMCA building, and threw in a charming little park by the new railroad's depot south of Congress Street and west of Granada. In time, however, the SP bought up the El Paso & Southwestern, ending its planned expansion to the coast and making Tucson once again a one-railroad city.

The expansion of railroading was only one aspect of a rapid and dramatic development of transportation in Tucson. In 1898, the streetcar line connecting the downtown area with the university opened for business, the first permanent intracity public-transport system in Tucson's history. Until the summer of 1906, mules supplied the motive power; occasionally, they also terrified passengers by running away. This threat vanished when the trams were electrified, but it was replaced by the obvious inconvenience of being stranded during a power outage. By and large, however, the system provided workable, efficient service until the last day of December 1930, when motorman Dallas E. Smith took Car 10 out on its final trip to the university. Thereafter, the rails were paved over and Tucsonians looked to the bus and the automobile for transportation.

The automobile first appeared in Tucson soon after the turn of the

Above
One hazard of mule-drawn streetcars was that the power supply might not cooperate. This one decided to take a nap on Maiden Lane near the corner of Stone Avenue in 1905.

Left
This group of dignitaries assembled at the Elysian Grove in the summer of 1906 to celebrate the electrification of the municipal streetcar line. The festivities did little to move the people on the right of the table, but those on the left, though uninvited, managed to get into the picture.

Opposite:
Top
Built in 1912, the El Paso & Southwestern Railroad depot was one of the most handsome of Tucson's public buildings. It stood behind a charming little park full of rare trees and shrubs. The depot, long out of use, was about to be converted into an office and restaurant building in 1980.

Left
A vice president of the Southern Pacific Railroad, Epes Randolph was primarily responsible for building the rail line from Tucson to Nogales, which made Tucson the terminus of an international railroad. He also procured the land for the municipal park in Tucson that for many years bore his name.

century, providing wonderment, excitement, and sport to the city's citizens. Speedway Boulevard got its name from the fact that Barney Oldfield, America's most famous race-car driver, and Harold Steinfeld, Albert's son and heir, raced down it far out in the desert east of the university. Before long, the city began to experience other effects of this technological marvel. The fragility of tires and the notorious roughness of most of the streets became two excellent arguments for street paving, which began in earnest after 1910. Far more significant, the automobile gave its owner unprecedented mobility. Suddenly a person could live far from his job, and far even from the streetcar line. Tucson began to sprawl.

The great empty space between the railroad tracks and the university that would have greeted a traveler in 1890 soon filled up. Within little more than three decades, the streetcar traveled through settled, largely residential neighborhoods all the way to the main gate, and settlement had begun to spread north and east of the university. Between 1904 and 1924, Tucson's urbanized area expanded almost threefold, from 1.4 to 3.4 square miles. Within the next 12 years, it more than doubled again, and the pace of growth has accelerated steadily ever since. For this achievement, Tucson has the automobile to thank—or blame.

But for pure excitement and fascination, no part of Tucson's twentieth-century transportation revolution equaled the coming of the airplane. This marvelous contraption made its first appearance on the Southern Arizona desert on February 16, 1910—arriving, knocked down and crated, at the SP depot. The city nearly turned itself inside out welcoming the aviator, Charles K. Hamilton, and his wonderful machine. Three days later, Hamilton took off from the Elysian Grove to the cheers of a crowd estimated by the *Star* as "thousands." It probably was no exaggeration, the SP having offered special excursion rates to attract people from communities far and near. Businesses closed and schools let out so everyone could "See Hamilton—the Bird Man fly."

"Following the strains of music rendered by the Tucson band," the *Star* reported on February 20, "the aviator stepped into his biplane and made ready for his ascension, and gliding gracefully over the ground for a short distance, the machine caught the wind and ascended on one of the prettiest flights ever seen in the West." The flight was four miles, the average speed 35 miles an hour, and the maximum altitude 900 feet.

Hamilton and his machine had come to Tucson to participate in an "aviation meet," the inspiration for which originated with Emanuel Drachman and George T. Kitt, president of the Chamber of Commerce. For his participation, Tucson's business community guaranteed Hamilton the princely sum of $2000. Despite the crush of spectators, gate receipts fell far short of the guarantee, and the businessmen had to pony up nearly $1200 to

settle the account.

Nevertheless, reported the *Star,* "the aviation meet was one of the most successful yet conducted in point of excellence of the aviator's work"—an excellence not marred by four accidents, two on each of the two days of the meet. "In both instances, his machine ran into the fence around the racing course now being constructed at the grove," the paper noted. Whatever bruises Hamilton received from his encounters with Drachman's fence, they probably did not equal the bruises Drachman's ego sustained when he first was offered a chance to fly in the plane, then was refused because he weighed 23 pounds more than the 200-pound maximum a passenger could weigh.

Stirring events periodically nourished Tucson's fascination with aviation, itself an echo of the national mood. On November 1 and 2, 1911, two aviators flew into Tucson, bound in opposite directions. Robert G. Fowler came out of the West, trying to make the first transcontinental flight from the Pacific to the Atlantic, and landed on a vacant lot where the old University of Arizona Library stands. From the East, Calbraith Perry Rodgers flew in with his Vin Fiz Flyer the next day and landed on Ninth Street, about six blocks from where Fowler had set down. Rodgers was competing for a $50,000 prize that newspaper magnate William Randolph Hearst had offered for the first successful Atlantic-to-Pacific flight in 30 days or less. Unhappily, he had 15 accidents and so many breakdowns that his trip lasted 84 days, so he collected nothing—except the honor of being the first man to fly across the United States. In 1915, Tucson was thrilled by the arrival of one Katherine Stinson, a teenage flier, who treated the citizens to a three-day exhibition of aerial acrobatics—including the loop-the-loop—as part of the entertainment at the Pima County Fair. She also carried the first airmail in Arizona, from the fairgrounds to a vacant lot behind the post office, where she dropped it from her airplane.

World War I put flying to its first practical test. It also put Tucson firmly on aviation's map. Army fliers stationed at fields in California and Texas praised the city's year-round flying weather lavishly. Leaving nothing to chance, the Chamber of Commerce in 1917 appointed a committee of five civic leaders to greet the aviators, truck gasoline to their planes, and provide overnight lodging and meals. The committee also oversaw first the leasing, then the grading of Tucson's first airstrip, off Oracle Road near the present site of Amphitheater High School.

Fliers were impressed, and word spread in official reports about Tucson's hospitality. The reputation paid off in the spring of 1919, when the famous Army Flying Circus came to the city to perform in behalf of the government's Victory Liberty Bond sale. The very day the military aces flew in, Army General Billy Mitchell addressed a letter to Mayor O. C. Parker notifying him that the government had designated Tucson as one of 32 official landing places for military aircraft in the United States.

The honor, though welcome, carried a cost. The city was to provide an adequate airfield primarily for military use, but also for airmail service, forest-fire control, and civilian aviation. The preparation and maintenance of the field would be entirely a city expense. Enthusiastic though the city government and the Chamber were about this recognition, they balked at the cost, informing Washington by letter that Tucson would provide an airfield for the Army's use, but that Uncle Sam should bear all charges of installing and maintaining it.

These terms proving acceptable, the council and the Chamber jointly scouted the best location for the field, settling finally on nearly 83 acres on South Sixth Avenue, the present site of the rodeo grounds, then far south of the city. When Levi Manning, who owned the property, consented to sell it for $30 an acre, the council agreed to borrow money from the Consolidated National Bank to buy it. The purchase price, together with the cost of fencing and grading the property, came to about $5000, a sum the Chamber raised by popular subscription. The field, the first municipally owned and operated airport in the United States, was officially dedicated November 20, 1919, when City Councilman Randolph E. Fishburn took off from the north side airstrip in a Curtiss biplane piloted by a stunt flier then performing in the city, and landed on the new field.

The airport on South Sixth Avenue served Tucson's needs for only eight years. The city grew like a boom camp in the 1920s. Military and civilian aviation grew even faster. Army air traffic increased because Tucson became a regular refueling stop; and Charles W. Mayse, Arizona's most famous early aviator, arrived in the city and set up its first flying school at the municipal airfield. By 1925, it was clear Tucson had outgrown the facility and needed a new one.

That same year, the federal government released several sections of land southeast of the city for homesteading. The city promptly secured one, near what is now South Craycroft Road, then went to the state for another adjoining it. With 1,280 acres available, work began immediately on a new municipal airport, named Davis-Monthan Air Field for two Tucson pilots who had lost their lives flying for the Army. Public interest in the project ran so high that it was completed by September of 1927—the largest municipal airport in the United States, and the one with the longest runways.

The new airfield was dedicated by no less a person than Charles A. Lindbergh, the "Long Eagle" whose solo nonstop flight from New York to Paris four months earlier had electrified the world. Tucsonians knew several weeks ahead of time that Lindbergh would arrive on September 23, and were beside themselves with anticipation. That whole day, special trains arrived from Nogales, Phoenix, and Douglas, bringing dignitaries of all sorts— foreign, state, and local. Tucsonians had decorated their city. Schools were closed, and the county court recessed at noon in order to give everyone from judge to clerks time to get to the airfield by 2 p.m., when Lindbergh was due to arrive.

Tucson's love affair with the automobile, vintage 1926. The cars at this show came in many makes and models. The "Big Six" Studebaker roadster in the foreground sold new for $1,050.

At 10 minutes before two, the assembled crowd saw the long-awaited plane approach. "On reaching the field," wrote Edwin W. Hammer, an Eastern visitor, to his son, "he flew around it several times, close to the fence, where thousands of cars were parked, so that we had a close-up of the 'Spirit of St. Louis' with Lindy at the controls. His landing was beautiful and he taxied right up and inside the hangar." The crowd then flocked to the road to catch a glimpse of the official party as it headed toward the new Veterans Administration Hospital then under construction on South Sixth Avenue. Hammer returned to the Old Pueblo Club—and was amazed to find that Lindbergh had the room next to his. "I had the best sort of close view of him. He is a daisy," Hammer wrote. Downstairs at the banquet that evening, "I could not have been closer to him unless I had sat on his lap! The general opinion seemed to be that voiced by one fine-looking young girl: 'Isn't he adorable?'"

Davis-Monthan remained the city airfield until after World War II. By this time there was regularly scheduled passenger service and airmail. From 1940 on, however, civilian aviation had to share the airport with the Army, which took over most of it for an air base. Tucson had eagerly sought the base for the revenue it would bring and had sent Monte Mansfield, a leading businessman and one of the original Chamber Aviation Committee, to Washington to lobby for it. Tucson won over intense competition from other desert cities. With the Army ensconced, however, the handwriting was on the wall, and the city fathers had to worry about finding a site for the third municipal airfield. After scouting the possibilities, the city in 1940 bought about 4000 acres some two miles south of the original airport and reserved 2500 acres for a new field. During the war, the Consolidated-Vultee Aircraft Corp. built three huge hangars at the new site for use in its B-24 modification program. These buildings now form part of the airport industrial center. In

Above
By the late 1920s, Citizen Auto Stage Co. was offering bus service from Tucson to Nogales, and giving the railroad a little healthy competition.

Right
Charles K. Hamilton — "Hamilton, the Bird Man," as the local press dubbed him — astounded and delighted Tucsonians in February of 1910 by his two-day flying exposition at the Elysian Grove. It was the city's first air show.

Bottom Right
After dedicating the new Davis-Monthan Air Field, Lindberg flew the "Spirit of St. Louis" over to the old municipal airport on South Sixth Avenue, where the rodeo grounds now are located. A crowd was there to see him off the next morning.

Opposite
With advertisements such as this one, which appeared in The Literary Digest late in 1934, the Sunshine Climate Club sought to attract tourists and health seekers — and their dollars — to Tucson. Even in the Depression, the campaign worked.

1947, the municipal airfield moved to the new location, thanks to the efforts of the Tucson Airport Authority, founded at the urging of the Chamber for the purpose of running the airport. It has done so ever since.

The airport's move deprived Tucsonians of at least one pleasant summer recreation. On hot evenings, many people liked to go out to the civilian edge of Davis-Monthan, where it was grassy and cool and there were lawn chairs. There they would watch for the one regularly scheduled evening plane to arrive. It was a cheap, enjoyable, and comfortable way to spend what might otherwise have been an unpleasantly oppressive evening.

Tucson's civic boosting did not confine itself to promoting new and exciting transportation projects. In the fall of 1922, at the urging of Jesse James, the local Dodge dealer, a group of 82 local businessmen launched the Tucson Sunshine Climate Club, an organization whose sole purpose was to attract tourists to the city. Depending entirely upon funds raised in the community by an annual campaign, the club advertised nationally, emphasizing Tucson's benign climate. At first, air conditioning of any sort being still in the future, the advertisements boosted only the winter season, but by the 1940s the club sought tourists for a season that lasted from midfall to late spring. In its first 28 years, the Sunshine Climate Club spent more than $520,000 on advertising, which brought a total—documented by the club—of 24,448 tourists to Tucson. These vacationers generated business conservatively estimated at $275 million in the local economy.

To promote tourism effectively, however, Tucson needed a first-class tourist hotel. In 1922, it had none. The Santa Rita was nearly 20 years old, and past its prime; other hotels catered to commercial travelers, bachelors, or residents. In addition to liabilities of age and clientele, most Tucson hostelries were downtown, cheek by jowl with the business district. It was clear to members of the Sunshine Climate Club, as well as to boosters at the Chamber, that Tucson must do better.

Since no outside interests came forth to build a deluxe hotel, the Tourist Hotel Committee of the Chamber early in 1925 took the bull by the horns. The committee itself, it was announced, would see that the hotel was built, and it would sell $300,000 worth of stock in the community to finance the undertaking. The stock went on sale early in May. Nearly half the issue sold out the first day; within a week, it was oversubscribed by more than $40,000. Despite official optimism, few investors expected a direct return on their money. Instead, they believed the community as a whole would benefit from their investment. Those attending a "victory banquet" at the Santa Rita on May 16 heard themselves and their city congratulated on "the happy discovery that a representative body of Tucson business and professional men had been gathered together and solidified in this enterprise, which [body] could be depended upon to get out and put over anything that Tucson may require in the future in the way of civic betterment and progress."

Flushed with success, the stockholders organized themselves into the Tucson Tourist Hotel Company and elected a board of directors, whose first charge was to choose a site for the hotel. Several offers of free land were received: 130 acres northwest of the university; 300 acres southeast of the Tucson Golf and Country Club (located where Broadway Village now stands); and 120 acres adjacent to the municipal airport on South Sixth Avenue, together with a $10,000 bonus if the offer were accepted. Levi Manning, who owned the property and made this munificent gesture, pointed out that a rail spur could be run directly to the hotel to accommodate

Above
Paul Kuiper took this view of the elaborately carved facade of the El Conquistador Hotel just before its demolition in 1968.

Right
Tourists on horseback posed in front of the hotel during its heyday.

those arriving in private cars, while the proximity of the airport would be a drawing card for those who might fly to Tucson.

Eventually, however, the board settled on the first tract it had been offered—120 acres a little east of Country Club Road and a little north of Broadway, in what was then open desert. By early summer, a well site was chosen and a rig positioned to start drilling; the hotel would be outside the reach of the city water system. Once the location was settled, the board sponsored a community contest to choose a name for the hotel. The response was an astonishing 6000 entries. Ralph E. Ellinwood, editor and co-owner of the *Star*, submitted "El Conquistador," which won. "El Conquistador Name Chosen for New Tourist Hotel Here; Pronounce it 'Conkeestador'," a headline in the *Citizen* announced rather snidely on July 31.

Henry O. Jaastad, a local architect chosen to design the hotel, submitted drawings for the main building at the end of September. He conceived it in the grand manner. Designed in mission style—Jaastad specialized in church and school architecture—its facade would measure 280 feet across and be surmounted by a tower 65 feet high. Guest cottages would be dotted around this imposing edifice.

Even in the design stage, it became clear the hotel would cost more than the $341,000 the company had raised. Since construction contracts were not let until late May of 1926, it also was obvious the board's prediction of an opening the next January was overly optimistic. Still, the company remained determined to do the project right, whatever the cost. There would be a "spacious lounging room," sun parlors, promenades for enjoying the view, and 46 guest suites in the main building, each of them with individual tiled baths and sun porches. The tower would be surmounted by a huge copper dome; palm trees would line the drive up to the front of the hotel. Grounds would be landscaped with 1000 flowering plants and 80 varieties of ornamental shrubs; the rose garden would have 350 varieties of roses. There would be a swimming pool—and later, the directors planned, a golf course.

All this cost money. By July of 1927, the Tucson Tourist Hotel Co. was broke and needed to raise $175,000 to continue construction. Now a kind of inertia set in; not until December did the board go once again to the community. This time the results were very different. Though the new offering carried eight percent interest and was secured by a first mortgage on the whole hotel property, Tucsonians bought up less than half the notes. With its capital source dry, the company could not continue building, so it began looking for outside investors. Early in 1928, as a result of the board's efforts, the United Hotels Co., one of the nation's largest chains, agreed to take over the splendid white elephant and complete it. The Tucson Tourist Hotel Co. went out of business, to be succeeded by the El Conquistador Hotel Co., which duly gave United a 30-year lease on the property. The new company contracted with Tucsonian John Murphey, then a young land developer, to finish construction with all the grandeur that originally had been planned.

On November 22, 1928, the El Conquistador finally opened, with the main building and four cottages. It was sumptuous and elegant. It attracted the wealthy and the famous: General John J. Pershing, author John Galsworthy, financier Henry Morgenthau, Jr., movie mogul Louis B. Mayer, the Sears and Roebuck families. Unfortunately and ironically, it also accommodated too few people to be profitable. It opened with only 70 guest rooms, and grew only slightly thereafter. Moreover, it operated on the American plan, for which reason it lost the meal trade of affluent Tucsonians, and it was open only during the winter season. Even had the Depression not begun before the hotel's second season, it is not likely the El Conquistador ever would have been a financial success. As it was, the hotel went bankrupt in 1935.

Reorganized and placed under new management, the El Conquistador modernized in the late '30s, adding more rooms and a cocktail lounge, as well as a stable with 50 horses. During World War II, it became almost a country club for officers stationed at Davis-Monthan Army Air Base. After the war came a succession of sales and, in 1959, the start of the El Con Shopping Center on what had been the eastern half of the hotel's property. When the center proved to be successful, as it did almost immediately, it was clear the hotel would have to give way. By then surrounded by the city, it closed its doors on the first day of 1964. Four and a half years later, it fell to "progress" in the guise of a wrecker's ball. Within a year, the new Levy's, now the westernmost building of the center, was rising to take its place. Although the hotel's dome, some of its architectural detailing, and some parts of its woodwork were removed and are preserved in other buildings, the only surviving relic in its original place is the water tower, remnant of the most pedestrian, least glamorous part of the great hotel.

If the El Conquistador focused many Tucsonians' eyes east of the city in the late 1920s, some citizens continued to concentrate on the downtown. One such was T. N. McCauley, who came to Tucson about 1927, bringing the headquarters of his Dos Cabezas Mining Co. with him. Nobody knew much about McCauley, who had migrated from the East, but rumors circulated that he had built his considerable fortune by selling worthless stock to rich, gullible Eastern investors. Whatever animosity Tucson may have felt for this new arrival vanished, however, when he announced he would build a 10-story building on the corner of Congress Street and Stone Avenue to house the Consolidated National Bank (which he had acquired,

together with the Santa Rita Hotel) and provide the most prestigious office space in the city. Overnight, McCauley became a municipal hero. He would give Tucson its first skyscraper.

McCauley announced his plans on January 10, 1928. Just three days later, it became known that an option had been taken on land at the northeast corner of Pennington Street and Stone, a spot then occupied by doctors' offices and a fruit stand, for a hotel. When the city learned that Albert Steinfeld and his son Harold were principals in the project, expectations rose, although some Tucsonians wondered whether a hotel could succeed so far from the center of town. When the Steinfelds announced that their hotel would have 11 stories—and that Tucson, as a result, would have not one but two skyscrapers—the city was ecstatic.

Unlike the Tucson Tourist Hotel Co., both McCauley and the Steinfelds had adequate financial backing. The twin skyscrapers went up on schedule, each at a cost of about $1 million, a fact that stirred municipal pride inordinately. Both opened in 1929. McCauley found banking not to his liking, and soon sold the Consolidated Bank and its new home to the Valley National Bank. The Steinfelds kept the hotel, though they chose to lease it rather than operate it themselves.

Left
A wonder of its age, the new Consolidated National Bank Building, built by T.N. McCauley at a cost of $1 million, opened in 1929 — when Tucson photographer Albert Buehman took this photograph.

Opposite:
Top Left
With its graceful renaissance architecture the Consolidated National Bank was one of the ornaments of Congress Street. When this photograph was taken about 1903, it also was the city's commercial hub.

Bottom Left
The fragility of automobile tires and the notorious roughness of many Tucson streets were compelling arguments for street paving. This photograph shows Congress Street east of Scott, paved in the 1920s.

Top & Bottom Right
As late as 1897, winter rains still turned West Congress Street into a sea of mud through which men drove their horses and wagons at their peril. Completion of the streetcar line the next year led to the paving of the street, and an entirely different, "modern" look for the downtown area.

The Pioneer Hotel opened amid gala festivities on December 12, 1929. The name, the press explained, honored Albert Steinfeld, who had put together the financial partnership that built it. With 250 rooms, a "presidential suite" believed to be one of the finest such accommodations in the West, and its own orchestra, the Pioneer truly seemed to be what a special newspaper supplement published the day of its opening proclaimed: "A crowning achievement in the annals of Tucson's civic and commercial growth of the past decade and a harbinger of future unremitting progress."

Although the Depression brought hard times to the Pioneer, forcing a mortgage foreclosure in 1932, the hotel did consistently better than its more elegant counterpart to the east. One reason was the fact that it was a commercial, rather than a resort, hotel, and as such operated year round. When commerce moved north along Stone Avenue and east along Pennington Street, the Pioneer became the hub of the central business district. For this fact Harold Steinfeld was largely responsible, since his own store was on another corner of the same intersection, and he built one for Alex Jácome, Sr., his commercial rival, on a third. This development effectively guaranteed that any traveler with business downtown stayed at the Pioneer.

For 41 years, the hotel was host to personalities as diverse as General

Above
In 1930 Isabella S. Greenway founded the Arizona Inn, partly to house the "extra furniture" that disabled World War I veterans produced in the Arizona Hut, which she had launched the year before.

Opposite:
Top Left
North Stone Avenue in the 1930s, with the two great glories of the downtown: The Pioneer Hotel, with eleven stories, and the Valley National Bank building, with ten.

Top Right
In 1940, when this photograph was taken, there still was a lot of empty space between the Arizona Inn and the Catalina foothills, where John Murphey and Josias Joesler were already building.

Bottom Left
With beer at five cents a glass, beds at twenty-five cents and rooms at fifty cents a night, the Red Front Hotel on South Meyer Street between McCormick and Ochoa was not one of Tucson's fancier hostelries when this photograph was taken about 1932.

Bottom Right
"Would you think me mad if I built a hotel to house my extra furniture?" Isabella Greenway asked a friend in 1929. The friend did not, and Mrs. Greenway went ahead with the plan.

Jonathan Wainwright, Knute Rockne, Liberace, Eleanor Roosevelt, Zasu Pitts, Tom Mix, Lyndon B. Johnson, Will Rogers, Spiro T. Agnew, and the Cleveland Indians. The tragic fire that ended its great days on December 20, 1970, also claimed the life of Harold Steinfeld.

The last great hotel built in Tucson in the years between the wars resulted quite unexpectedly from a charitable work. The charity was the Arizona Hut, a workshop set up to employ disabled World War I veterans. Its founder was Isabella Greenway, the widow of John Campbell Greenway, Arizona's premier mining engineer and a distinguished veteran of two wars. Mrs. Greenway built the Arizona Hut on land she owned about two and a half miles north of the city in the desert. The workers produced a variety of goods—clothing, novelties, and especially furniture—under her benign care.

Evidently, however, she had no market for the things they produced. In 1930, a year after the Arizona Hut began, Mrs. Greenway musingly asked a friend, "Would you think me mad if I built a hotel to house my extra furniture?" The friend did not discourage the idea. Mrs. Greenway took a rough sketch of what she planned to M. J. Starkweather, a prominent local architect who had designed her home, and he drew the plans for what became the Arizona Inn. By the standards of the day, it was spacious but not extravagant, occupying one city block. The main building and the first four cottages opened the same year, clustered around the gardens that would be the Inn's crowning glory.

The Arizona Inn was a success right from the start. "Mrs. Greenway's idea that winter visitors want exclusive individuality in a restful yet stylish atmosphere where they can enjoy the Tucson climate to the utmost, has been carried out," reported the *Citizen* in October of 1931, at the start of its second season. Additions that year and in 1940 enlarged the Inn's guest capacity to 140. Like the El Conquistador, it operated first only during the winters, but the advent of air conditioning made year-round operation feasible.

Mrs. Greenway, meanwhile, found a broader scope for her talents. In 1933, when Franklin D. Roosevelt named Arizona Congressman Lewis W. Douglas, a Tucsonian, to be director of the budget, Mrs. Greenway took his place in the House of Representatives. She served there four years—the first, and so far the only, woman to represent Arizona in the federal Congress.

The Arizona Inn still flourishes, the only one of the three hotels to do so. As the demise of the El Conquistador and the Pioneer chronicled the shift of Tucson's commercial center to what had been suburbs or raw desert when they were built, the Inn's continuity stands as a monument to the fact that Tucson, rapidly growing and fast-paced as it is, still relishes the sense of civility and comfort that drew people to the city half a century ago.

In the late 1890s, young Tucsonians of both sexes could play serious music in Mariner's Orchestra. Boys, on the other hand, had a choice between the Orchestra and Mariner's Juvenile Band, which did more traveling and may have been more fun. Both organizations were founded by Barney Mariner.

REFINEMENT, RECREATION AND DEPRESSION

Mexican-born Fred Ronstadt came to Tucson in 1882 at the age of 14 to learn the carriage-maker's trade. In 1898, he organized the Club Filarmónico Tucsonense, a forty-member band that provided music for all sorts of occasions, from political rallies to funerals. Ronstadt, a clarinet player, directed the band, as well as writing and scoring most of its music.

On a bright, chilly day at the end of November 1926, Amelita Galli-Curci, the Metropolitan Opera's famous coloratura soprano, stood with a party of Tucson's cultural elite on a vacant lot on South Scott Avenue. After the group paused to pose, smiling for press photographers, Mme. Galli-Curci, dressed fashionably in black velvet, was handed a spade. She gingerly turned over a little dirt. The assembled dignitaries applauded. The diva then graciously accepted a sash of cured rattlesnake skin, presented by Edith R. Holbert, who—it was explained—regularly caught and killed rattlesnakes for their skins; and a Papago basket presented by Madeline Dreyfus Heineman. Donning the sash and placing the basket where it would show to good advantage, Mme. Galli-Curci smiled bravely and the cameras clicked again. Then the ceremony ended.

It was, said Mrs. Heineman, the "greatest day in Tucson's artistic history." For her, it was the culmination of nearly two decades of hope, planning, and hard work. She had every reason to feel proud and pleased. The future, to this indomitable lady, seemed brighter that November afternoon than it had since she reached Tucson as a young bride a quarter century before.

Just 19 years earlier, Mrs. Heineman had entertained 16 women at her home for the purpose of discussing the formation of a musical club. Like their hostess, all the women were amateur performers and music lovers; the club's purpose would be to foster group musical study, including discussion of composers and performances of their work. Though the organization would be peripatetic, moving for its meetings from one member's house to another, its schedule was set. It would meet on alternate Saturday mornings. Not surprisingly, it became known as the Saturday Morning Musical Club.

Although they pioneered the way for serious music in Tucson, members of the Saturday Morning Musical Club were by no means the city's first performing musicians. Leaving aside the "Sonoranian buffoons" of J. Ross Browne's account and other itinerants who drifted in and out of the city, the honor of founding Tucson's musical tradition belongs to a group of Sonorans known as Las Tres Ratas—the three pickpockets. History records neither their names nor what music they played, but they were the first regular instrumental group: a trio of violin, cello, and flute. They appeared in Tucson in 1895.

Two years later, Fred Ronstadt took a hand in promoting music in Tucson, when he and A. V. Grosetta formed a 10-man band in the Southern Pacific shops where they worked. Ronstadt, who had come out of Mexico to learn the carriage-maker's trade, had great musical ability and patience to match. He wrote the band's music, then taught the members how to read it, directing them while playing the piccolo. When his brother, also a piccolo player, joined the band, Ronstadt learned to play the clarinet. At first, he

Above
Although Scotty Gray was not much larger than his cymbal, no one can doubt that playing it and wearing the uniform of Mariner's Juvenile Band gave this boy much to be proud of.

Opposite:
Top
These elegantly attired members of the Club Filarmónico Tucsonense posed for a studio portrait in Los Angeles when they toured southern California in 1898.

Left
This mule-drawn streetcar advertises a concert by the Club Filarmónico the same evening at Emanuel Drachman's Elysian Grove. The driver, however, has other things to do before he can attend; the mule has pulled the car off the tracks.

Right
In 1898 business at Fred Ronstadt's blacksmith and carriage shop, located at Scott Street and Broadway where the Roskruge Hotel now stands, was leisurely enough so its proprietor could organize a band and join the National Guard. When business grew livelier after the turn of the century, Ronstadt had to give it full time, and the band collapsed.

said, the group "could have qualified for a circus burlesque, but in time it got better."

Ronstadt moved on to greater things in 1898, organizing the 40-member Club Filarmónico Tucsonense. This band was not merely larger than its predecessor; it also was more elegant and kept busier. Led by Ronstadt's clarinet and marshaled by his baton, members played at numerous parties, political rallies, serenades, weddings, and funerals. They also gave concerts in Levin's Park and in the municipal park opposite city hall on Meyer Street. When they played at night, as they did every Thursday, they had to read their music—composed and scored by Ronstadt—by the light of small kerosene lanterns, until the city at last agreed to furnish them electricity.

One summer, the Southern Pacific engaged the club to tour southern California and Los Angeles. Once the offer was accepted, it turned out that no salaries would be paid; indeed, the limit of the SP's involvement was to offer the musicians half-price fares. The club played its first benefit concert to raise money for the trip. Although members sweltered all the way over to the coast and all the way back, no one suffered ill effects, and there was a bonus: a handsome studio portrait, done in Los Angeles, of most of the players in uniform with their instruments.

When the Spanish-American War broke out in 1898, the entire Club Filarmónico trooped down to the recruiting station and joined the National Guard. Ronstadt became sergeant major of the company. Fortunately, the war ended before they saw action, but they did their patriotic duty playing at rallies and keeping enthusiasm high on the home front.

The Club Filarmónico stayed together for seven years. By then, Ronstadt's carriage business was so flourishing that he had no time for music-making, so he resigned. Soon after, the organization disbanded, to be succeeded by the Old Pueblo Band, whose percussion and brass kept the city humming before and during World War I.

In the late '90s, when the Club Filarmónico was getting going, a man named Barney Mariner put together two companion musical organizations for young people. Mariner's Juvenile Band included only boys; Mariner's Orchestra was open to both sexes. The boys may have had more fun. Like their successors down through the generations, they wore dashing uniforms—red and gold—and enjoyed special privileges. One was a railroad car placed at their disposal when they went to play in neighboring towns. Many of Mariner's Juveniles graduated to the Club Filarmónico.

For all their worthy efforts, all these bands played unabashedly popular fare. So, in a city with a burgeoning sense of cosmopolitan culture, the Saturday Morning Musical Club filled a definite need. It did so quickly. By the end of its first season—during which membership had grown from the

Smaller members of Mariner's Juvenile Band were dwarfed by the size of the instruments they played, but they persevered. Out-of-town trips on a special railway car compensated for a lot, and the prospect of joining the Club Filarmónico in a few years was irresistible.

original 16 to 50—the club had presented recitals of music by Grieg, Schubert, Chopin, Beethoven, Chaminade, MacDowell, Liszt, and Gounod, in addition to two progams of miscellaneous offerings and one of music from grand opera. All talent was local, and attendance remained limited to members, but already Mrs. Heineman and others had begun thinking about the inevitable expansion of the club's role as the purveyor of culture to the mass of Tucson's citizenry. In pursuit of this mission, the group brought Freida Langendorf to Tucson for its first "artist recital" in January of 1910, and opened its doors to the public. This event, in turn, led Mrs. Heineman to think about a permanent home for the Saturday Morning Musical Club.

By this time, the group had become somewhat anchored, having shared with the Women's Club in the rental of rooms at the Old Pueblo Club. When the Women's Club opened its own building in 1914, the Saturday Morning Musical Club hired the auditorium for its meetings. But these arrangements were imperfect, if only because the accommodations were small, and the lack of a permanent home tended to discourage the growth of satellite groups—a choral society and a young people's organization. In 1916, the musical club got together the money to buy the lot on East Ochoa Street where Wheeler W. Williams' mansion once had stood, but it was too small for the theater Mrs. Heineman envisioned. So the lot was sold to the York Rite Masons, who built their temple there, and Albert Steinfeld arranged for the purchase of a larger one on Scott Street north of Cushing.

Although the musical club continued to grow—by the mid-1920s, membership totaled nearly 1000 and included most of Tucson's cultural leaders, male and female—a suitable theater and auditorium remained financially beyond reach until 1926. Then Mrs. Heineman persuaded Alexander Berger, a businessman and Tucson winter resident, to interest himself in the project. Both were widowed, and Mrs. Heineman probably made an excellent case for a major donation to the cause of Tucson's arts as a memorial to the late Mrs. Berger. Philanthropy was nothing new to Berger or to his brother, Harry; the latter had given the University of Arizona the fountain west of Old Main as a memorial to his son and other university students who had died in World War I. But Alexander Berger's gift was truly munificent. He offered Mrs. Heineman $100,000 for the club's theater and headquarters. She accepted gratefully. The musical-club board commissioned architect Arthur Hawes to draw the plans for an elegant Spanish-style theater with auditorium and numerous other rooms. Mrs. Heineman then capitalized on her extensive artistic acquaintance to prevail on Mme. Galli-Curci to come to Tucson and turn the first spadeful of earth. The $180,000 Temple of Music and Art opened the following year, encumbered by a heavy mortgage but buoyed up by hope.

Financial troubles followed soon after, compounded by the onset of the Depression. The month after the stock market crashed in 1929, Mrs. Heineman (who by now had become Mrs. Harry Berger) announced that the Saturday Morning Musical Club was facing total financial failure, and with it the loss of the Temple of Music and Art. An attempt to put the club back in the black by selling life memberships had failed wretchedly; though the fee was a modest $250, only 57 persons had bought them. Moreover, the city, county, and state governments, all of which had promised the Temple tax exemptions, chose this time to revoke them and demand payment.

Somehow the intrepid board weathered these financial storms. Money came in—enough to pay off the $50,000 balance on the mortgage, retain a resident orchestra, and present a weekly series of free concerts. For these accomplishments citizens could thank Mrs. Berger, whose steady hand guided the club's destinies for 30 of its first 34 years. The city appreciated her thoroughly. When she finally stepped down in 1940, 150 prominent citizens gathered in the ballroom of the Pioneer Hotel to pay their respects and show their appreciation for the contributions she had made to the city she loved.

Long before this, another serious musical group had taken root in Tucson. The Tucson Philharmonic Orchestra—later and better known as the Tucson Symphony—was organized in September of 1928. The idea for it originated with Harry O. Juliani, a native of Italy, lover of music, and prominent local attorney. Camil Van Hulse, a Belgian-born composer,

Above
Madeline Dreyfuss Heineman founded the Saturday Morning Musical Club in Tucson in 1907. Nineteen years later, she saw her major dream come true when ground was broken for the Temple of Music and Art, the club's permanent home.

Top Left
The Temple of Music and Art, the dream of Madeline Heineman and the hope of Tucson's cultural elite, was built on South Scott Avenue in 1927. More than half a century later, it remains one of Tucson's favorite downtown landmarks.

Italian-born Harry O. Juliani spearheaded the formation of the Tucson Symphony in 1928, and became its first manager.

became its first conductor.

"Juliani did all the hard work—he had the first idea for the symphony," Van Hulse remembered years later. The lawyer telephoned "quite an imposing list of musicians," most of whom expressed an interest in the project. The organizational meeting occurred at the Pima Theater on West Congress Street; between 50 and 60 musicians came. "The enthusiasm was very great—he [Juliani] put his aims and ideas forth," Van Hulse recalled. Then he asked how many were interested in forming a symphony. The show of hands was nearly unanimous. The musicians took a secret ballot and elected Van Hulse conductor. Juliani became manager. Then the hat went around for donations to buy sheet music.

These duties disposed of, Van Hulse took the podium and launched the newly formed symphony into an impromptu performance of Schubert's *Rosamunde Overture*. Six men got up, said they hadn't counted on the new orchestra's playing such heavy stuff, and excused themselves from it for good. Despite their defections, the symphony proceeded to prepare for its first concert, which took place in the auditorium of Tucson High School on January 13, 1929. Public response was excellent. The house was full and the newspapers published rave reviews.

The symphony has flourished ever since. In 1930, at the start of its second season, high-school youngsters went door to door around the city selling tickets. There was plenty of response. Later years saw such performers as Rudolph Ganz, Julia Revell, and Mme. Elenore Altman appear with the symphony, which also undertook "pops" and children's concerts as part of its regular schedule. In the 1938-1939 season, however, hard times arrived, and symphony members learned to their dismay that the orchestra would either have to find a sponsor or go out of business.

At this juncture, the University of Arizona extended the hand that saved the symphony. The university had been in the process of organizing an orchestra to provide music students with experience and offer a vehicle for credit in performance courses. Symphony and university officials agreed instead to merge the two groups. The symphony retained its name and continued drawing its musicians from the community—local business people, professional musicians, housewives, and students. The university became the sponsor, and concerts were held on campus. This arrangement continued for many years.

In 1948, one more musical group made its appearance on Tucson's scene. Called the Arizona Friends of Music, it began as an affiliate of a Los Angeles organization known as Evenings on the Roof. Its purpose was to bring Tucson a series of first-rate chamber-music concerts, and it has done so regularly ever since. One of its organizers and charter members was Sybil Juliani Ellinwood, Harry Juliani's daughter.

Important though music was to the development of a cosmopolitan culture in Tucson, other arts blossomed forth as well. From a modest beginning in late 1923 as a committee of the Tucson Women's Club, the Tucson Fine Arts Association became a nucleus of men and women interested in recognizing local talent in painting and drawing. After the Temple of Music and Art opened, the Fine Arts Association located its gallery there and sponsored monthly lectures on subjects related to the graphic arts. After a short stint at the university, where it used the marvelous second-story reading room in the old main library as a gallery, the association returned downtown, inhabiting in succession the Temple, the Chamber of Commerce (located then in the old *Citizen* building on South Stone), and the Kingan House on West Franklin Street. There it remained—under the name of the Tucson Art Center—until the present Tucson Museum of Art was built in the 1970s.

Other, lesser organizations contributed their share to Tucson's cultural life in the period after statehood. About 1915, a society calling itself the Tucson Rimers burst upon the scene, with the evident purpose of encouraging poets as the Saturday Morning Musical Club encouraged musicians and the Fine Arts Association would encourage painters. Most charitably viewed, the Rimers' production was mixed, though some distinguished younger poets helped raise its tone. Typical, however, were offerings such as the following, which bespoke a greater love for Arizona than skill in expressing it:

> O my Arizona bedroom
>   Is beneath the Milky Way
> And the moon is in its ceiling
>   And the star that tells of day,
> And the mountains lift the corners
>   And the desert lays the floor
> Of my Arizona bedroom,
>   Which is large as all outdoor.

These poems appeared sometimes in newspapers, more often in obscure regional publications of poetry. From there, members of the Rimers meticulously clipped them and pasted them in scrapbooks, together with notices of the Arizona Poetry Society, which appeared in the 1920s to give heart, and annually a $20 prize, to more serious poets.

History came in for its share of attention in May 1933, when Francis C. Lockwood, a professor of English at the university and an inveterate amateur historian, organized a group known as the Desert Rats. Lockwood, who had begun researching and writing Arizona history almost as soon as he reached Tucson from Pennsylvania in 1916, knew very well that the most valuable—and most ephemeral—sources for the subject were unfortunately mortal. He grounded his research in interviews with pioneers; it was only natural that he should seek to find and fix the facts of early history by assembling a genial group of men whose memories extended far back into the territorial period. Will C. Barnes, frontiersman, soldier, and compiler of the state's place names, became a charter member, joining rancher John A. Rockfellow, lawman Jeff Milton, scientist Godfrey Sykes, historian James H. McClintock, and Catholic priests Bonaventure Oblasser and Victor Stoner. Although the purpose was serious, the conduct of business left room for recreation. Members trooped off in caravans to such historic spots as Apache Pass and Cochise's Stronghold, where they walked over the ground, listened to the lore written and told of the sites, and camped amid the ghosts of the past. Frequently women shared in these expeditions, sometimes as participants, more often as spectators at the very throne of history.

Tucson's culture found many other expressions in the years between the wars. The movies had made their appearance in the century's second decade, and during the era of the silent film, they often were accompanied by stage entertainment. Vaudeville acts came to town weekly. Traveling musical and dramatic shows also came to Tucson, generally en route to or from California. Before the Temple of Music and Art opened, Paderewski, Mme. Pavlova and her troupe of Russian ballet dancers, Sir Harry Lauder, the Hungarian National Chorus, and the Sistine Choir all performed at different times in the Rialto Theater, on Congress Street just west of Sixth Avenue. They offered Tucsonians a varied exposure to the world of the arts not available to residents of most other cities of 25,000.

Impelled by the rapid population growth of the 1920s, Tucson spread, its expansion spurred by the automobile. Elegant neighborhoods began growing up on the fringes of the city. The first homes in El Encanto, just west of the El Conquistador, were built during the late '20s, and development of Colonia Solana, east of the old country club, began about the same time. So did building in San Clemente, south of Broadway and just across Alvernon Way from the city's park and golf course. Homes in all three neighborhoods were large, substantial, and costly. Property owners in El Encanto and Colonia Solana protected their milieus and investments with 50-year covenants specifically prohibiting resubdivision and any commercial land use.

Development also spread northeast of the university, not far from where Tentville once had stood. Here John Murphey and Josias T. Joesler, a Swiss-born architect, built the Old World Addition, a development that spanned both sides of Campbell Avenue between Mabel and Elm streets. At a time when Tucson's predominant architectural influence was the pseudo-Spanish style popular in California, homes in the Old World Addition suggested a variety of European models. Tudor half-timbers stood adjacent

to French renaissance towers, Moorish arches, and Germanic castles in miniature. Murphey and Joesler built solidly and well. Until the late 1960s, most of the Old World Addition stood intact, but since then the building of University Hospital, as well as other university expansion, has doomed much of the neighborhood to the wrecker's ball and bulldozer.

By the time the Old World Addition was finished in 1929, Murphey and Joesler already had begun to develop land north of the Rillito River that Murphey had homesteaded earlier in the decade. Here, in the Catalina Foothills, the particular sensitivity of both men showed to best advantage. Murphey and his wife, Helen, had traveled extensively through California and Mexico, studying architecture and ornamentation, and acquiring numerous art objects that they later incorporated into the homes Joesler designed and Murphey built. Both men agreed that the foothills development should be Mexican in architecture. Joesler's designs called for the use of native materials only, and adobe predominated. He also understood that American workmen, schooled in building symmetrical structures, could never capture the irregularity of authentic Mexican building, so he insisted on employing Mexican laborers. He regularly surprised these men by appearing at the job sites to inspect every detail of construction, which he discussed in fluent, heavily accented Spanish.

Murphey and Joesler developed the foothills throughout the 1930s, but they also found time for some nonresidential building as well. Early in the decade, they built shops along Fourth Avenue north and south of Sixth Street, but the buildings stood vacant for some time because of the Depression. In 1936, Joesler designed and Murphey built St. Philip's in the Hills, generally conceded to be Tucson's most beautiful church; wags promptly nicknamed it St. John Murphey's in the Weeds. Three years later, the two men collaborated in the building of Broadway Village, one of the city's first shopping centers, which Joesler designed after shops in Patzcuaro, Mexico. When World War II began, the two men shifted to the design and construction of military bases.

As Tucson expanded its boundaries in the 1920s, the downtown also changed. The central business district moved north and east from Meyer Street to center somewhere near Pennington and Stone. The downtown commercial area spread east along Broadway after an epic civic battle ended with the building of an automobile underpass below the Southern Pacific tracks. Other subways along Fourth, Sixth, and Stone avenues breached the "Chinese Wall" to the north, inviting development in that direction.

Much of the activity downtown centered on Litt's Drug Store at the northeast corner of Congress Street and Stone Avenue, whose soda fountain made it a natural gathering place. The proprietor, T. Ed Litt, was as familiar a figure on the sidewalk outside his business as he was indoors, for

THE ARIZONA POLO
ASSOCIATION
(A non-profit community organization)
PRESENTS
IN COOPERATION WITH PIMA COUNTY
AND CITY OF TUCSON

ANNUAL MID-WINTER

RODEO
FEB. 22 - 23 - 24
1929

"La
Fiesta
de los
Vaqueros"

PIMA COUNTY

FAIR
FEB. 21-22-23-24

PROGRAM OF EVENTS-PRIZES
RULES AND REGULATIONS

TUCSON, ARIZONA

Since it was founded in 1925, Tucson's annual "Fiesta de los Vaqueros" has been a famous and well-loved event in the city's winter season, and a perennial magnet for tourists from all over the United States.

Litt's corner, like the store itself, seemed to attract people for a few moments of conversation between errands. A block to the north and on the other side of Stone was Steinfeld's grocery and lunch counter. If Litt's was the place for a cup of coffee or a soda, Steinfeld's lunch counter was the mecca for the noonday meal. It drew Tucsonians and tourists alike; on any winter day, such famous men as flying ace Eddie Rickenbacker, the doctors Charles and William Mayo, financier and former U.S. Vice President Charles G. Dawes, and novelist Sinclair Lewis might be found there, hobnobbing with the leading lights of Tucson's business community.

Two downtown businesses appealed especially to Tucson's youth. One was Jimmy Rand's Smoke Shop, which stood next to Litt's; probably its popularity derived as much from its second-story room with a poker table as it did from Rand's merchandise. During baseball season, Rand also ran a daily betting pool, whose pot could run as high as $400 or $500. Even more popular than Rand's was Dooley's Varsity Shop, located on Stone between Congress and Pennington. Julius Bookman (called Dooley), the proprietor, had come to Tucson to play drums in Emanuel Drachman's theater orchestra at the Elysian Grove, and he later played timpani for the Tucson Symphony, but his shop became his true calling. He sold cigars. He also served sodas and sandwiches, and he had four pool tables in the back. Roy Drachman, Emanuel's son, who grew up in Tucson in the 1920s, remembered that boys of school and college age came to Dooley's as if it were their private club. Dooley kept the atmosphere pleasant by excluding the rougher element. In the evenings, the youngsters gathered there before and after their dates. Dooley lent a sympathetic ear to their tales, and became a father-confessor to many a disappointed young swain.

Every Halloween, Dooley staged a mardi gras for Tucson's children. This event took place in Stone Avenue between Congress and Pennington, a stretch of street the city closed off for the occasion. The youngsters came in costume, as did Dooley, differently attired every year. Since he was a very small man, standing only five feet two inches, he could easily be mistaken for one of his young guests, and he offered a prize to the first child who could identify him. There were other prizes too—toy spurs, dolls, and the like—along with music and free ice cream. Everyone had a good time, but when the festivities ended, the older children still managed to find a few garbage cans to overturn on their way home.

Youngsters of school and college age frequented a number of spots around the edges of the city that had swimming pools and dance floors, though the most popular one of all, the Blue Moon, at the corner of Stone Avenue and Drachman Street, had no pool. Younger children looked forward to Saturday mornings, when they could go to the brand-new Fox Theater and see a movie, a serial, and a stage show and get free popcorn or

Opposite Top
Ben J. McKinney, longtime Pima County cattleman and Tucson lawman for twenty years, was one of the organizers of the Fiesta de los Vaqueros in 1925.

Top
The "bicycle squad" of *Tucson Citizen* newsboys gathered outside the newspaper's building on South Stone Avenue and Jackson Street to pose for photographer Albert Buehman in the 1920s. The bosses of the squad rode motorcycles.

Left
As early as 1916 Steinfeld's grocery, then at 17 W. Congress Street, was the best food market in Tucson, and the lunch counter in the store the choicest spot in the business district to eat the noon meal. The store later moved to the corner of Pennington and Stone.

Below
Polo became a popular sport among affluent Tucsonians in the 1920s. The Arizona Polo Association, formed in 1925 to sponsor the Fiesta de los Vaqueros, later fielded the Sonora Tigers, shown in this 1927 photograph.

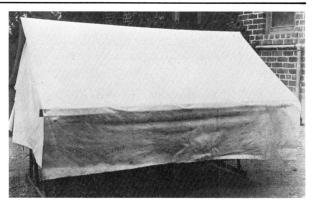

Top and Opposite Top
An "Arizona bedroom ... beneath the Milky Way," specifically on South Third Avenue. When the summer rains came, the "bedroom" was watertight; on clear evenings, it opened up so the occupants could enjoy the air and the sight of the heavens. Shoes and stockings hung from the ridgepole, away from scorpions and spiders.

Right
Founded in 1929, the Southern Arizona School for Boys projected an image of outdoor informality. One of the most successful private schools in Southern Arizona, SAS continued to operate until the mid-1960s.

gifts—all for a dime.

In the years before 1934, when the invention of evaporative coolers made Tucson's summer weather bearable, men whose business kept them in town sent their wives and families to the mountains or the coast to escape the worst of the heat. The predominantly male character of the city's summer society gave rise to the Agnes party, a famous—and notorious—Tucson institution.

The party began with the friend of an unsuspecting bachelor or grass widower touting the charms of Agnes, always described as an attractive young woman married to a loutish railroad man who was often away. When she was alone, the bachelor learned, she was always willing to show a lonely man a good time. Once the bachelor was hooked, his friend would suggest a date with this paragon. When the evening came, the friend would pick up the bachelor and drive him to the house where Agnes was supposed to live, then walk up to the door with him. The house was always dark, and when the date knocked and asked for Agnes, a heavy, angry voice within would ask "Who wants her?" The door then would swing open and a man—the cuckolded husband, of course—would fire a volley of blanks from his pistol. The friend of Agnes' hapless escort would pretend to be shot, and would fall dramatically. The shots were the signal for the neighbors, all of whom were in on the joke, to turn on all the lights, revealing the duped swain for the amusement of everyone. In the rare case where the victim of this hair-raising prank asked for explanations, he would learn that no Agnes existed or ever had, and that he had become part of a summer ritual. Then, even with Prohibition in force,

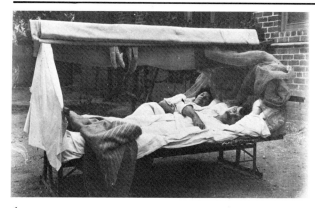

the perpetrators would invite him in to calm his shattered nerves with a libation.

By the early 1930s, Tucson had established itself not merely as a mecca for health seekers but as a center of tourism as well. The success of the tourist industry reflected in part the diligent efforts of the Sunshine Climate Club, in part the El Conquistador's attractions, and in part a Southwestern ethos that canny Tucsonians had begun to recognize as one of their city's drawing cards. Quite naturally, they did what they could to foster it for the benefit of winter tourists. One of the most conspicuous—and successful—results of their efforts was the Fiesta de los Vaqueros, Tucson's annual rodeo.

The idea came from Leighton Kramer, a ranch owner, who invited a number of local worthies to discuss it at his Rancho Catalina in 1924. The men agreed to the concept, then formed the Arizona Polo Association to sponsor it. Both the association and the rodeo made their debuts the next year, with the enthusiastic support of the Chamber of Commerce. But the real work of organizing the first rodeo fell to two cattlemen, Ben J. McKinney and Ed Echols, both of whom later became sheriffs of Pima County. Echols had done his share of rodeoing already, and later claimed to have conceived the idea of the Tucson rodeo while performing in England.

Tucson and the surrounding country, north and south, demonstrated their western-ness in other ways too. By the late '30s, the region had become the nation's guest-ranch capital. More than 115 ranches, most of them small, operated in Southern Arizona. Tucson was their supply point and the railroad terminus for their paying guests. The spreads varied greatly, from working outfits with room for a few guests to full-scale tourist establishments replete with every convenience, where the only reminders of ranch life were the horses and the patient wrangler who guided mounted greenhorns along the trails, warning them of the perils of cacti and rattlesnakes.

Guest ranches catered, of course, to the rich who fled cold winters in Northern cities. Their decor was rustic, though comfortable, and their style casual. One ranch brochure warned against wearing expensive trousers for riding, since the chaparral and cactus would tear them; denim and corduroy jeans were acceptable for men and women on all occasions. Food was abundant and regional, and the atmosphere calculatedly informal. The whole experience was a counterfeit of a West that never had existed, but it sold.

At the same time that guest ranching reached its apogee in southern Arizona, independent schools flourished as never before or since. Shortly before the beginning of World War II, 15 private boarding schools dotted the landscape around Tucson. All were ranch schools, and horses and the outdoors ultimately counted more at most of them than did solid academic

Advertising the open spaces of the last frontier, Southern Arizona's guest ranches in the 1930s and later sought to attract prosperous Easterners fleeing cold winters and urban formality. By the late 1930s, the region had more than 115 guest ranches. Tucson was their supply point and the rail terminus for their guests.

Left
Scenes like this, taken at an unidentified Southern Arizona guest ranch, leave no doubt of the lure this kind of vacation held for wealthy Northerners fleeing the cold winters at home. With their studied informality, rustic decor and regional food, guest ranches counterfeited a West that had never existed.

Right
The *Arizona Daily Star* sponsored this promotion, doubtless one of the strangest in the history of Tucson, to tell the business community that "It pays to advertise in the Star." Evidently the writer of the sign, who was suspended by his feet from a rope and steadied by ropes on either side, wrote the patriotic message backwards, from the bottom right to the top left, concluding with the newspaper's plug. It's not hard to understand why a crowd had gathered.

Opposite
Around 1929, the *Arizona Daily Star* organized the Happy-Dayites, a club for shut-in invalids. A column for them appeared periodically in the paper, and big parties occurred about twice a year. This photograph was taken at their Christmas party in 1937.

curriculum. Like tourists at the guest ranches, students in ranch schools came largely from wealthy Eastern families. Many came for health reasons, and most grew better from living in the fairly Spartan outdoor environment. The same could not be said for the schools themselves. With a few notable exceptions, private education did not flourish in southern Arizona, largely because the tradition that nourished independent schools in the East never sank roots in the Southwest. For generations, Easterners with money or determination sent their sons and daughters to private schools, which traditionally provided better education than public institutions. In the West, however, public schools grew up with the region, and became part and parcel of the Western tradition.

The tourist industry and the schools helped buffer Tucson's economy against the Depression, but the community suffered nevertheless. "It was tough," recalled Oliver Drachman, Mose's son. "It was damned tough. Everybody owed everybody money. I owed the bank, just like the others, and I couldn't pay them, and it was taken for granted. Everybody was in the same boat." The benign winter climate attracted not only tourists but also luckless tramps, who camped in "hobo jungles" near the railroad tracks despite the best efforts of police and charitable institutions to send them back where they had come from. "We didn't have to worry about snow, or overcoats, or big employers collapsing, because there weren't any," John Talano remembered. But when President Roosevelt declared the bank holiday early in 1933, Talano saw men and women lined up in front of a bank on Congress Street "weeping 'cause they couldn't get any money and many of them were going to have to do some jobs they weren't used to doing."

Various federal relief agencies provided employment in Tucson during the Depression. Young men in a Civilian Conservation Corps camp on Mount Lemmon built the Catalina Highway up the mountain from the south side; earlier, those intrepid enough to make the trip had to approach through Oracle, then go up on the old and dangerous fire-control road. Workers for the Works Progress Administration graded and paved streets, built culverts and water mains, laid sidewalks (still some of the best in the city), put up schools and garages, and operated a rock-crushing plant. Scholars on the Federal Writers Project put together a state guide. Artists working for the Public Works of Art Project and the Federal Arts Project of the WPA produced murals, paintings, and designs for public construction.

Under the leadership of the indefatigable C. Edgar Goyette, Tucson Organized Charities bore a far greater share of the load. The group operated community houses for jobless and destitute men and women, and offered what assistance it could in finding them work. It filled food baskets and helped poor Mexicans return home, since they were unemployable in Tucson. During the winter of 1930-1931, Goyette and Harold Bell Wright

raised $15,000 from local residents for relief. As the number of transients grew, and the federal government began urging communities to send them back to their homes so the burden of caring for them could be spread nationally, Tucson Organized Charities undertook to feed the vagrants. But Tucson became a "one-meal town." A transient could get one free meal in return for an hour's work on the city's rock pile. Then, unless he was ill, he was expected to catch the next freight out of town.

The hard times also spurred many individuals to charity. Chief among these was Harold Steinfeld, whose Christmas gift to the community during every Depression winter was a free pair of shoes to any child needing them. Steinfeld's bounty extended further; the *Citizen* reported in January of 1931 that the store had given away $5000 worth of merchandise in the Christmas season just ended. The gifts were practical—clothing, material, shoes, and underwear—but they must have been extraordinarily welcome. The store also extended credit to the jobless on their good names, and nearly went broke carrying the accounts of those who could not pay.

Somehow, the community staggered through the Depression. As misfortunes do, the hard times strengthened loyalties and brought the community closer together. They also produced incidents that, in retrospect at least, made people laugh, and so lightened the memory of darker days.

Such as the story of George H. Smalley and the morning paper.

Smalley had grown up as a newspaperman and had come to Tucson in 1898 to take over the editorship of the *Citizen*. He stayed on the job only three years, leaving when the paper's politics turned Democratic; he founded another paper, the Tucson *Post*, then became a free-lancer, then went into other occupations. He remained, like many news people, a newspaper addict who wanted at least two papers a day. When the Depression squeezed his family budget so severely that one had to be sacrificed, he gave up the *Star* with great reluctance—and became a bear at his breakfast table.

After two or three days of gloom, the *Star* reappeared. Smalley asked his hired man, Octavio Salgado, where it had come from. "De un amigo," Salgado replied—from a friend. Smalley felt better until, one morning, the hired man failed to turn up. No one knew where he was. Smalley and his wife telephoned everywhere they could think of, but got no answer until they called the police station. Yes, they learned, Octavio Salgado had been arrested and was in jail. The charge? Stealing newspapers.

Smalley got into his car and drove down to the jail, where he posted Salgado's $10 bond—a larger sum, incidentally, than the cost of a year's subscription to the *Star*. Driving home, he lectured Salgado severely on the evils of stealing newspapers. The hired man listened contritely; then, as they pulled into the driveway of Smalley's house, he jumped out, went around to open Smalley's door—and handed him a copy of that morning's *Star*.

Top
Tucson Mountain Park, west of the city, has hiking trails, campgrounds, and lovely vistas to charm Tucsonians and visitors alike.

Bottom Left
In the spring, melting snow from the Catalina Mountains gives the brief illusion that Tucson has all the water it needs.

Bottom Right
Cactus blossoms are part of Southern Arizona's springtime color.

Top Left
Tumacacori National Monument, located about 45 minutes south of Tucson, was built by Franciscan priests around 1800. The grounds feature the original, partially-restored adobe mission, a burial site, and a museum. The mission had been abandoned before it was completed and was later pilfered by Apache Indians and others.

Top Right
Throughout the Barrio Historico, located downtown, there are many fine examples of Sonoran architecture that have been painted in bright colors.

Left
The DeGrazia Gallery and Mission in the Sun, nestled in the Catalina Foothills, features the work of renowned Tucson artist Ted DeGrazia. DeGrazia and the Pima Indians built the gallery (his former home) and mission in honor of Our Lady of Guadalupe, the virgin saint of Mexico.

Opposite:
Top
Columbia University's Biosphere 2 Center, located in Oracle, about half an hours drive north of Tucson, is a 100-year experiment in enclosed eco-systems.

Bottom
Tourists flock to Tucson to enjoy its desert climate, slow pace, golfing and premier resorts. Loews Ventana Canyon is one of several "destination resorts."

Above
This statue of Pancho Villa, the famous Mexican revolutionary, stands in the Veinte de Agosto Park in downtown Tucson.

Left
The Pima Air and Space Museum covers the area of three football fields with military, commercial and Presidential aircraft representing America's history. The museum is open daily and also conducts tours of Davis Monthan's AMARC facility.

Above
Built around the turn of the century for the Owl's Club, this gracious mansion was sold first to Levi H. Manning, then to Albert Steinfeld. Currently an office building, it remains one of the treasures of Main Avenue.

Top
The Carnegie Free Library was designed by architect Henry Trost and built in 1900. Currently the building houses the Tucson Children's Museum. The marble bench in front of the building was built in 1919 with funds bequeathed for the purpose by Merill P. Freeman.

Top Right
Mission San Xavier del Bac, "the white dove of the desert," is probably the finest example of Spanish mission architecture in the American Southwest. The mission, completed in 1797, has served continuously as a parish church for Pima and Papago Indians ever since.

Right
The 10-story Bank One building, at the corner of Stone Avenue and Congress Street, was the city's tallest when it was built in 1929. Now, other buildings downtown tower over it.

Above
The elegant Manning home, built in Snob Hollow on the Paseo Redondo early in the 20th century, served at one time as headquarters for the BPO Elks Lodge No. 385.

Left
Reflecting two eras: A window in the Bank One building reflects the Bank of America building downtown.

Far Left
The Bank of America building on Stone Avenue, built in the 1970s in the heart of the old central business district, thrusts concrete and glass skyward. Though massive, it is light and airy as a breeze.

Top
Young dancers, resplendent in their regalia, at the International Native People's Pow Wow in Tucson, a yearly celebration of native dances, trade goods, and cultural demonstrations lasting several days.

Bottom
Climbers in the Catalina Mountains north of Tucson encounter rough country but splendid scenery.

Top
The Tucson rodeo, formally known as La Fiesta de los Vaqueros, began in 1925 as a tourist attraction. In 2001 it was still going strong.

Bottom
Locals and visitors alike enjoy the refreshing pools of cool water in Sabino Canyon's stream, the only continuous source of water in the surrounding area.

Above
The elegant house built by rancher John Zellweger for his German bride about 1884 was remodeled and restored more than 90 years later, and is now one of the jewels of downtown Tucson.

Right
Mirroring history: The windows of the Bank of America Plaza downtown, built in the 1970s, reflects the Bank One building, built half a century earlier.

Far Right
The stone portico that once adorned the first San Agustín cathedral was salvaged when the building was demolished in 1936. Nearly 40 years later, it became the facade of the Arizona Historical Society.

Above
The Veteran's Administration Hospital, built in 1928, is a classic of the Spanish mission style that came to Arizona from California in the second decade of the 20th century. The third Pima County Courthouse, built a year after the hospital, is another example.

Top Left
St. Phillip's in the Hills Episcopal Church, generally acknowledged as Tucson's most handsome church, was designed by Josias T. Joesler and built by John Murphey in 1936.

Top Center
El Tiradito, Tucson's folk shrine, is more than a century old. Although its origins are shrouded by myth, the shrine supposedly marks the grave of a murdered sinner who could not be buried in consecrated ground. Over the years, devout men and women who have gone to the shrine to pray for his soul have come to believe that their wishes there may be answered by a special providence.

Center
The 1908 Rockwell house in Snob Hollow has been restored for use as an office building. The house is noteworthy as an example of Tucson's eclectic taste at the turn of the century.

Far Left
A building shaped like an inverted glass pyramid, on Wilmot Road and Speedway in Tucson's eastside, houses the 5/3 Bank.

Left
Details like this archway at Broadway Village are eloquent testimony to the architectural vision of Josias T. Joesler.

Above
Ted DeGrazia's original watercolor and oil paintings can be found hanging in the DeGrazia Gallery, as well as painted on the walls of the Mission in the Sun chapel.

Right
Visitors may take a guided tram or hike through beautiful Sabino Canyon Recreational Area in the Santa Catalina mountains. This stone bridge, which crosses a stream, is one of nine along the 3.8 mile paved road.

Above
Kitt Peak National Astronomical Laboratory has helped Tucson earn the title "Astronomy Capital of the World."

Left
The giant saguaro, found in Sabino Canyon and Saguaro National Monument in Tucson, can grow upwards of 50 feet high and have more than 20 upturned branches. The cactus is a night-blooming Cereus whose large white, fragrant flowers bloom in June.

Right
As the sun moves westward, the Cochise Stronghold area of the Dragoon Mountains is thrown into high relief. A short drive east of Tucson, the Dragoons are another image of the majestic beauty that is an enduring part of the experience of Tucson and its desert environment.

Top Left
A piece of downtown Tucson in the springtime.

Top Right
The third Pima County Courthouse nestles comfortably into a downtown that has grown tall around it.

Center
Built in 1967, Tucson's city hall dominates El Presidio Park. The space both occupy was once enclosed by the Spanish presidial wall.

Bottom Left
The Casas Adobes Shopping Center, in northwestern Tucson, preserved the Spanish colonial feeling that many people consider the hallmark of the Southwest.

Top Left
After historic preservationists managed to defeat a cross-town freeway right through a section of the Barrio Historico, restorations such as this one turned the barrio into one of the most handsome areas of downtown Tucson.

Top Right
A wrought iron gate leads to a walkway between two restored adobe buildings in the Barrio Historico, Tucson's oldest neighborhood.

Center
In Tucson, the desert is never very distant. Surviving in a dry, hostile environment has been a constant challenge to human inhabitants of the Santa Cruz Valley for thousands of years.

Botttom Left
The Music Hall of the Tucson Community Center is the permanent home of the Tucson Symphony and the site of many other musical events each year.

Bottom Right
The El Con Water Tower, the most pedestrian part of Tucson's great hotel enterprise, is its only surviving relic. The tower was designed by Josias T. Joesler and built under the supervision of John Murphey. It is one of Tucson's most distinctive landmarks outside the downtown area.

A modern work of sculpture stands in front of the new City of Tucson Library, showcasing the downtown business district.

TUCSON AT THE MILLENNIUM

The Temple of Music and Art is home to the Arizona Theater Company, a group bringing dramatic works to both Tucson and Phoenix. The company brings the best in stage entertainment to Tucson with a yearly season running from September through March of each year.

In August 1975, Tucson marked the bicentennial anniversary of its founding with a five-day fiesta that included everything from the display of historic photographs to native cookery, and from ceremonial raisings of the flags under which the city had lived to a grand bicentennial ball. Although overshadowed somewhat by the approaching national bicentennial 11 months later, Tucson's festivities were, as the *Citizen* remarked, the "greatest civic celebration in the city's history."

Tucson's bicentennial gave its people a chance to look back into the mirror that was their past, and congratulate themselves on how far they had come. As a snapshot of history it showed a joyous city growing fast but remarkably unbothered by racial and ethnic turmoil. The bicentennial, however, was only an instant in local history. What the city had become by 1975 was the fruit of 35 years of development that began before the United States entered World War II.

The 1940 federal census had found 36,818 people living in the Tucson metropolitan area. This was an increase of more than 4,000 souls over the number reported by the 1930 census, and mirrored a population trend that would be constant throughout the 20th century. But the total had another significance as well, for the 1940 census was the last to report Tucson as Arizona's largest city. In the years right after World War II, Phoenix overtook the Old Pueblo in population, and the intervening decades have only increased the capital city's lead. Maricopa County—Phoenix and the cities around it—remained the state's population center at the beginning of the 21st century, its conservatism dictating state policy toward both local and national issues.

By the time the war came, Tucson was as fully integrated into the nation as any other community across the land. Its population had come from all parts of the United States and from most countries around the globe. Curiously, the vegetation around the city gave clear proof of its population's pedigree. The University's lovely olive trees, together with its date palms, were imports from Egypt early in the century. Lawns and flowering plants native to the East, the Midwest and the Pacific Coast grew in soil that a century before had supported only desert growth.

Public and private architecture also bespoke Tucson's diversity. Streets in the oldest sectors of the city were lined with adobe houses like those that had greeted the first Anglo settlers who came to the Gadsden Purchase, but a few blocks east there were homes built in high Victorian style, while others to the north showed the influence of the California cottage and mission styles. The old city hall had been an elegant building in the classical style; the beautiful second courthouse, with its elegant mosaic dome, represented the mission style. The farther one moved from the city core, the more modern was its architecture.

The railroad, which had reached Tucson in 1880, had provided the city's first significant connection with the rest of the country. Just under a half-century later, Standard Airlines, a predecessor of American Airlines, completed the connection by establishing regularly scheduled air service in 1928. Meanwhile, a net-

Left
The desert in spring bloom, with typical Sonoran desert biotypes, including mesquite trees, barrel cacti, and saguaro cacti.

Right
A saguaro cactus in bloom.

work of roadways stretched to link the city with states on three sides of it and Mexico to the south. So it was predictable that Tucson should participate in the changes that transformed the country in the last half of the 20th century.

Postwar America became a country on the move. Roads improved and postwar automobiles became larger and more reliable than their prewar counterparts. The rich began discovering the pleasures of automobile travel, while middle-class men and women found gasoline and lodging were not as expensive as they had feared. Americans began traveling, and before long the person who had relocated from east to west, or south to north, ceased to be a curiosity, finally becoming the rule rather than the exception. The great federal highway program begun in the 1950s, which built the extraordinary network of interstate routes crossing the country, made travel, and thus relocation, easier than it ever had been.

As cities, especially in the West, gained population, suburbs grew up around them offering more open space, newer schools and better roads than the cities themselves could offer. Newcomers were drawn to these new communities, and so were many of the cities' more affluent people. Services followed them—streetlights, sewer systems and paved roads. More important to the cities, retail trade also moved. Groceries, drugstores and department stores left the old city cores and moved to where the people had gone. Finally, within a couple of decades, the old central business districts became

virtual ghost towns, while the inner cities remained home only for the poor
who had not been able to afford the move to the suburbs.

The entrance to the Sanctuary at
St. Phillip's in the Hills Episcopal
Church, designed by Josias Joesler.

In many cities, urban decay was slowed, then reversed, largely through
the efforts of local governments spending federal dollars. New tax structures
encouraged businesses to return to the central cities. New parks were created, hotels built and cultural facilities such as museums brought in to lure
visitors back to the city cores. Sometimes these efforts succeeded, sometimes
they failed. The best of them created new downtown zones where local
history provided the theme and public-private partnership the ambience. But
such places were as far from the old downtowns they were meant to recall as
the automobile from the stagecoach.

Tucson's great sprawl outward began in the 1960s. At the beginning
of the decade, downtown was intact. The major national and local department stores and specialty shops were still located there; so were the banks,
real estate offices, hotels, restaurants and theaters. Local governments, both
city and county, as well as the courts, from city to federal, were concentrated

there as well, along with the offices of the law firms that did business before them. By the end of the decade, however, everything but government, courts and lawyers had left, and what had been the old downtown business district was visibly dying.

Growth had been almost constant in Tucson since the days when the first farmers settled outside the Spanish presidial wall in the late 18th century. As Tucson's Anglo population surged after the Gadsden Purchase, the community grew accordingly. First, in the 1890s, it expanded north of the railroad toward the infant University of Arizona. Then, in the first decades of the 20th century, growth accelerated as the area north of Speedway Boulevard was developed. Later, development spread eastward, though as late as the time the war began, university ROTC cadets still practiced cavalry maneuvers in the vicinity of Tucson Boulevard and Speedway. After the war, people came in unprecedented numbers; as the late historian C. L. Sonnichsen observed, "The basic ingredient in Tucson's history during the '50s and '60s was newcomers." They continued coming in a steady stream in the '70s, '80s and '90s, as growth focused on the areas northwest and southwest of the city. Typically, the city annexed the land occupied by the new developments, though some new areas resisted annexation or chose to unite instead with suburban communities outside the city.

The key ingredients in the calculus of expansion were the availability of relatively flat, and cheap, land, and a means of transportation to link those who lived out of the city with their jobs within it. First came streetcars, then buses. But in the early 20th century the automobile became the preeminent tool of growth, and continued in that role for more than 90 years. What the car made possible was what its opponents called urban sprawl. People who loved the open spaces and who, in later times, would be called environmentalists, loudly deplored it. Replied longtime Tucson developer Roy P. Drachman, "Everyone hates urban sprawl except the people who live in it."

That the city's growth was unstoppable became evident before the end of the 1930s, when developer and businessman John Murphey began building in the Catalina Foothills. There the land was far from flat, but for Murphey, at least, it was cheap; he had acquired his first 1,700 acres under the Civil War-era Federal Homestead Act for $25 an acre. In the development, he had two essential associates: Josias T. Joesler, a Swiss-born architect whose adobe home designs entranced all who saw them; and Helen Murphey, the developer's wife, whose skill in collecting Mexican artifacts was apparent in the numerous homes where they appeared. Joesler designed other homes in the city, especially in what was known as the Old World Addition north of Speedway Boulevard. He also designed St. Phillip's in the Hills Episcopal Church on Campbell Avenue, widely viewed as the city's most beautiful church; and Broadway Village, the city's first shopping center, on Broadway and Country Club Road.

Broadway Village opened in 1940, when its location still bordered on the

A gaily decorated house in one of Tucson's barrios is itself a history lesson.

open desert, the expensive precincts of the El Encanto neighborhood and the equally pricey El Conquistador Hotel. By war's end it was surrounded on all sides by city. El Encanto, whose residents had contemplated incorporation as a separate community in the mid-30s, was still the best in-city neighborhood, but after the war the hotel fell on bad days and soon only its bar remained open. In 1964, the whole complex of buildings that had made it up was razed, and El Con Mall, the city's first regional shopping center, opened in its place. Only the hotel's water tower, spared because it was south of Broadway, recalled its former glory.

The opening of El Con Mall marked the beginning of the end of downtown as a retail trade center. Development elsewhere came in stages. New shopping malls followed where development led, first east to what is now called Park Place Mall, on East Broadway; then north, to Tucson Mall, on Oracle Road; and finally, in the 1980s, to Foothills Mall, on West Ina Road in northwestern Tucson. Meanwhile, dozens of smaller shopping centers sprung up on most of the city's larger streets, bringing drugstores and grocery markets to residents of newly developed areas.

Downtown was losing its retail merchants just as the idea of urban renewal was about to take hold of the city. This plan, based on federal funding, had been proposed, and dropped, as early as 1957. When it was revived five years later, the decline of downtown was foremost in the minds of its backers. They foresaw not merely slum clearance but also the creation of cultural facilities that would attract citizens and tourists. They also wanted convention facilities, to give Tucson a share in an increasingly lucrative market.

But urban renewal was highly controversial, and among its most vocal opponents were people who stood to lose their homes and businesses if the plan were enacted. The issue generated enough heat that the City Council

first opposed it, then reversed itself to allow a vote by the people. Voters similarly disapproved, then reversed themselves, allowing work on only a small area. Later decisions enlarged it.

Work began when federal funds became available in mid-1972. The results it produced justified both the optimism of its backers and the pessimism of those who had opposed it. The city did eradicate slum neighborhoods where living conditions were abysmal and crime high. Tucsonians also got a new art museum, and a community and convention center with an arena that has accommodated activities as diverse as ice hockey and giant truck racing. They also got a first-class music hall, a little theater; and a sparkling new office and shopping center. The latter development, ironically, was named La Placita; the original Placita de la Mesilla had been a little square in the center of the old, now vanished, neighborhood.

But these new facilities were built only at a terrible expense. Urban renewal and the companion federal Model Cities program resulted in the destruction of 319 homes and the forced relocation of more than 1,000 people. Among the buildings leveled was a lovely architectural anomaly: a two-story Victorian adobe, once the home of Lionel and Barron Jacobs, pioneer merchants and early Tucson bankers. This house had stood on Alameda Street, north and outside the oldest part of the city. But most of the homes that fell before the bulldozer lay to the south in the city's historic core, the site of Mexican Tucson and the place where Anglo settlers first came more than a century earlier to begin new lives on what was then the American frontier.

The approach of urban renewal had brought together a group of people intent on preserving what they could of the past. They targeted landmarks such as El Tiradito, the old Plaza de la Mesilla, the ruins of old Fort

A late afternoon view of suburban Tucson and the City Center. Tucson is encompassed by a number of high desert mountain ranges forming a large natural basin 30 to 40 miles in diameter.

Above
The rear of the Jacobs House in 1965.

Opposite:
Top
From left Sidney B. Brinckerhoff, executive director of the Arizona Historical Society, and Carlos Ronstadt, society president, stand in front of the Sosa-Carrillo-Fremont House with Ann-Eve M. Johnson and Emil Haury, who stood between the old house and the bulldozer that had come to destroy it.

Bottom
The Sabino Otero House in 1963.

Lowell, and other historical and architecturally significant properties. One image speaks to their anguish and their determination. It is of Ann-Eve Mansfeld Johnson, one of the city's best known civic leaders and head of the Tucson Heritage Society, and Emil Haury, Arizona's most famous anthropologist, standing one rainy morning in front of the bulldozer coming to level the Sosa-Carrillo-Fremont house, the last remaining structure identified with a governor of Arizona Territory.

This part of the story, at least, ended well. The bulldozer stopped, and the house was saved, ultimately to become an elegantly furnished museum interpreting city life on the Southwestern frontier. This victory delighted the preservationists, who all too often found nothing on which to congratulate themselves.

Sometimes this struggle to shield some remnants of historic Tucson produced darkly humorous results. The Sabino Otero house on South Main Avenue was reprieved, but street engineers insisted that it be moved to accommodate the realignment of Granada Street. Unhappily, the house was made of adobe, a material that, unlike wood, does not move easily. When the movers came, the house crumbled, leaving only its wooden porch. This was moved to the Arizona Historical Society, where it stands as part of a patio depicting Tucson in the 1880s.

If the preservationists had failed to save most of the urban renewal area, they were largely responsible for saving much of what remained after the work was done. They forced the city to pass an ordinance in 1974 permitting creation of historic neighborhoods in the city. Within these areas homes and other buildings received limited protection from demolition, while new buildings were subject to a review process to assure their architectural congruity with the older structures. The first neighborhood to be designated historic was Armory Park, which had been developed in the 20 years after the railroad had reached Tucson in 1880; others that followed were the El Presidio neighborhood north of downtown, the Barrio Viejo south of it, the area near old Fort Lowell, and the West University neighborhood.

Somewhere amid the crises of growth and the ongoing battle between those who wanted it and those who opposed it, Tucson moved from being the small city its natives fondly remembered to a metropolis where, suddenly, everyone did not know everyone else. In this new, big city, politics ceased to be a matter decided by homegrown aristocrats and became subject to such forces as economic needs and ethnicity. Groups, especially Hispanic, who had been quiet in the old days now became vocal in demanding a larger piece of the common loaf. To the surprise of old-timers, people whose parents had been maids, nannies and gardeners now held professional positions and became interested in the quality of education they received and the opportunities before them. Everyone acknowledged the rightness of this new society, but it seemed uncomfortable to many people.

Big-city Tucson had an economy based on four pillars. Among them the defense industry took pride of place. Hughes Aircraft (later, Raytheon

City of South Tucson's new municipal complex houses the mayor, city offices, courts, police and fire departments.

Missile Systems) came to the city in the early 1950s and instantly became Southern Arizona's largest manufacturer and private employer. Postwar development of large-scale copper mining south of the city continued the trend of industrial growth. The University of Arizona provided a second source of economic strength. The third column represented local government, and the fourth the federal government, exemplified in Tucson by Davis-Monthan Air Force Base.

Of these enterprises, the university and local government were the most stable economically. Hughes, on the other hand, built missiles and parts for other weapons; if the government found it necessary to cut back on these, Tucson would feel the change immediately. And Davis-Monthan seemed even less reliable. What if Uncle Sam should decide, in a fit of fiscal responsibility, to close it? Air Force fliers had more than 300 days a year of clear skies, possibly the best situation to be found at any base in the continental United States. But the awful possibility of Davis–Monthan AFB closing brought delegations of Tucsonians, figuratively on their knees, to Washington whenever the subject came up. In other words, when Uncle Sam sneezed, the city caught cold, and sometimes the disease approached pneumonia.

Predictably, there were both up and downsides for Tucson as a big city. In the negative column, the planners' decision in the 1960s not to carve the metropolis up with freeways resulted as early as the next decade in paralyzing traffic delays. Major streets needed to have at least six lanes to carry traffic east and west, but most had only four. In the county the situation was often worse. The decision against freeways meant that both governments

Top Left
Kitt Peak National Astronomy Laboratory, one of the world's leading observatory complexes, is located approximately 56 miles west of Tucson atop the Quinlan Mountains nearly 7,000 feet high. The observatory holds the world's largest collection of optical telescopes for solar, stellar and planetary research.

Top Right
The Pima Air and Space Museum houses more than 250 aircraft, including President John F. Kennedy's Air Force One, early commercial planes, fighter planes, cargo planes and more. The museum also conducts tours of Davis Monthan's AMARC facility.

Left
Santa Cruz Church, an imposing landmark in the city of South Tucson, is a focal point for the almost exclusive Hispanic and Catholic populations of this part of greater Tucson.

continued for the next 30 years playing an expensive game of catch-up, trying and always failing to widen roads sufficiently to meet needs five or 10 years ahead.

Regional planning in general did not do well in the Tucson metropolis. Numerous attempts had been made since the 1930s to plot rational growth within the city and metropolitan Pima County, but all failed. In the 1970s, in the wake of urban renewal, a new comprehensive plan appeared, but it fared no better than its predecessors. The best the city could do in many cases was to establish overlay zoning on existing developments, which was the equivalent of locking the barn after the horse was stolen. The power of developers generally proved limitless, and new housing areas continued to grow up ever farther from the city limits.

The automobile had been the instrument of Tucson's expansion; in the decades after the war it continued to be indispensable for moving around within the metropolitan area. Nowhere was population density great enough to make light rail a viable transportation alternative. Even a municipal bus system was only marginally effective; its reach, which had to be as wide as possible, was expensive, and voters repeatedly defeated higher subsidies to enlarge it. Municipal tightfistedness put pressure on ticket prices, thus threatening to put mass transport beyond the economic reach of many of the city's poorest citizens. Many of these, as a result, were obliged to use their cars, all old, to get around, and the exhaust from these automobiles helped degrade municipal air quality.

Automobile exhaust, plus the dust that blew from every unpaved road in the metropolitan area, made for an air pollution problem that Tucsonians in the past had associated only with Phoenix and Los Angeles. It was never that bad, of course, but especially when the area was under high atmospheric pressure, the air turned visibly dirty and a rust-colored haze threatened to blank out the surrounding mountains. Under federal mandate, state and local governments undertook to limit pollution. Cleaner-burning auto fuels were mandated and the legislature required annual automobile inspections in Maricopa and Pima counties to test for harmful emissions. By the beginning of the new millennium Tucson's air had begun to improve.

Another uncomfortable aspect of big-city living was a growth of crime of all kinds. There had, of course, been considerable lawlessness at the end of the 19th century, when Tucson was still a frontier town, although it was never as lawless as Old West storytellers had made it out to be. Occasionally, county and city law enforcement got the spotlight for efficiency, as they did in 1934, when Tucson police arrested the nationally infamous bank robber John Dillinger in the old Congress Hotel, where he and several members of his gang had been staying.

But the crime that bloomed in Tucson after World War II seemed different and somehow more sinister. Some feared the infiltration of the East Coast mobs, one of whose reputed leaders, Joseph Bonanno, had moved to

Tucson in 1966. The city's proximity to the Mexican border made it one of the capitals of the international drug trade in the 1970s, and surprised citizens would hear frequently of the seizure of thousands of pounds of marijuana and spectacular quantities of cocaine and other drugs. Marijuana, at least, had been available in Tucson for decades, but not so visibly and not on such a grand scale.

Gang violence, largely among the young, was perhaps the most visible manifestation of crime as the century ended. Gangs found their members among the poor. The hot summer months produced epidemic violence, with drive-by shootings and muggings the most common actions, especially in poorer parts of the city, and in South Tucson. Often, too, violence accompanied drug sales, another crime area dominated by youths. Arizona's prisons, where most of the lawless youths ended up, also were divided into gangs that continued the wars inside. Captive gang leaders also saw to it that drugs made their way into prisons, where their control reinforced the leaders' power. The possibility of prison rehabilitation seemed ever more remote.

If the problems of bad roads, air pollution and crime seemed part of the package that was big-city life, there were advantages to offset them. The sheer increase in population inevitably brought cultural institutions the city had not yet seen. The 1920s had witnessed the building of the Temple of Music and Art, child of the longing of Madeleine Heineman Burger, and the birth of the Tucson Symphony. The Tucson Boys Chorus, the city's world-ranging "ambassadors in Levi's," came into being in 1939. The years after World War II had brought the Tucson Friends of Music Society in 1948. Three years later came the Arizona Sonora Desert Museum, now world famous for its preservation and display of Sonoran desert flora and fauna.

In 1966, following the example of many another theater group since territorial days, the Arizona Civic Theater was established in Tucson, but unlike its predecessors it succeeded. Even before the Temple of Music and Art had been restored for the group's use, the theater had begun performances

The Arizona-Sonora Desert Museum is a world-famous zoo, natural history museum and botanical garden featuring living animals and plants native to the Sonoran Desert.

in Phoenix, and—succeeding there, too—became the Arizona Theater Company. The city also was home to other, smaller companies, of which the Invisible Theater became the most famous. Two other arts organizations, both born in Tucson, followed the path of the Arizona Theater Company to become regional. The Tucson Opera Company came into being in 1972, while the Tucson Ballet Company appeared four years later. Both now prosper as state arts groups, performing in both Phoenix and Tucson.

As Tucson accoutered itself with cultural institutions, the University of Arizona also grew in size, reputation and purpose. In the 1950s, Arizona's land grant university was widely considered a "party school" whose undergraduate men spent most of their time getting suntanned, while their opposite numbers plotted endlessly to marry them. A half-century later, no shred of this reputation remained. At the start of the new millennium, the University of Arizona was among the nation's top research institutions, receiving millions of dollars annually from government and private sources for research in fields as various as astronomy and medicine, anthropology and optics. More than 31,000 students, both undergraduate and graduate, made up the student body. The bartender who in 1886 decried the university's coming to Tucson because it would bring the town neither business nor wealth would have been amazed to see how wrong the years would prove him to be.

The transition from provincial party school to first-rate university was the result of many factors. As the school grew, the faculty improved, though this did not occur automatically. Successive university administrations sought distinguished scholars to perform their research and teach in the sunny desert. The momentum they generated attracted other scholars, and students followed. New areas of faculty expertise led to the establishment of other academic departments, which in turn led to wider studies at the frontiers of scientific knowledge. Meanwhile, university sports programs brought another kind of fame to the school, and Tucson fans became their most fervent supporters.

The University of Arizona was the city's first institution of higher learning, but the postwar years brought others. Pima Community College, another tax-supported school, opened in 1966 in a rented building near the airport. Tucsonians, having waited patiently for a year to see what sort of institution it would be, were amused or dismayed according to their wont that its first act was to build a "graffiti wall" on which students might express themselves. Soon, however, administrators and faculty began shaping curricula that would satisfy degree programs and provide a background for students who wished to continue their education at the University of Arizona or elsewhere. Pima Community College also provided training in specific areas needed by industries opening in Tucson, and added to the general training of the area workforce. At the beginning of the new millennium, the college had three campuses in the metropolitan area and the equivalent of nearly 18,000 full-time students.

Finally, the University of Phoenix opened the first of its two Tucson campuses in 1981. This school, which in the 1990s became the largest privately

owned university in the United States, offered curricula designed for students who already had full-time jobs, and therefore needed evening and weekend classes, as well as instruction on the Web. In the year 2000, the University of Phoenix had more than 3,500 students in Southern Arizona.

Since the beginnings of Anglo Tucson, health—or, rather, the pursuit of better health—had been a consistent reason for people's migration here. Early health seekers came to find cures for pulmonary illnesses, especially tuberculosis. Tucson and Southern Arizona's first hospital, St. Mary's, had opened in 1880. Many others, among them a Southern Methodist hospital, a sanatorium for Indians, an osteopathic hospital and a hospital for Southern Pacific Railroad employees, came and went with the years. The first veterans' hospital was founded after World War I; it got its permanent home on the city's southside in 1928. Tucson Medical Center, the city's largest hospital, started in 1907 as the Desert Sanitarium, located in the desert then far northeast of Tucson where the air was drier and cleaner than it was nearer the city's center. When tuberculosis ceased to be the great threat it had been at the start of the century, the old sanitarium became the nucleus for a new non-profit hospital, built in the 1940s entirely by community support. As the city spread east, then west, new hospitals, some specialized, others general, followed to serve the needs of people who moved there.

Of all hospitals in Tucson at the beginning of the new millennium, however, the most famous was University Medical Center. This institution opened in 1971 as University Hospital, only four years after the University of Arizona College of Medicine had been launched. The hospital later became part of the larger Arizona Health Sciences Center, which also embraced the university colleges of medicine, nursing, pharmacy and public health; and the School of Health Related Professions.

The hospital and its related academic colleges achieved national reputations in several areas. The medical school's Arizona Cancer Center did pioneering work in cloning cancer cells to test potential therapies on tumor tissue. The late Dr. Sydney Salmon, founding director of the Cancer Center, led these experiments in the 1980s. Other researchers have done high-profile work in cancer prevention and bone marrow transplantation.

At the beginning of the new millennium, the medical college's Sarver Heart Center was, if anything, even better known than the Arizona Cancer Center. Here, in 1985, Dr. Jack Copeland for the first time made successful use of an artificial heart as a bridge to the transplant of a donor heart. Within the next 15 years, Copeland got more experience with artificial hearts than any other surgeon in the country, but he also became famous for the successful outcome of numerous donor heart transplants.

Finally, the Arizona Health Sciences Center became famous for its work in the study of arthritis and for creating the first comprehensive gerontology program in the United States. Work in these areas reflected, at least in part, the large number of elderly people in the state's population.

That Arizona's only medical college and teaching hospital should be located in Tucson rather than in Phoenix was difficult for residents of the capital city to concede, and for several years in the 1970s there were rumblings about building equal facilities in Maricopa County. But the costs of such an ambitious undertaking made it unlikely the notoriously stingy legislature would approve, and in time the state Board of Regents finally put an official end to the talk.

The 2000 Census reported a population of 486,699 within Tucson's city limits; including the entire metropolitan area, the total came to 843,746. Just 10 years before, the greater Tucson area population had been 666,880, of whom 405,390 lived within the city. These figures came as no surprise, since in the United States, Arizona was second only to Nevada in the rate of its growth.

Present Pima County buildings dwarf the old county courthouse downtown.

But its distribution around Tucson was surprising, since population within the city had risen 20 percent in the decade of the '90s, but Marana, Oro Valley and unincorporated areas southeast of the city had experienced a 36 percent increase. Most of this suburban growth occurred in developer-planned communities like Rancho Vistoso, north of Oro Valley, and Dove Mountain, above Marana.

The census showed one other significant shift. Tucson's Hispanic population increased by 46.6 percent between 1990 and 2000; statewide the increase over the same period was 88 percent. Given the fact that censuses generally undercount ethnic minorities, the data were a significant portent of Tucson's future.

But what sort of future would that be? Water was always short over much of the American West, and Tucsonians have been negotiating for it since the city's founding. Spanish presidial soldiers and settlers had contested the Pima Indians' share in the 1780s. A century later, Anglo landowners tried to banish Chinese agriculture along the Santa Cruz River in order to save water for their own farms. In the last three decades of the 20th century, Tucson and Pima County governments battled the Tohono O'Odham (once called Papagos) and Anglo farmers alike for the water they used in agriculture.

Tucson, however, had a unique distinction: until the Central Arizona Project water reached the metropolitan area in November 1992, Metropolitan Tucson was the largest community in the nation to be entirely dependent on ground water. In the 20th century, the water table under central Tucson fell at least 200 feet. One study estimated that the city had used between nine and 11 percent of the water below the Tucson and Avra valleys between 1940 and the dawn of the new millennium.

Alarm about persistent overdrafting—taking more water from the aquifer than was replaced by natural means—led the state Legislature to enact a statewide groundwater law in 1980, the object of which was to achieve a

balance between water withdrawn and water replenishing the aquifer. With this impetus and with the leadership of successive city councils, Tucsonians learned to conserve. Developers found themselves pressed to limit the number of golf courses they built in new subdivisions, and the ones they built were to be watered with reclaimed effluent. Water bills went up summer by summer. Houses were replumbed with low-flow toilets. The lawns that grew, summer and winter, in front of many city homes in the 1960s vanished, to be replaced, by the start of the new millennium, by gravel or native desert vegetation. People learned to reuse "gray water" to water outdoor plants. Swimming pools construction fell off during the 1990s, though it seemed to be making coming back in favor at the beginning of the new millennium.

No one believed Tucson would use up all its water resources and blow away like dust, but it was clear that shortages would continue. The metropolis, therefore, had to make its policy of conservation permanent, and anticipate long-term changes in the lives of its citizens. Against the certainty of continued population growth, and the additional stress the increase would put on water supply, Tucson would almost certainly have to continue buying agricultural land to take it out of production. Even more important would be large-scale recharge of CAP water through streambeds and settling ponds, a process still in its infancy as the century ended. And, certainly, water rates, especially during the hot months, would continue to rise to discourage heavier use than was necessary.

Ultimately, Tucson, like other cities in the American West, may be able to supplement its water supply with desalinated seawater. Desalinization technology is available, though it is slow and very costly, and piping desalted water from California or Mexico would likely make it prohibitively expensive.

On the other hand, who knows? A century ago, no one could have foreseen what technology would accomplish by the end of the millennium. We should be humble as we wait for history to unfold further.

CHRONICLES OF LEADERSHIP

I n the two centuries since Spanish soldiers established Tucson as an outpost on the northernmost frontier of Spain's sprawling New World empire, the settlement—first a presidio, then a village, then a growing city, and finally a sprawling metropolis—has played a key role in the economic history of present-day Southern Arizona and the American Southwest.

Even before the Civil War broke out in 1861, Tucson was an important supply center for ranchers, miners, and soldiers in the Santa Cruz and Sonoita valleys, as well as a refuge for early-day health seekers. As its importance increased during the era of the Indian wars, the town became the economic hub of the Southwest's last frontier—the center of commerce, transportation and finance. The coming of the railroad in 1880 further enhanced Tucson's importance, and brought a dynamic population ready to exploit the rich business opportunities the region offered.

This generation of frontier entrepreneurs presided over Tucson's transformation into a main-line American town, with conveniences like gas works, electricity, telephones and a municipal water system. They built hotels, recreational facilities, and theaters; they founded new commercial ventures, built railroads and streetcar lines, and, with pleasure and mild surprise, watched the University of Arizona begin to grow into an institution in which first the territory and then the state could take pride.

Yet only since the beginning of World War II did Tucson's economy start developing in the directions that have made it so successful. The war began the city's involvement with the aircraft industry as well as with the U.S. Army Air Corps, which became the U.S. Air Force. Large-scale manufacturing and defense contracting came with the arrival of Hughes Aircraft, the predecessor of Raytheon Missile Systems, in the 1950s. Copper mining and agriculture both expanded, while new industries, notably electronics, also developed here. At the dawn of the new millennium, the optics industry seems poised to grow significantly in Tucson.

Meanwhile, postwar mobility, a benign climate, and the lure of the Southwestern lifestyle made Tucson one of the nation's fastest-growing cities, and growth in turn underlay strong development industries, notably construction and real estate. And as the University of Arizona grew to national significance in scientific research, Tucson became a center for high-tech manufacturing.

At the beginning of a new century, Tucson looks forward to a future seemingly limited only by the imagination of its citizens and the ambitions of its business leaders.

John Bret-Harte

ABRAMS AIRBORNE MANUFACTURING, INC.

Abrams Airborne Manufacturing, Inc. was founded in 1965 by Harold L. "Bud" Abrams. The company is a family-owned business and is managed by first, second and third generations. Harold L. "Bud" Abrams is C.E.O.; Gary L. Abrams, president; Jenny Abrams Wilson, vice president; Barbara H. Abrams, secretary/treasurer and Christopher R. Abrams is plant manager. A younger daughter, Julie Abrams Shepard, left the company after 30 years to move to her husband's new job location.

Bud had worked in general sheet metal for 20 years, but wanted to get into the precision part of the business. He started a business in his garage in 1964 and enlisted the help of his wife and three young children. Everyone worked and helped the business

to grow, and a year later he was able to secure financial backing, move into a small building and hire three employees. Abrams Airborne Mfg. is still located at the same address and has expanded to over 120,000-square feet with over 160 employees.

Abrams Airborne Mfg., Inc. has supported the aerospace and electronics industries since 1965, specializing in precision sheet metal fabrication, CNC machining, aluminum dip brazing and other related processes. Abrams' precision manufactured products orbit the planet on International

Home base. The front view of Abrams Airborne Manufacturing, Tucson, Arizona.

Space Station Alpha, communication satellites and space shuttles. Company produced components and antennas are on naval ships, tanks, military and civilian aircraft. Commercial products for the computer and medical fields are also manufactured by the Abrams.

The company has received many awards, including the "1991 Family Business of the Year," "Excellence for Protection of Wastewater," "Small Business Contractor of the Year," and "Certified Supplier" awards from many customers.

The Abrams family, owners of Pima Aviation, Inc., are leaseholders of the Marana Northwest Regional Airport. The family also owns and manages Tucson Aeroservice Center, Inc., the Fixed Base Operation which offers flight service, pilot training, charter service, and aircraft sales.

The Sky Rider Coffee Shop, located at the airport, is another family operation.

Bud and Gary are both private pilots and fly their collection of warbirds whenever time permits. Bud was a pilot in World War II

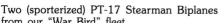
Two (sporterized) PT-17 Stearman Biplanes from our "War Bird" fleet.

in the 5th Combat Cargo Squadron flying C46's in the South Pacific. He taught Gary to fly, and father and son enjoy restoring historic aircraft as a hobby.

Bud is a founding member of the Pima Air and Space Museum. He served for nine years on the Tucson Air Museum Foundation Board, three of those years as president of the board. He also served as a Trustee on the Arizona Aviation Hall of Fame Board and he designed the cabinets that hold the portrait and memorabilia of the nominees elected to the Hall of Fame. Gary Abrams also served as secretary and then president of the Tucson Air Museum Foundation Board.

A tree farm in Cochise, Arizona, growing apples, pecans and pine trees is another family enterprise.

The Abrams family. Front row: Barbara and "Bud" Abrams. Back row, from left to right: Chris Abrams, Gary Abrams, Jenny Abrams Wilson, and Julie Abrams Shepard.

Harold "Bud" Abrams flying his 1941 vintage Stearman PT-17 Biplane.

The Abrams family members are longtime residents of Tucson and are deeply rooted in Arizona. Barbara's family arrived in Tucson in 1928, Bud's in 1935 and their three children Gary, Jenny and Julie are Tucson natives. Other family members employed at Abrams Airborne Mfg. include Bud's nephew Chris Abrams, great nephew Scott Abrams, and grandson Cade L. Wilson, all Arizona natives.

The second and third family generations will continue to expand and add new technology to Abrams Airborne Mfg. Inc. in future years—a goal that Bud and the family have worked toward since he started the business in his garage so many years ago.

ARIZONA DAILY STAR

The Old Pueblo held fewer than 6,000 souls and statehood was still 35 years down the road when Louis C. Hughes and Charles H. Tully published Tucson's first *Daily Bulletin* on March 1, 1877. It lasted 28 days.

The fledgling paper was soon revived as the Arizona *Tri-Weekly Star*, closely followed by a new name—the *Weekly Star*. On January 12, 1879, the paper finally settled on a name that would last awhile—The *Arizona Daily Star*.

Stagecoach arrivals and details on the latest gunfight filled its pages. Editor Hughes even kept a Colt .45 nearby as a way to dissuade disgruntled readers. Close to 200 newspapers would come and go during Arizona's rough and raw territorial days.

Among the survivors were the Arizona *Daily Star*, which today is Southern Arizona's largest news-gathering operation.

While still serving local readers in the traditional print medium, its stories also reach out electroni-

By around 1915, women had become part of the Star, but the men still wore their hats indoors.

cally to a worldwide readership. Its founders could have hardly imagined it.

Though Tully left the business toward the end of its first year, Hughes carried on. During the early years, the *Star* held forth at a succession of downtown offices, including one in Tucson's notorious red-light districts. Its overzealous inhabitants soon had Hughes seeking better quarters.

In 1881, he moved the paper to a new, two-story building near Congress Street and Church Avenue. Hughes was appointed territorial governor in 1883, leaving the paper in the hands of his wife Josephine. An early feminist and ardent teetotaler, Josephine often pushed her causes in the paper.

After his political career collapsed in 1886, Hughes returned to the *Star*, selling it in 1907 to father and son George and William Kelly. Three years later, the Kellys sold the paper to the Copper Queen Consolidated Mining Co., which eventually became part of the Phelps Dodge Corporation.

Not long after, many noticed a slight slant in the paper toward mining interests. By then, the *Star* was churning out its editions from a building in the middle of

In the late 1800s, the Star was located in this building downtown near Congress Street.

the block on Church Avenue, between Pennington and Congress streets.

It moved again in 1917 to a multistory building at 33 West Congress Street—next door to what would later rise as the Fox-Tucson Theatre.

In 1924, wealthy Phoenix attorney E.E. Ellinwood and California newspaper business manager William R. Mathews bought the *Star* from Phelps Dodge. The deal was that Ellinwood's son Ralph would run the newsroom and that Mathews would run the business end. Each partner would own 49 percent, with copper scion Lewis W

Douglas owning the remaining two percent. Mathews' initial investment was $4,000, with Ellinwood advancing him the remainder of the loan. Mathews paid it off in a few years.

In 1930, however, Ralph Ellinwood, just 37 years old, died of a heart attack. Though his widow Clare became the paper's new owner, it was Mathews who ran it with an iron fist from then on. Struggling to keep the paper afloat during the Great Depression, Mathews also had to deal with a disastrous fire in 1933 that charred the *Star's* entire plant.

In 1940, Mathews and Tucson *Citizen* publisher William A. Small agreed to create Tucson Newspapers, Inc., a common agency to oversee production, advertising and distribution for both publications. Both papers moved into a new building at 208 North Stone Avenue, but Mathews still ruled the *Star* newsroom.

Unencumbered by even a beginning class in journalism, he interviewed world leaders, predicted the surprise bombing of Pearl Harbor, and witnessed the Japanese surrender aboard the *USS Missouri*. A conservative Democrat, Mathews would routinely make or break candidates for office during his four decades of running the *Star*.

In 1965, Mathews and Clare Ellinwood sold the *Star* to *Citizen* publisher Small for $10 million. Mathews still held on to editorial control until 1968, when he took ill. He died the following year.

On April 8, 1971, the *Star* was sold again, this time to the Pulitzer Publishing Co., owners of the St. Louis *Post-Dispatch*.

Michael E. Pulitzer became editor and publisher. Two years later, the *Star*, along with the *Citizen* and *TNI*, moved to a new building at 4850 South Park Avenue. Even more exciting than the spiffy new quarters was the loan of two computer terminals, for the staff to use as "a space-age substitute for the typewriter."

Champagne flowed in the newsroom in April 1981 when *Star* reporters Clark Hallas and Bob Lowe won a Pulitzer Prize— the paper's first—for exposing the alleged misuse of funds within the University of Arizona football program.

Just a year later, tragedy struck when a series of electrical explosions rocked the South Side plant on July 22, engulfing seven men. *Star* business manager Frank Delehanty died from his injuries. Also seriously injured were *Star* executive managing editor Frank Johnson and veteran *Star* photographer Jack Sheaffer. Despite a crippled plant, the *Star* published the next day.

The *Star* continued to move forward. Typewriters were trashed and the entire newsroom became computerized. Writing, editing, design and layout were all done on the ubiquitous computer screen. Even photographers gave up the darkroom as digital photography jumped to the forefront.

In 1991, Bobbie Jo Buel, an 11-year veteran of the *Star*, became the paper's first female managing editor. Eight years later she was joined by the *Star's* first female publisher and executive editor, Jane Amari.

The *Star* took a giant leap into cyberspace in March of 1995 with the creation of StarNet, the electronic version of the Arizona *Daily Star*.

Today, readers around the world can log on to a myriad of stories, as well as link to other news and information sources. The Arizona *Daily Star* and its readers have come a long way since that first edition of the *Bulletin*, back in 1877.

From its current home on South Park Avenue, the *Star* circulates in Pima, Cochise, Santa Cruz and Pinal counties. It is the largest newspaper in Southern Arizona.

ACS HEALTHCARE SOLUTIONS–MIDAS+

MIDS, Inc. was founded in 1987 by James E. Peebles and Christopher J. Heller, MD. Jim Peebles and Dr. Heller became acquainted during the 1970s, when Jim was the director of information systems at the University Medical Center and Dr. Heller was doing a study of emergency room services. It was this early meeting and subsequent relationship that led to the founding of this successful Tucson-based healthcare software company.

Dr. Heller maintained a strong interest in the changing direction of healthcare and the need to measure and monitor the quality and outcome of services provided on a continuing basis over an expanded period of time. Jim Peebles' interest lay in the development and application of information systems with a strong emphasis in the healthcare area. After 11 years at UMC, Jim co-founded Sunquest Information Systems and served as its CEO from 1979 to 1986.

During a casual conversation in 1987, Dr. Heller expressed his interest in designing a system to support quality management activities in acute care hospitals. Jim was looking for a new challenge after the success of Sunquest and, jointly, they decided to pursue a new startup company. MIDS was incorporated and development was underway.

Later in 1987, the first employee was hired even though there was no formal office. Jim was doing development from a home office and collaborated with others at either the hospital or by phone. During this startup period, neither Jim nor Dr. Heller received any compensation so payroll requirements and expenses were minimal. After successful implementation of the initial product at two Carondelet facilities in 1987, three additional employees were hired in 1988 and a national advertising and exhibit program was undertaken. Several new clients were acquired during that period.

In 1988, MIDS moved to office space at 8835 East Speedway and occupied approximately 8,000 square feet including training facilities for the next several years. The product continued to grow to meet client demands and, in 1998, MIDS relocated to approximately 20,000 square feet at its current location, 2500 North Pantano Road.

Several events contributed to the growing market for MIDS primary product, MIDAS+, a system to monitor and improve healthcare quality. First, during the 1980s there was a growing interest in continuous quality improvement (CQI). Second, the Joint Commission on Accreditation of Healthcare Organizations (JCAHO) required hospitals to monitor healthcare outcomes and to perform peer review activities. This created a desire for automation and time saving processes. MIDAS+ was designed from its inception to provide this capability.

The nature of the products and services provided has changed over time to meet the evolving needs of healthcare. In addition to the MIDAS+ product that was initially conceived, services now include extensive data analysis incorporated with concurrent national comparative data.

MIDS was acquired by BRC, a Texas-based company, in early 1998 and became part of ACS when it acquired BRC later that same year. The company is now known as ACS–MIDAS+ and has over 100 employees and over 500 hospital clients. Its success was built on always putting the customer first with exceptional service. As a result, the company is now recognized as the premier leader in informational tools that analyze and improve the quality of healthcare.

Founders Jim Peebles and Chris Heller, MD.

ARIZONA HISTORICAL SOCIETY

Predating statehood by 28 years, the Arizona Historical Society was founded in Tucson on January 31, 1884 as the Society of Arizona Pioneers by a group of saloonkeepers, merchants, freighters, and other citizens who were concerned about the preservation of their pioneer heritage in the Arizona Territory.

One of the criteria for membership was arrival in the Arizona Territory by no later than 1870. As a result, over the next decade the pioneer membership and financial support dwindled, and the Society was reorganized into the Arizona Pioneers' Historical Society with broader membership categories and an annual appropriated sum of $3,000.00. By 1971, the Arizona

Pioneers' Historical Society had become the Arizona Historical Society.

In the 1970s and 1980s the AHS, in its roles as both a trustee agency of the state and a nonprofit educational institution, expanded geographically from its Tucson origin to form additional chapters in Tempe, Yuma and Flagstaff. The Arizona Historical Society is a Smithsonian affiliate. Anne I. Woosley is the executive director of the Arizona Historical Society, whose headquarters are in Tucson.

The Society's Publications Division was awarded the "Rounce & Coffin Award" for excellence in design and production. The award-winning *Journal of Arizona History* provides academic and lay readers with informative articles on the people and events that have shaped the history of the state and region. The AHS's Field Services Division serves in

Anne I. Woosley, PhD, executive director of the Arizona Historical Society.

an advisory and support capacity to an impressive roster of 47 statewide organizations.

The Society's educational programs and exhibits are defined by the AHS mission statement to collect, preserve, interpret and disseminate the history of the state of Arizona and northern Mexico as it pertains to Arizona. Three-dimensional, photographic, and manuscript collections serve to document the time period represented from the arrival of the first Europeans in 1540 to the present.

The Arizona Historical Society's work is supported by hundreds of volunteers and by an involved statewide membership. Throughout its 117 history, the AHS has remained the primary historical agency in the state.

Pioneer Historical Society meeting room. Courtesy, AHS, #2660

ARIZONA MORTUARY UNIVERSITY CHAPEL

During the early 1920s, less than 30,000 people called Tucson their home. The center of town was East and West Congress Street. Stone Avenue was the main route used when traveling north and south and "through town." The city's only red and green traffic signal guarded the intersection of Congress and Stone. Eight blocks north of Congress Street, Third Street crossed Stone Avenue and continued east for about a mile to the University of Arizona. The intersection of North Stone Avenue and East Third Street was considered prestigious. Grace Episcopal Church, a gothic edifice built of stone with beautiful stained glass windows, stood on one corner. A family-owned market and a small drug store on another corner met basic neighborhood needs. There were brick homes with shade trees, neat lawns and wrought iron fences. A barbershop, Earl's Café, and a Mobil gas station were just down the street. Streetcars ran from Stone Avenue, east on Third Street, to the University campus.

The rails remained long after the streetcars were replaced by a city bus system.

In 1926, Lee C. Yocum established Arizona Mortuary on the choice northeast corner of Stone and Third. Mr. Yocum, who had owned a funeral home in Logan, Ohio, moved to Tucson with his wife Verna and their two young children, seeking, like many others in those days, a dry climate for health reasons. After initial opposition and court battles involving neighbors, zoning was changed and construction began. Throughout the years, Arizona Mortuary proved to be a stabilizing influence for the neighborhood. Quality went into its construction and furnishings, the grounds were professionally landscaped and manicured, and its fleet of funeral cars were kept up to date and polished.

By 1930, there were six funeral homes in Tucson, all located in or near the downtown area. When Lee Yocum died in 1939, Verna Yocum became president and director of Arizona Mortuary. World War II brought many changes. For several years, Davis Monthan Air Force Base and Tucson Veterans Hospital awarded Arizona Mortuary the contracts

Front Entrance, 1965.

to care for their dead, and honored the mortuary with official letters of commendation for their outstanding services. The funeral home's reputation spread, the volume of cases increased annually, and the company was invited to become a member of National Selected Morticians, as well as of the Order of the Golden Rule. Arizona Mortuary became a highly respected institution in the community, and expanded in the 1960s through the purchase of a second location east of town, Arizona Mortuary Eastside Chapel. Both locations enjoyed enviable success that continued through the years.

After Verna Yocum's death in 1972, Verna's son-in-law Robert Long, took over as president of the corporation. The two funeral homes continued to prosper, but the local scene was changing due to growth in all directions. The neighborhood of Stone and Third

Hand-laid brick patio between Yocum residence and the funeral home.

(now named University Boulevard) lost its unique character, the Episcopal Church had been torn down, and all the old brick homes on Stone Avenue were destroyed in favor of used car lots. The small grocery store and pharmacy were gone. Stone Avenue became a street lined with vacant buildings, falling in disrepair. In 1977, Service Corporation International (SCI), the largest death care corporation in the world, bought both Arizona Mortuary locations. SCI acquired East Lawn and South Lawn Cemeteries in 1981 and soon built funeral homes on the property to provide full-service death care to their client families. The Eastside Chapel was closed and sold, but SCI added other funeral businesses to their death care "family," including Palms Mortuary and Heather Mortuary & Chapels. Changing times and ownership brought new programs for the future, including pre-planned and funded funeral and cremation services and pre-need sales of cemetery property and merchandise. Many of the same employees, as well as many new employees, continued providing caring, professional services to the citizens and visitors of Tucson.

As Arizona Mortuary celebrates its 75th year in business, all of the "old-time" employees of the funeral home, some of whom had worked there 20 to 40 years or more, have retired or died. Although Arizona Mortuary's appearance has changed over the years, it keeps its vigil on the corner of North Stone and University Boulevard. When visitors enter, they almost feel like they're stepping back in time. The domed

The building in 2001. Seventy-five years of compassionate service.

ceiling in the intimate chapel has been restored to its original splendor, and graceful arches and French doors join the various rooms furnished with lovely antiques, such as an historic 300-year-old grandfather clock. The early history of this walnut case and its clock movement is not certain, but it is known that the clock arrived in Tucson during the 1800s when a prominent citizen who had purchased it in Los Angeles sent it to Tucson on the train. Soon after World War I, O.C. Parker, Tucson's mayor and undertaker, bought the clock. Throughout the years the clock has kept vigil in a funeral home. In 1962 Arizona Mortuary acquired the clock for its Arizona Mortuary East Chapel, but in 1978 the clock was moved to Arizona Mortuary on Seven East University Boulevard after a vandal fired a bul-

let through a window of the funeral home. The bullet shattered the glass door of the case, and ripped through its back panel. The bullet missed its intended target and the pendulum continues to swing to and fro, ticking away the minutes of each hour, as it has done since its arrival in Tucson more than 150 years ago.

Today, Arizona Mortuary University Chapel's dedicated employees are proud to continue the funeral home's 75-year legacy of compassionate and professional service to families facing the most difficult event of their lives—the death of a loved one.

Chapel with old-world charm.

AVILA CONCRETE CONTRACTOR

Avila Concrete Contractor is a commercial and industrial concrete sub-contractor, which specializes in the "big box" tilt-up type of construction. Rosendo "Ross" Avila had years of experience in this high tech type of construction before establishing Avila Concrete in 1973 with only a few paychecks and the desire to go out on his own. Mr. Avila started with a Ford pick-up truck as his office and a small pad of paper as his accountant. Surviving the turbulent times for the construction field in the late-'80s that eliminated many of his fellow companies, he has become one of the most respected, admired and successful commercial concrete owners in southern Arizona.

Born in the agricultural community of La Union, New Mexico, Mr. Avila was eldest son of Mexican-born migrant workers. The family eventually settled in Eloy, Arizona where the fields of cotton soon became the family's main source of income. Mr. Avila enjoyed school but had to quit after the eighth grade to help sup-

port his six siblings. This helped instill the hard work ethic that is very much part of his character. In 1955, at the age of 20, he moved with his new wife Grace to the fast-growing city of Tucson, where he soon found a job as a laborer for Wendell T. Decker, general contractor. In 1962 Ross joined the Finisher's Union where he learned to enjoy working with concrete and achieved the status of finisher. Five years later he moved to the Carpenters Union to learn the carpentry field. Mr. Avila had worked his way from laborer to superintendent but felt there was something more he could accomplish for himself, his family and his community.

The Avila family had now reached seven, with three daughters and two sons that were living in a home that he built on Tucson's east side. At the insistence of Wendell T. Decker, Avila hired a few local men and started his very modest company. They began with a few homes and continued on to gas stations, convenience stores, and small commercial buildings. Knowing the quality of work done by Avila Concrete, Mr.

Wendell T. Decker and Rosendo "Ross" Avila.

Decker utilized them for all of his concrete services within his growing developments. Soon Avila Concrete was laying the foundation for grocery stores, apartment complexes, shopping centers, high rises and large industrial projects. Avila Concrete grew to 25 full-time employees and Mr. Avila knew that he had finally made it as a principal contractor within the Tucson community. Tucson was rapidly growing in the early-'80s and so was Avila Concrete, but when the recession hit and the savings and loan fiasco occurred, real estate and the construction industry took a big hit.

Development in Tucson came to a crawl in the latter part of the 1980s; companies unable to weather the financial storm went bankrupt. A few general contractors filed bankruptcy, creating a domino effect for other subcontractors and suppliers. Avila Concrete was struggling with non-fulfillment of contracts totaling over $100,000, a tremendous amount

Avila Concrete's first "official" office.

Avila Concrete's new office building at 4320 East Illinois, Tucson, Arizona.

or this small company run by one man, along with the assistance of his children, in a make-shift office with a newly-hired accountant. With the success of his business so far, Mr. Avila believed he could ride out the storm, and refused to declare bankruptcy. Unfortunately, the market was no help and did not offer the opportunities on large buildings that the company had been used to. Avila Concrete took any job that came along, mostly on small homes and small businesses that were also risky, due to the instability of the market. There were times when Mr. Avila would request that his highest paid workers not cash their paychecks until he was paid on a job. Only a few companies, mostly corporations outside Tucson, fought to have Avila Concrete liquidated to regain some of their possible losses. Just when all seemed bleak and foreclosure eminent Avila Concrete filed reorganization in 1993. Mr. Avila felt that he must repay his debts to the community that brought prosperity for him only

a few years prior, even though he was never paid the money owed to him. With many of his suppliers and his employees behind him, Avila did something only a few companies have accomplished—pay back all debts and return many times stronger.

Once again Tucson is booming. Mr. Avila takes his company to a new level, utilizing new technologies that allow for hundreds of more yards of concrete poured at once, machines and techniques that make for super flat floors, and larger cranes to accomplish faster tilting of panels. In the past 30 years, Avila Concrete Contractor, has poured the concrete for a large part of Tucson, including custom homes in the foothills, shopping centers, grocery stores, technology campuses, high rises, manufacturing plants, schools, the Fine Arts buildings at the University of Arizona, hospitals, public works buildings, hotels, recreation facilities, airports and manufacturing warehouses. The success of Avila Concrete is now exhibited through Mr. Avila's donations to public works for the community, schools and sports activities for his grandchildren. Projects completed as of 2001 are a $1.3 million contract for a new casino and a 7,500-square-foot tilt-up hous-

Tilt up "panel."

ing a new office and warehouse for Avila Concrete. It is certainly true, that as much as Tucson is a part of Mr. Avila, Avila Concrete Contractor is a part of the Tucson community.

America Online at Williams Centre tilt-up building.

BREAULT RESEARCH ORGANIZATION, INC.

Robert P. Breault, founder of Breault Research Organization, Inc., traces his passion for optics and space-based astronomy back to 1954, when he was a 14-year-old admiring the night heavens from his bedroom window in Naugatuck, Connecticut. Inspired by several astronomy books, young Bobby Breault plotted his life's path: a mathematics degree, a stint as an Air Force fighter pilot, and a graduate degree in astronomy—all to prepare him for a career as a space-based research scientist. He had his future lined up three years before Russia launched the space race in 1957.

The roots of his company were first started around 1972 when, as a graduate student at the Optical Sciences Center at the University of Arizona and its and part-time employee, Bob Breault performed a computerized stray light analysis on what is now known as the Hubble Space Telescope. He improved its optical stray light performance by a factor of 100,000, which drew the attention of many major aerospace and defense companies. Breault's part-time work at the Optical Sciences Center quickly grew to full time, but not take up all his time. In 1975 he formed the sole proprietorship, Breault Research Organization and, with assistance from Alan Greynolds, took on some requested optical stray light analyses for these and other leading aerospace companies as a private consultant. The company's abbreviated name, BRO, was chosen to help customers phonetically pronounce Bob Breault's name.

In May 1979, the month he graduated, Bob Breault incorpo-

Bob Breault, founder of Breault Research Organization, Inc.

rated the company as Breault Research Organization (BRO), Inc. to serve the aerospace and defense industries. BRO grew from a one-person operation to one that now employs 50 people at its 6400 East Grant Road facility. BRO also expanded from its founder's academic specialty area of stray-light analysis and suppression—essentially controlling stray light in optical devices—to include a wide array of optics areas. BRO established itself as the premier authority on optical challenges for a variety of industries including automotive, display, medical, semiconductor, and telecommunications. The company leverages its R&D heritage to provide innovative answers to these industries' most difficult optical and illumination problems. It also continues to work on defense projects—something Breault takes very seriously because of his stint as an F-100 Wild Weasel pilot in

Vietnam. At that time, Breault's life depended on his equipment and skill, which helped him perform and return safely home following missions deep into enemy territory.

BRO has stayed close to its roots as an engineering house. Its staff includes two dozen engineers with experience in optics, physics, and engineering (over 80 percent have masters or doctorate degrees). The BRO team is world renowned for its experience in all aspects of optical and illumination system design, simulation, performance analysis, tolerance specification, prototyping and support through testing. Bob Breault developed and sold as a BRO product a stray light analysis program called APART™. Al Greynolds developed ASAP™ as one of the world's most recognized and comprehensive optical software programs. Hardware capabilities allow BRO to take projects beyond theoretical design and into the marketplace.

Named one of the top 50 fastest growing high tech companies in Arizona in 1997, 1998, 1999, and 2000, BRO continues to aggressively expand to meet industries' increasing demand for optics. As the leader in the optics industry, businesses look to BRO for cutting edge optical technology.

In 2000 Bob Breault, his Chief Operating Officer Charlie Luebbering, and Information Systems Manager Wayne Hall, collaborated to found Inqutec, an optics startup holding company. In turn, Inqutec founded LightSharp, a specialty company that has proprietary technology for removing stray light from commercial digi tal cameras. Also in 2000, Bob and Kathleen Perkins, BRO's vice presidents of marketing and sales, respectively, started OpticsReports™, a financial newsletter about optics companies, targeted to investors at all levels.

Over the ensuing years, BRO has performed stray light analyses on the Hubble Space Telescope; the Infra-Red Astronomy Satellite (IRAS); the Diffuse Infrared Background Experiment (DIRBE); part of the COBE (COsmic Background Explorer) mission Galileo that went into orbit around Jupiter; Cassini launched to Saturn, many of the "Star War" weapons of the '80s; European Space Agency's Infrared Satellite Observatory (ISO); Xray Multiple Mirror Telescope (XMM); all the ground-based 8-meter telescopes of the late '90s; GOES (one of the weather satellites), and many more.

BRO is considered one of the leading companies in Optics Valley, a term applied to the location of the Arizona cluster of optics companies and the Optical Sciences Center at the University of Arizona. BRO provides optical engineering software and consulting services to customers around the world. The company is now recognized as a superior technical organization that "pushes the envelope."

Bob Breault is also the recognized evangelist of clusters. A cluster consists of a coalition of the public sector, the educational system, and the private sector to promote science, technology, and education for the economic benefit of the local region. In 1992 Breault helped form the Arizona Optics Industry Association

(AOIA), the first Optics Cluster in the world. By mid-2001 AOIA included about 200 optics companies in Arizona.

The optics cluster is a multipronged approach about how to inform public and private sectors about high technology, how these sectors can best work synergistically, and how to enhance science and math education. For example, the governor of Arizona and Arizona's legislators are active participants in the Cluster, as is the mayor of Tucson, and the presidents of all the universities and the community colleges in Arizona. Employee volunteers from Raytheon, Breault Research, and other companies go into the classroom to talk about and demonstrate science. Members in the Cluster motivate children from grades K-12 to foster an interest in science.

There are now, literally thousands of people in the state of Arizona who were involved in the Cluster creation process. They include the governor, head of the Arizona Department of Commerce, head of the Governor's Strategic Partnership for Economic Development, executives from Northwest Development Bank, and various executives from Arizona's venture capital firms.

The following excerpts are from articles on the optics cluster by Alan Fisher of the *Arizona Daily Star* in 2001:

Breault retains the sense of wonder he had as a 14-year-old who shot off homemade rockets. "I'm still a young kid, still a pioneer beyond my age. There are new areas to explore. The pilot aspect of risk-taking is still there. It hasn't diminished much, to the dismay of some of my employees and people in the community." The work never stops, but Breault feels it's been worth it. "My careers have been very, very fun. Packed with challenges, even with death-defying challenges in some cases. But it's been very satisfying, from the people I've worked with to the projects I've been asked to do. I plan to work until two days after I die. For real."

The Breault Research Organization building in Tucson, Arizona.

THE ARIZONA INN

The story of the Arizona Inn and its founder, Isabella Greenway, is the stuff that legend is made of. It is a story that starts at the beginning of the 20th century and involves many fascinating, well-known national figures. The creation of the Inn is a story of altruism, resourcefulness, pioneering spirit, passion, and valor.

Isabella Greenway, an only child born in 1886, lost her father when she was nine years old. She and her mother divided their time between a great-aunt's Kentucky farm and her grandfather's home in Minneapolis. At the age of 15, she and her mother moved to New York to live with an aunt and uncle. Isabella came out as a debutante in 1903, a time in New York that Edith Wharton portrays in her novels. She forged a lifelong friendship with Eleanor Roosevelt, was a bridesmaid in Franklin and Eleanor's wedding, and married one of their great friends, Robert Munro Ferguson, who had been one of Theodore Roosevelt's Rough Riders.

Isabella's early married life was difficult. Robert Ferguson was

The entrance to Arizona Inn, circa 1930. The opening date was December 18, 1930.

stricken with tuberculosis, and the family, with two small children, moved from New York and homesteaded in New Mexico. When Ferguson died, Isabella married John Greenway, also a Rough Rider, family friend, mining pioneer, and a World War I hero. In a tragically short time, she was widowed again. Undaunted by hardship, upon moving to Tucson in the 1920s, Isabella created the Arizona Hut to give jobs to World War I disabled veterans who could be trained to manufacture and sell furniture.

Initially, the Arizona Hut furniture sold in shops across the country. By 1929, when the Great Depression hit, sales plunged. Most of the furniture went unsold, and someone told Mrs. Greenway that she had enough furniture to "build a hotel." And, so, she did. Today the Hut furniture is still in use at the Inn, and two on-site cabinetmakers maintain and reproduce the pieces.

The Arizona Inn, on a luscious 14-acre property, was built in 1930. It is listed on the National Register of Historic Places, cited for its role in developing tourism in Tucson, its Spanish Colonial revival architecture and Mrs. Greenway's political career and humanitarianism.

Volunteers in front of the "Arizona Hut."

By the early 1930s Isabella Greenway had become politically prominent. In 1932, she seconded Franklin Roosevelt's presidential nomination. In 1933 she was elected by an overwhelming margin to Congress, and became Arizona's first Congresswoman. In 2000 she was inducted into the Arizona Business Hall of Fame and is currently being honored by various exhibits, films and an upcoming biography from University of Arizona Press.

Now in its third generation of family ownership, The Inn is run by Mrs. Greenway's granddaughter, Patty Doar, and is nationally-recognized as a premier resort. It houses 86 individually-decorated rooms and suites, and two private guest residences. The award-winning dining room is considered one of Tucson's best restaurants. More than seven decades from its inception, the family-owned Arizona Inn remains a monument to the integrity, energy, and compassion of an extraordinary Arizona citizen, Isabella Greenway.

CONTROL ENGINEERING INC.

Mr. John P. Benson, P.E., C.E.M originally founded Control Engineering, Inc. as an Arizona corporation in 1982. After graduating with a degree in Mechanical Engineering from the University of Arizona (Tucson) in 1961, Mr. Benson went on to serve in the Armed Forces as a First Lieutenant in the United States Army. Mr. Benson then continued his career in the mechanical engineering field, specializing in automatic building temperature control systems. He was the Arizona branch manager for several years with one of the worlds largest temperature control system manufacturer's before moving on to an Arizona-based consulting engineering firm.

In 1982 Mr. Benson decided he would like to own and operate his own control contracting business. He researched several brands of control system products to represent in the Arizona market before selecting Staefa Control Systems, due to their innovative products and leadership in the HVAC (Heating, Ventilating and Air Conditioning) controls and building management systems industry. Now an offering from Siemens Building Technologies, Inc., Staefa primarily utilizes independent distributors to market their products. Control Engineering is Staefa Control Systems' exclusive independent distributor for the state of Arizona.

When Mr. Benson founded Control Engineering, and as his business grew, his goal was always to ensure that Control Engineering was an enjoyable place to work. Company Christmas parties and spring or summer family picnics were common every year. Additionally, Mr. Benson strived to provide all of Control Engineering's customers with the best products available, the best service possible, and to complete all projects to the customer's satisfaction and expectations, no matter the cost.

As a result of Mr. Benson's industry reputation, dedication, knowledge, and ability to find and keep valuable employees, Control Engineering has grown to be one of the most significant and influential control contractor/manufacturer's representatives in the Arizona market.

While Control Engineering's office was located in Phoenix, with literally hundreds of customers in Arizona, their presence in southern Arizona began to grow. In order to provide a growing customer base with customers such as Davis-Monthan Air Force Base, Tucson's Arizona Air National Guard facility, and Fort Huachuca Army post near Sierra Vista more timely and local service, Mr. Benson decided it was time to open a branch office in Tucson.

In 1994, Mr. Benson officially opened the Tucson branch office under the management and direction of Mr. Keith Metzger. Mr. Metzger entered the HVAC "controls" business with Control Engineering during its first year of operations in 1982. Prior to Control Engineering, Mr. Metzger served in the U.S. Air Force as an electrical mechanical technician in the Strategic Air Command, and other miscellaneous electrical/mechanical trades until he found the love of his career life with HVAC controls.

The Tucson office started with Mr. Metzger and two part time field employees. Today, the Tucson office has grown to a maintained level of 16 full-time employees, including journeyman electricians, technicians, project engineers, managers, sales, service and other administrative staff.

Today the Tucson branch has expanded its customer base in southern Arizona to the likes of Kartchner Caverns State Park near Benson, Douglas School District, Cochise Community College District, America Online, University of Arizona Agricultural Campus, and the tallest building in Tucson—the Unisource Energy Tower, among others.

John P. Benson, founder and president of Control Engineering, Inc. (2001)

ENGINEERING & ENVIRONMENTAL CONSULTANTS

Engineering and Environmental Consultants, Inc. (EEC) was founded by John "Chuck" Hollingsworth, PE, and Frances L. Hollingsworth in March 1987. Chuck's vision was to provide quality environmental engineering and consulting services to the Southwest region. Since its inception, EEC has grown to a company of 75 plus employees, providing not only environmental services but also civil engineering, transportation, land surveying, landscape architecture, and natural resource planning. The company sees its role in society as being integral to the quality of life in the communities it serves by ensuring that residents have cleaner air and water, better transportation, and housing developments with adequate infrastructure to meet current and future needs.

Companies willing and able to perform environmental consulting services were not available in the community in 1987, and EEC was the first Tucson-based organization dedicated to providing this much-needed expertise. EEC was founded on Chuck's vision of establishing an environmental and engineering services company that was sited locally and could provide the services necessary to satisfy a demand created by several newly enacted federal hazardous waste laws. At start-up, EEC's focus was on hazardous waste consulting and wastewater engineering, which fueled the rapid growth that made the company successful in its early years. As business increased, the company moved to its first office in 1988, located at 4400 East Broadway.

In 1989, Michael J. Murray joined the firm to oversee what had become a burgeoning Underground Storage Tank (UST) problem. Mike has since managed UST projects for large corporations and military installations, and now directs the Environmental Services Department at EEC. Most notably, Mike has been the program manager for the past eight years for two major environmental management contracts at Fort Huachuca, Arizona. These projects have included Hazardous Waste Remediation, UST Management, and the removal and cleanup of unexploded ordnance and ammunition at military installations. Mike's department also performs environmental assessments of real property and risk assessment modeling, and has designed and operated landfill gas mitigation systems for the City of Tucson. The Environmental Group pioneered the use of mobile laboratories for on-site investigations and clean-up projects.

The first engineering design service that EEC added was Civil Engineering and Land Development. Ryan Bale, PE, was hired in 1995 to oversee this department, and brought more than 20 years of private and municipal experience to the company. In addition, James L. Dean, RLS, joined the firm in 1996 to establish a Survey Department. Ryan now oversees the Civil/Survey Division and has provided engineering and surveying services to many of the community's largest developments, including Riverside Crossing, and the Slim Fast production plant. Likewise, Jim manages four full-time survey crews, which use total station and global positioning system equipment, as well as standard ground-based survey techniques.

EEC established a Public Works and Transportation Department in 1997 with the addition of R. Craig Allison, PE, PLS. Craig brought extensive experience to the firm in the areas of roadway, drainage, and highway design. The group also designs water and wastewater infrastructure projects for the City of Tucson and Pima County. With the anticipated need for infrastructure design, Craig positioned EEC for the award of major roadway design projects in Pima and Maricopa Counties, and the cities of Tucson and Phoenix. EEC's Transportation Group is providing planning and design services for the widening of 2.5 miles of Craycroft Road from the Rillito

Tucson managers, from left to right, James L. Dean, Ryan G. Bale, Chuck Hollingsworth, Michael J. Murray, and R. Craig Allison.

EEC headquarters building in Tucson at 4625 East Fort Lowell Road, since 1994. Courtesy, David Bean Photography

River to Sunrise Drive. MicroStation and GEOPAK computerized roadway and drainage design systems are used to model the proposed improvements.

To strengthen its Public Works Group's position throughout the state, EEC purchased the assets of McLaughlin Kmetty Engineers in Phoenix, Arizona. The acquisition provided EEC an opportunity to establish its presence in the Phoenix market. Mark Gavan, PE, was hired in December 1997, to oversee the Phoenix Civil Engineering effort and to manage the newly-acquired office. Mark brought considerable experience to EEC with more than 20 years of civil and drainage engineering expertise in the Phoenix area, including such projects as the widening of Bell Road to six lanes, the Oak Street Storm Drain, and the Gila Bend Area Drainage Master Plan. Shortly thereafter John Barker, LA joined EEC. John started the Landscape Archi-

tecture Division and was responsible for Paseo Highlands Park design and several ADOT highway landscape projects.

EEC continued to grow, and in 1999 Michael Collins was hired to launch the Natural Resources Department. Mike brought experience in environmental planning and regulatory compliance for the Department of Defense. As a result, EEC established an office in Sierra Vista to better serve the needs of clients in southeastern Arizona. In 2001, Mike became vice president of business development for EEC, and Steven Fairaizl was hired as the natural resources department manager. Steve brought more than 25 years of expertise to the company. His department now specializes in biological and cultural resources, environmental planning and geographic information system (GIS) consulting.

An engineering company must identify the needs of the community and develop the personnel and equipment to meet these needs. As needs change, a firm must constantly re-engineer the company business model and expand the expertise of the

staff. This challenge awaits all engineers in today's society. What communities want—and demand—-for quality of life, will inevitably result in asking the engineering community to provide new solutions in a cost-effective and dependable manner. Chuck believes that engineers truly do "build our society." Service to the community is also a vital aspect of being an engineer; they must contribute their time and efforts to all aspects of making life better for the residents of their community. Teaching children about leadership and responsibility has been one of Chuck's goals for many years. He has served on the boards of the Red Cross, the Marshall Home for Men, the San Pedro Foundation, and the Boy Scouts of America. He believes people should be given the tools and training to do their job well, provide them with guidance, and empower them to make the right decisions.

Phoenix managers, from left to right, Mark T. Gavan, John E. Barker, Steven D. Fairaizl, and Michael G. Collins. Courtesy, Bob Wilcox Photography

DATAFORTH CORPORATION

In November of 1984 Dataforth Corporation was formed as a joint venture between Burr-Brown, a maker of electronic operational amplifiers, digital to analog and analog to digital converters, and other electronic products. Dataforth was the idea of Lee Payne, who had been a product design engineer and engineering manager at Burr-Brown for 13 years since attending graduate school at the University of Arizona.

In the early 1980s Burr-Brown, under the leadership of Jim Burns, CEO, and Tom Brown, chairman and founder of Burr-Brown, was looking for new market areas. The first effort was to start an internal systems division. To target the then emerging personal computers for industrial use, Jim Burns and Gene Toby, Burr-Brown marketing manager, started an entrepreneurial company called Intelligent Instrumentation, Inc. A second spin-off occurred under Larry McDonald, another Burr-Brown engineering and marketing person. As a trend was developing, Dataforth submitted its initial business plan to Jim Burns and it was accepted.

The first products were limited distance modems and a communications tester. Later products were to be communications multiplexers. The first sales were in 1985. In 1986, after 18 months in operation, with three employees, the company turned profitable. Since that time, it has remained on a growth path, posting regular, annual profits.

Since the start of the company until the present, Tucson subcontractors have been used for basic assembly of printed circuit boards. In the early years this was invaluable, allowing personnel to concentrate on new products, marketing, and company organization. In 1988 Bob Smith, former product design engineer, engineering manager, and marketing manager at Burr-Brown joined the company as vice-president of marketing and sales. At that time the company was housed in a small, leased space which was expanded twice. The second expansion was when Burr-Brown's line of STD, computer Input-Output cards was acquired. These products had once been the products of another small Tucson company, Applied Microsystems, Inc. Sales of these products financed the second major line of products. These are signal-conditioning amplifiers used in

---

Dataforth building.

industrial test and measurement applications. With these products the company had returned to its roots in analog circuitry. Additional space was needed immediately. The company moved to another leased facility near the Tucson International Airport. Growth was brisk with the new product line. In 1994 even more space was needed. At that time a building in the Tucson International Business Center was purchased.

There are presently over 1,500 active customers located in all major developed areas of the world. Thirty percent of sales are international. Most of these are European; however, sales in Asia, Japan, Central America, and South America are growing. Sales and distribution are now under the company's own network of national and international representatives and distributors set up by Bob Smith, vice president of sales and marketing.

Factory automation is a current project. An automated assembly line has been successfully installed, and the economic benefits are readily apparent. Larger machinery is now scheduled for acquisition.

The company now has annual sales of $6 million with 45 employees in a 12,000 square-foot building. An active program for new product development is being pursued. These will include microprocessor-driven data acquisition systems utilizing the successful line of signal conditioning modules.

GALLERY IN THE SUN

In the foothills of the Santa Catalina Mountains north of Tucson, Ettore "Ted" DeGrazia built the Gallery in the Sun. It was quiet and beautiful there. His dream began in 1951. Built with his own hands and those of his Indian friends, together they made hundreds and hundreds of adobe bricks. One by one these bricks became the Gallery walls.

It is a large gallery, containing six smaller sections of original oils and watercolors. The work contained in these galleries dates from 1925 to 1978. DeGrazia spent all his life researching his subjects, which include the story of Father Kino; the Papago Indian legends; Cabeza De Vaca; the first non-Indian in Texas, New Mexico and Arizona; the Yaqui Easter; and the bullfight. This treasure trove of creativity also includes all of his sculptures, ceramics, jewelry, enamels and books. The Gallery is open every day, and everyone is welcome. The Gallery in the Sun is often

thought of as a haven for those seeking a quietness of beauty.

Beside the Gallery is the Mission in the Sun in honor of Our Lady of Guadalupe, the beloved virgin saint of Mexico. Her image is at the altar. Murals are painted on all of the walls along with colorful Indians bringing flowers. The Mission is dedicated to Father Eusebio Kino. Father Kino was a Jesuit priest who in 1537 brought kindness to the Indians, who in turn, loved him. His memory is revered to this day.

In between the Mission and the Gallery is a simple grave. This is where DeGrazia is buried. At the head of his resting place is a cholla cactus cross with an inscription—Ad Infinitum—meaning "forever."

The following is a vignette in DeGrazia's own words:

"My first trip to the Navajo reservation took place in the late 1930s. I have always been inter-

Entrance to DeGrazia's Gallery in the Sun, located at the foot of the Santa Catalina Mountains, north of Tucson. Courtesy, Mary R. Gianas

ested in Indians...that first trip was a revelation to me almost as if I had discovered the new world...the high plateau country was a palette of color...all shades of red and gold burned by the bright sun that glowed out of the brightest blue sky I had ever seen. It is the Trading Post where I came to know the Navajo best. They travel miles to trade their wool and to meet friends. I have learned much, and much admired the Navajo."

DeGrazia was born in a small mining town of Morenci, Arizona territory, in 1909. It was there that he learned about the rich colors of the earth. He spent many hours prospecting for gold in the Superstition Mountains northeast of Tucson. He was successful most of the time and the Gallery in the Sun holds many beautiful pieces of gold and gold jewelry. DeGrazia's love of the desert southwest and the native people who live there is evident to all who visit. He was a maverick, a good guy, and a man of the people who painted for the masses.

DeGrazia's "Mission in the Sun," next to the Gallery. The Mission was built in honor of Father Kino and Our Lady of Guadalupe. Courtesy, Mary R. Gianas

GRG CONSTRUCTION CO., INC.

Glen R. Greer, president and CEO of GRG Construction Co., Inc. acquired his experience and work ethics while working for his father's construction company; starting as a laborer and working his way up to foreman and finally project manager.

Glen "grew up" in the construction industry, one of four sons of the late Bruce E. Greer, owner of Bruce Greer Construction Co., who contributed such local landmarks as The Tucson Auto Mall and Rita Ranch to name just a few. Glen first acquired his contractor's license in 1989, doing mostly small sewer jobs to get started. He did most of the physical work himself by day and his evenings were spent doing paperwork, including bids. GRG Construction Co., Inc. specializes in site development of subdivisions typically completing all grading, underground utilities, paving, and drainage protection phases of a project. GRG has been providing these services since 1994 when Glen began site development projects for The Estes Company, among others, and seeing steady growth ever since.

The company has experienced a healthy growth rate exceeding $11 million in gross sales in the year 2000. GRG currently has over 100 employees with over 50 pieces of operating equipment worth approximately $3 million at their disposal.

GRG Construction's growth is attributable to over 100 years of cumulative construction experience gained by key company individuals, including some of the loyal employees "inherited" from Bruce Greer Construction Co.

Glen Greer reviews his daily paperwork.

GRG paves a parking lot north of Tucson for a professional office complex.

that included his brothers Thomas M. Greer II and Bruce Greer Jr.

Often, one can find Glen working side-by-side with his employees as well as developers to get the job done. Glen understands that the future growth of GRG Construction Co., Inc. depends on a quality product and the ability to remain on schedule and within budget. His estimating staff has demonstrated a meticulous eye for detail and competitive pricing when submitting bids; his field supervisors are seasoned professionals, taking pride in the quality of their work.

Glen has worked, and continues to work, for some of the most reputable companies in southern Arizona, taking an active role as part of Tucson's development—as was his father's wish.

CLIFTON GUNDERSON LLP

The accounting firms of Clifton Gunderson LLP and Cotton, Parker, Johnson & Co., P.C. announced an agreement to merge effective August 1, 2000. The Cotton, Parker, Johnson employees in Tucson and Phoenix, AZ, and Dallas, TX, became part of the multi-regional Clifton Gunderson organization. Clifton Gunderson LLP, formed in 1960, is one of the most successful and rapidly growing accounting and consulting firms. In just 40 years, the firm has grown to be the 11th largest CPA and consulting firm in the United States with over 1,300 total personnel, including 500 CPAs. With offices in 13 states and Washington, DC, they have the resources and experience to help their clients get where they want to be. Their mission is simple, "... growth of our people and growth of our clients...all else follows."

In Tucson, where Clifton Gunderson already has an office (since 1983), the combined staff will be located in expanded office facilities at 335 North Wilmot Road, Suite 300. They provide traditional auditing, accounting, and tax services for a variety of clients. The company also provides many non-traditional services, such as systems design and assistance, internal procedures, development, budgeting and forecasting, and counsel in management decision-making.

In making the announcement, Carl George, Clifton Gunderson CEO said, "We are very excited about joining forces, since both firms bring so much value to the table. Clifton Gunderson will provide a greater range of consulting services and a national network

Ron Parker, CPA, partner in charge.

of well-established offices. Together, we are the third largest credit union specialist and we will continue to grow that practice."

Cotton, Parker, Johnson was established in 1977 in Tucson, AZ. Over its 23-year history, the firm achieved professional distinction by providing specialized accounting services to credit unions, not-for-profit organizations, small businesses and individual clients.

Ron Parker, president and managing partner of Cotton, Parker, Johnson said, "We made the decision to merge because we feel we can serve our clients better by having access to the resources of a larger firm. By joining Clifton Gunderson, we are able to continue building our leadership position in the credit union

niche, while expanding our services to other key client groups."

It was 22 years ago when the two-year old accounting firm of Cotton, Parker, Johnson & Co. secured its first engagement with a credit union.

Ronald T. Parker, CPA says he obtained this client by a referral from an existing client in another field. "We felt at the time that auditing credit unions could be an extremely lucrative niche for a young firm. Consequently, we became involved in the credit union area on a serious level by having our partners serve on credit union supervisory committees and boards as well as speak at many credit union conferences. This was, of course, before we obtained our first client."

Now, more than two decades later, Clifton Gunderson currently provides professional services to over 225 credit unions and related entities nationwide, ranging in asset size from $1 million to over $2 billion.

The Clifton Gunderson Tucson Partners celebrating their 40th Anniversary in November 2000. Left to Right: Richard Fellner, Ron Parker, Jay Buck, Rick Goldenson, John Sheehan, Tom Johnson, and John Cotton.

HARLOW GARDENS

John M. Harlow, Sr., operated a landscape architecture and contracting business in Duluth, Minnesota in the 1930's, but the area's short growing season did not adequately support the operation, so the enterprising businessman sought a more suitable location. Tucson looked promising.

After a couple of years of winter residence in the desert community, Harlow and his family moved to Tucson full time in 1940. He worked out of an office in the Old Adobe Patio at 40 West Broadway Boulevard in 1952.

One of the first landscaping jobs was in Phoenix; another was at the Ely Ranch near Nogales. In the 1940s the Harlows purchased some property on east Pima street, set up a quonset hut, and grew their own plants. That location became the company's sole outlet around 1957, and remains so today. Mary Louise Harlow, John Sr.'s wife, ran a flower shop out of the Pima location for several years.

The Harlow landscaping firm has handled many interesting projects, including this 1948 tree-moving operation.

All four Harlow children worked in the business from a young age. Ten-year-old twins, William C. and John M. Harlow, Jr., rode with their father to Bisbee many Sunday mornings, where they sold rosebushes from the back of their truck. The senior Harlow, who wrote a "Weekend Gardener" column for the *Tucson Citizen* for ten years, was a member of the city planning and zoning commission.

Through the years, John M. Harlow and Associates Landscape Architects was the professional arm of the business, specializing in residential and commercial landscape design. The other portion of the business, Harlow's

Landscape and Nursery Center, took in the retail, landscape contracting, and horticultural maintenance operations.

During the 1980's Harlow's phased out its commercial landscape contracting and landscape architecture business to concentrate its efforts with its retail garden center, residential design/build landscaping, and quarterly maintenance.

Harlow's has won 75 local, state, and national awards for landscaping excellence. The firm has completed work at the University of Arizona, Davis-Monthan Air Force Base, and Tucson Medical Center. Harlow's estimates it has been involved in over 2,200 residential projects.

In the year 2001, Harlow's took on a new name—Harlow Gardens—to better reflect the garden/park-like setting that customers are treated to when shopping at its retail garden center.

John Coventry Harlow, William's son, is the third generation involved in the business.

William and John M. Harlow, Jr., owners of Harlow Gardens, posed with their father, John M. Harlow, Sr., founder of the corporation, about 1941.

HORTICULTURE UNLIMITED, INC.

Since its inception in 1980, Horticulture Unlimited, Inc. has steadily grown over the last two decades into one of Tucson's top landscape design, construction and maintenance firms, dedicated to providing innovative and quality landscaping to hundreds of residential, commercial, and corporate clients. A.F. Sterling Homebuilders, Raytheon Corp., IBM, Diamond Ventures, Inc. Pima County, The City of Tucson and Honeywell Corp. are some of their notable clients.

The company, founded by a desire to beautify and shape landscapes throughout the city of Tucson, is expected to achieve gross sales of over $4 million this year. Owners David Morris and Dawn Fried have articulated their vision of their firm through steady growth, innovative business planning and customer satisfaction. Their success is evident in their ability to keep pace with the burgeoning population of Tucson and steadily meet customers' specific landscaping needs.

The firm offers a wide range of landscaping, design and main-

Pima Canyon 'Desert Garden.'

tenance services, each supported by experienced design professionals, consultants and landscape teams. Services are headed by both Morris and Fried, who are married and met each other prior to college at the University of Arizona, where they both earned horticulture degrees. Fried oversees the maintenance end of the business and Morris manages the design and construction operations along with all administrative duties as president of the corporation.

Horticulture Unlimited's satisfied customers have been their most successful form of advertising and referrals have been the foundation for work since day one. The commitment to quality service and client satisfaction is apparent as soon as customers step into the company service headquarters at 3237 North Richey Boulevard. The office space, with land set-aside for both equipment storage and colorful landscaped gardens, was expanded in 1998, adding on offices and yard storage to meet the needs of this growing company.

Evident in a series of suites, as well as in the landscape plans laid out on design tables and in the awards hanging on the walls of

Horticulture Unlimited, Inc. headquarters in Tucson.

conference rooms at the Horticulture Unlimited headquarters, is an unwavering commitment to exceeding client expectations. Employees number about 125 and many of them have been with the firm for up to 10 years.

Outside of the company headquarters is a series of landscaped gardens providing customers an exciting display of new plant species and ideas for interesting design features that could dress up any property, commercial or residential. The staff stays abreast of new plant introductions, irrigation techniques and changing trends, so that they remain at the forefront of the industry.

Horticulture Unlimited is there to handle every phase of the project, from design and planning to installation, and from maintenance to complete landscape restoration. Because it's a service business, it takes leadership to deal with problems quickly and efficiently. It is the leadership at this firm that has given it a distinct reputation for being one of the best in the field.

IFS NORTH AMERICA, INC.

In the mid 1980s, a fledgling company named Industrial and Financial Systems married its specific expertise in relational database technology with its preventative maintenance knowledge acquired in the nuclear power industry. The result was *IFS Maintenance*, the very first software product in what is now an acclaimed portfolio of component-based business applications used by major industry leaders all over the world.

Founded in Linköping, Sweden in 1983, Industrial & Financial Systems today produces more than 60 enterprise application components used in industries ranging from manufacturing, financials and engineering to supply chain management, customer relationship management and maintenance and human resource administration. Its office in Tucson, Arizona, resulting from the partnering and subsequent acquisition of the former Tucson-based Avalon Software, is the largest IFS presence in North America, headquartering a major research and development facility, executive offices and marketing operations.

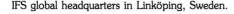
IFS global headquarters in Linköping, Sweden.

Terje Vangbo, IFS North American president.

Tucson is also home base for one of IFS's critical call center facilities.

With the singular goal of becoming one of the five largest global providers of enterprise applications, IFS maintains 72 additional offices throughout the world from Australia to Brazil to Greece and China, with representation in 43 countries including Saudi Arabia, Japan, Jordan and Taiwan. More than 3,500 employees steam the IFS engine that generated $256.5 million in total revenue for the year 2000, and its applications have been translated into no less than 22 languages. Listed on the Stockholm Stock Exchange (XSSE:IFS), it records on its 3,000-strong customer roster such respected companies as Volvo, NEC, Caterpillar, Saab, Nikon, Ericsson, National Semiconductor, General Dynamics, Rover and others.

The benchmark of IFS success has been its unwavering focus on the reliability of the e-business products and business applications it has designed and produced based on the most advanced component-based technology. Indeed, it was IFS that championed the component architecture system long before its merits were embraced by the general business software development community. Now in the fourth generation of IFS Applications, these products enable a user company to quickly add capabilities and specialized business applications to respond to its market demands, giving each IFS customer the freedom of action that is the ultimate weapon for the competitive edge in a highly volatile marketplace. To ensure successful implementation of its products, IFS professionals carefully monitor each customer project for quality control—to not only confirm that solution specifications have been met but to, most importantly, maximize customer satisfaction.

IFS also maintains and operates enterprise applications and e-business operations for many of its clients through a network of sales, implementation and support professionals based around the world. It is an organization of wholly-owned and jointly owned companies as well as a collaborative of distributors from the Czech Republic to India and Ireland. It is a worldwide partner of many market leaders including Hewlett Packard, IBM, General Electric, Deloitte and Touche, Rational Rose and Microsoft.

The alliances IFS has forged with global market leaders are an integral part of the company's goal of achieving a top five position in the arena of global business application suppliers and the number one position in specifically targeted segments. To reach the market for logistics, fleet management, repairs and maintenance in the defense aviation sectors a joint venture company was recently formed with BAE Systems. A distribution agreement with ABB Automation infiltrates the Industrial IT market with applications for service, maintenance, logistics, human resources and financials. A partnership with Cap Gemini Ernst & Young will enable both parties to jointly deliver business applications to customers worldwide, focusing on service and maintenance in the energy and utilities sector. And, while the IFS partner organization continues to grow, the company steadfastly retains its own delivery resources, guaranteeing the uninterrupted flow of vitally important end user feedback.

Credit for the success enjoyed by IFS is given to the company's focus on attracting, developing and retaining skilled personnel, utilizing the powerful combination of an ever-evolving dynamic industry environment with a corporate philosophy of recognizing and rewarding employee effort. This is especially critical in the rapidly changing IT industry, where a strong corporate culture based on core values of commitment, professionalism and simplicity creates the stable foundation that inspires great achievement. Each of the IFS branch offices operates autono-

mously, with individual responsibility given to IFS personnel who work in small project groups. This freedom to make decisions greatly influences each employee's development within the company, and, since it is company policy to recruit internally for advanced positions, each employee has the ongoing opportunity for increased knowledge about the company's products, organizational issues and internal processes. Another tremendous benefit of wearing the IFS banner is an exchange program called IFS Transfer, which encourages personnel to work in other countries for a limited period of time, creating advantages for personal and professional development and contributing to the sharing of knowledge within the IFS network of offices and subsidiaries.

In order to recruit the caliber of individual that will succeed on the career development paths that IFS encourages and supports through internal advancement and continuing education, the company has established a multifaceted program that actively involves local universities. The Tucson office, in particular, which

actively recruits young talent from the University of Arizona, among others, has helped develop a curriculum along with the school's MIS department for its e-business program and e-business lab. IFS has donated software and services to U of A as well as to San Jose State, so that students can realistically immerse themselves in the workings of the IT Industry, utilizing the real-world applications supplied free of charge by IFS.

The complex universe of Information Technology is a maelstrom of technological innovation, catapulting its players to the future with ever-increasing velocity and intensifying competition. Standing strong against IT Goliaths like Oracle, SAP and JD Edwards, IFS has played its David role with exceptional tenacity and inventiveness. With a global status spawned from confidence in its products and its people, IFS has well positioned itself to win the battle for preeminence in the business applications marketplace.

IFS western regional headquarters in Tucson.

LOVITT & TOUCHÉ INSURANCE

Nearly half a century ago, in 1953, after graduating from the University of Arizona and two years of military service during the Korean War, Carlos Touché started his insurance career with National Life Insurance Company. Two years earlier, D. M. "Mac" Lovitt had founded his independent insurance agency in Tucson.

A little more than 20 years later, Lovitt and Touché were the L and T of SLD&T—Snodgrass, Lovitt, Downey and Touché— which became one of Arizona's largest independent insurance agencies and is now one of the top 100 in the nation.

"I'm proud to say that during our entire history, we've remained a client-driven, hands-on kind of company. We don't just sell insurance. We solve insurance problems," said Touché, a member of the Million Dollar Round Table for more than a quarter of a century.

Touché credits much of the agency's success to James Spring, executive vice president and corporate secretary, who had been head of fire underwriting at Continental Casualty of California before joining SD&T when it merged with Lovitt in 1969.

"Jim is the smartest agent I've ever known," the senior Touché said. He also pays homage to Lovitt. "He helped establish the standards that maintain the company's position in the forefront of the industry," Touché said.

Lovitt was active in the firm, as well as in a lengthy list of community activities, until his death in 1998 at age 79. That same year, after more than four decades at the helm, Carlos Touché

Carlos Touché, chairman of the board, and "Mac" Lovitt, founder of Lovitt & Touché, Inc., (seated) with Charles Touché, chief executive officer, and Steven Touché, president. Portrait in background at left is of Marvin Snodgrass and at right, Hank "Buddy" Amos. Both were early-day partners in the firm.

turned over the agency's day-to-day operations to his two sons, Charles as chief executive officer and Steven as president. Although he retired as CEO, the senior Touché remains influential as chairman of the board and continues his day-to-day interest in the operation of the company.

Touché introduced his boys to the business while they were still in school. Charles, the older, graduated from his father's alma mater, the University of Arizona, with a major in finance. He gained experience at a subsidiary of Aetna Casualty Company in Los Angeles and C.T. Browning & Co. at Lloyd's of London. He joined his father's firm in 1976, and was elected president in 1990. A certified commercial property and casualty underwriter, he moved to the agency's Phoenix office in 1995.

Steven, a life member of the Million Dollar Round Table, graduated from Arizona State University with a degree in business finance and a minor in insurance. An expert in group life, health and pension plans, he gained experience in the business with Bankers Life in Cleveland before joining the firm in 1982. Charles and Steven became major stockholders in 1993.

The agency now has a staff of more than 120 highly trained professionals to meet the insurance needs of large and small clients throughout Arizona, the country and the world.

It is one of the main insurance brokers for the McDonald's Restaurant franchises nationwide and counts among its clients Kitt Peak National Observatory, Tohono O'odham Nation and CTI, Inc., and its subsidiaries.

What is today Lovitt & Touché has gone through a number of mergers and name changes over the years.

Marvin Snodgrass, a civic leader and well known for his charitable activities, started an insurance agency in the late 1940s. His agency quickly became one of Tucson's leading insurance firms, and in 1956 Jack Downey joined him as a partner.

Lovitt merged his company with Snodgrass and Downey in 1969. It became Snodgrass, Lovitt, Downey and Touché in 1973 when Snodgrass retired and Touché, who began his affiliation with the firm in 1956, became a partner.

The firm merged with Tucson Realty & Trust's insurance division in 1984. Tucson Realty traces its history to shortly after the turn of the last century.

With this merger, the company became Amos, Lovitt, Downey & Touché—the name of Hank "Buddy" Amos, owner of the realty company, replacing that of Snodgrass, who had retired in 1973.

Amos was one of Tucson's most successful fundraisers and an outstanding civic leader—serving on the board of Tucson Airport Authority and Tucson Community Foundation, of which he was a founder.

Carlos Touché has also been active in community affairs. He is a former tournament director of the Tucson Open and president of Tucson Conquistadors.

Noted for its innovative approaches to clients' needs, the agency was the first in Arizona to have a full-time safety engineer to help clients comply with OSHA regulations.

It created and manages thousands of customized property and liability plans, including self-insurance and self-funded plans when

James R. Spring, executive vice president and corporate secretary, has been a major contributor to the firm's success.

they best serve a company's needs.

Another Lovitt & Touché innovation was the establishment of Arizona's first pre-paid dental insurance company, Employees Dental Service—one of the first of its kind in the nation and one of the largest in the state.

Lovitt & Touché instituted a program of sending its young, new agents for training with Lloyd's of London. It formed a safety engineering staff to analyze client's claims records and work on-site to identify problem areas and reduce risks.

Jack Downey was instrumental in establishing the agency's own in-house adjusting de-

partment for quicker claims settlements—without the need for referral to New York or Chicago corporate offices for decisions. In the 1970s Downey spearheaded another company first—a separate department to handle property and casualty coverage for Arizona Indian tribes. It now writes coverage for numerous tribes.

Lovitt & Touché maintains contractual links with more than 100 of the world's largest insurance suppliers. These worldwide resources enable the firm to meet the specific needs of individuals and businesses with the best available coverage at the minimum available cost—and arrange for all support services any time and anywhere.

In addition to its corporate headquarters at 7202 East Rosewood in Tucson and a Phoenix office at 5050 North 40th Street, Lovitt & Touché has an office in Taylor, Arizona, at 650 North Main Street, under the direction of Eddie Hancock, vice president.

Lovitt & Touché Tucson headquarters

NANINI NORTHWEST, INC.

With the opening of Nanini Northwest Inc. in 1974, its mission was clear—assure the continuance of a family tradition of excellence in real estate development. Now, after more than a quarter of a century, company President Steven L. Nanini can proudly reflect on a track record of $95 million in past developments, as well as look forward to a bright future in the northwest Tucson area.

"We've always been quality oriented," says Nanini. "Throughout the years, our projects always have had aesthetic value—for the community or for the project. They have architectural character and good landscaping design. These are important factors."

Nanini, head of Nanini Northwest since its inception, cut his teeth in his family's multi-million-dollar road-building company in Chicago: Rock Road Construction Company.

His grandfather, the late Silvio "Sam" Nanini, had moved to Arizona in 1948, leaving Steve's father, Bill, to run Rock Road Construction Co. Young Steve started working in the Chicago business at age 16 and continued working there while earning his bachelor's degree from the University of Wisconsin in 1966. In 1970, Steve became one of the founders of LaSalle Partners, a full-service real estate firm. Then, in the mid-'70s, he agreed to move to Arizona to help his grandfather, who had become an icon in the Tucson community by developing the upscale Casas Adobes area, Tucson's first suburb.

The story of Nanini Northwest and the development of Casas Adobes really begins with Sam Nanini, who, at the age of 17, came to the United States from Florence, Italy, to make his fortune. Sam traveled across the country on the transcontinental Union Pacific railroad, working as a bootblack. Later, he found work as a hotel manager in Tacoma, Washington, but was drawn by the gold rush to Alaska, where he was a mule wrangler. Eventually, he earned enough money to return to Italy in 1911 to marry his childhood sweetheart, Giaconda.

Sam had intended to return to Tacoma, but they ran out of money and settled in Chicago. There, Sam drove a daily milk wagon delivery route from 1:00 A.M. to 9:00 A.M. and Giaconda worked with other Italian women sewing men's suits from piecework during evening sewing circles with her neighbors. After World War I, Sam and two other men started Rock Road Construction, which was to become the Chicago area's leading road-building company.

Sam and Giaconda first came to Tucson in 1938, after she was diagnosed with bronchial asthma and they were told she needed a change of climate.

Sam bought and sold land in the vicinity of the Arizona Inn,

Popular crooner Perry Como joined Sam and Bill Nanini in 1963 at Casas Adobes Plaza, in front of the fountain and lions imported from Carrara, Italy.

but later concentrated on the northwest area. He believed that the most important road into a city was from the north, as the Appian Way led into Rome.

When Sam first started developing land in Tucson, he platted one-acre lots over 12 square miles. He was adamant about homeowners having a full acre to enjoy the natural desert terrain.

The couple spent their winters in Tucson until 1948, when they moved to the city permanently. Bill stayed in Chicago to run the thriving companies until 1977, when he disbanded them and moved to Tucson to manage the Tucson National Golf Club and to assist his son Steve in the land-developing business.

In 1954, Sam developed three Casas Adobes subdivisions on about 300 acres—Casas Adobes Estates, Casas Adobes Heights, and Casas Adobes Country Club Estates. Casas Adobes North and Casas Adobes West were added later.

The original homes, as well as the first-class shopping center at Ina and Oracle roads known as Casas Adobes Plaza, actually were built of adobe bricks, in keeping with the Southwestern flavor of the area. The bricks, manufactured of adobe clay, straw, and asphalt by Sam's Casas Adobes Brick Co., were exceptionally sturdy, but each block was so heavy that workers refused to use them. Sam also imported a marble fountain from Carrara, Italy, and installed three statues in niches beside the fountain to give it an Italian accent.

The Plaza, as did every project that Sam Nanini touched, had an elegance about it that was unsurpassed in the Tucson area. His eye for detail has been passed down to his son and grandson.

"My father and grandfather were both perfectionists," Steve says. "Through them, I learned

---

Steve Nanini strikes a princely pose near the Duesenberg he restored. The classic auto originally was a birthday gift from Louise Astor for her fiancé, Prince Davani, in 1935.

to take the time to do it right the first time."

Some of Sam's northwest property continued to operate as a cotton and alfalfa farm but was not profitable. Bill purchased the farm from his father and, largely from his office in Chicago, developed Tucson National Golf Club and Tucson National Estates.

While many scoffed at the Naninis' plans to build a golf course in the desert—particularly in the northwest region of a city that lacked the population to support it—both father and son had the vision to see the value of their project. The critics were wrong; the Naninis were right.

The golf course opened in 1960 with much fanfare. Soon

afterward, a little-known golf professional, Jack Nicklaus, who had won back-to-back National Amateur Championships, became its first touring pro. In 1963, Tucson National became home to the Dean Martin Tucson Open, covered by NBC Television, providing national exposure. Nationwide television exposure in winter told the whole world that Tucson was the place to live. The addition of a hotel, restaurant, and condos—along with an extensive property upgrade and the opening of a luxurious spa and 176 guest rooms in 1985—has made Tucson National a popular destination resort.

At LaSalle Partners in Chicago, Steve had specialized in commercial, industrial, and office leasing; developing brokerage leads for numerous industrial parks; and corporate relocation in the area of Chicago/O'Hare field.

His frequent visits to Tucson heightened his interest in the family's real estate holdings. In 1974, encouraged by his grandfather, he moved to Tucson to help manage and develop the numerous family properties. His first project was Oracle Place, a 125,000-square-foot retail/office complex at Oracle and Ina.

Meanwhile, after Rock Road Construction posted its best year ever in 1971, it was dismantled and sold in 1974, and in 1975 Bill Nanini moved to Tucson, partnering with Steve and Sam in commercial, residential, and resort properties on the northwest side.

Nanini Northwest Inc. was formed in 1974 as a full-service real estate and development company to better service the Nanini holdings. The first office was in Casas Adobes Plaza, but it was moved to the Nanini Financial Center then to Oracle Place before moving into its current space in Foothills Office Plaza in 1983.

The Naninis' list of successful projects includes the Tucson National Resort and Spa, La Toscana Shopping Center, Casas Adobes Shopping Center, Oracle Place (One, Two and Three), Medici Park (land), Nanini Financial Center, Cigna Plaza, Mona Lisa Village, and Foothills Plaza.

The company's management division now operates several income properties, including Foothills Plaza and Mona Lisa Village, as well as several raw land properties. A proposed retail/office development on Magee and La Cholla is in the zoning process.

The extensive Nanini holdings are held in various entities and partnerships, all of which are serviced and operated by Nanini Northwest Inc. The company provides a full range of services, including property management, construction management, brokerage and leasing, venture capital, syndication and development.

While Nanini Northwest Inc. has grown with the territory, its roots remain deeply entrenched in Sam and Giaconda Nanini, who left their native land to pursue a dream of a better life in the New World. What they found and created in Tucson will provide a legacy for generations to come.

Before Sam's death in 1978 and Giaconda's in 1982, Sam created a "one-man Marshall Plan" in his hometown in Italy. It included an orphanage and water system as well as a concert hall. The couple played a key role in the growth of Casas Adobes Congregational Church on Oracle Road and also contributed land for the Nanini Library and the Nanini Botanical Gardens in Casas Adobes, along with other philanthropic endeavors.

Bill Nanini, who has never retired, maintains regular business hours in the corporate offices of Nanini Northwest. He continues to be the family's Patriarch, consulting with Steve on various aspects of the company's real estate development and other business investments.

Steve Nanini has had a long-time interest in classic cars and in 1986 and 1987 staged the Tucson National Concours d'Elegance on the 18th fairway of the Tucson National Resort. Steve has created award-winning classics, including Duesenberg, Mercedes Benz and V-16 Cadillacs.

The pride that he expresses in the cars he has restored, "creating something for future generations to enjoy," reflects the same feeling he has for his real estate projects, particularly the Tucson National Resort and Spa.

"My attention to detail has been the result of my tutelage from my Grandfather and my Dad," he says. "My Grandfather, a man of his word, always believed that a handshake was his bond. My Dad taught me to never give up. He is the most dogmatic, persistent person I've ever known and I respect him for it."

From their humble beginnings in Tuscany, the Nanini family story is a dream come true, much like that of Horatio Alger.

MOORE & MOORE, Attorneys at Law, P.L.L.C.

MOORE & MOORE, Attorneys at Law, P.L.L.C., is a mother and two daughters' law firm in Tucson, Arizona. The firm's roots began when Royanna Lebrecht Moore, the mother and senior partner, was a student at Rincon High School, participating in debate competitions and dreaming about law school.

Royanna graduated from the University of Arizona College of Law in 1981. After admission to the State Bar of Arizona, Royanna shared space with two other attorneys, taking some of their overflow work. Royanna's solo practice grew successfully over the years, and when her older daughter, Annalisa Moore, joined her in 1996, Royanna's law practice was situated in the building where the firm is currently located, at 4400 East Broadway.

Annalisa graduated from Rincon High School, received her degree in Entrepreneurship from the University of Arizona, and went directly to law school at the University of Arizona, graduating in 1996. Royanna and Annalisa formed the firm of MOORE & MOORE, Attorneys at Law, P.L.L.C., in January of 1998.

Royanna's younger daughter, Angela Moore, joined the firm in July 2000, after graduating from law school at Arizona State University, and receiving an advanced law degree in taxation (LLM) from the University of Washington. Prior to that, Angela received her degree in Finance and Accounting from the University of Arizona.

The firm focuses its practice in two primary areas. Royanna and Angela handle estate planning, including trusts, wills, probates, guardianships, and conservatorships. Annalisa handles family law cases, including divorce, custody, property settlements, paternity, spousal maintenance, and premarital agreements.

When Royanna went to law school, Annalisa and Angela were seven and four years old respectively, and it was a challenge to also take care of two small children. Royanna's goal of setting up her own practice, with the flexibility of working for herself, was important with a family. Annalisa and Angela started helping their mother in her office as teenagers. Both knew early on that they wanted to attend law school, as their mother had been the role model to show them that her career was one that was fulfilling, enjoyable, and provided a way to help people. Royanna was delighted when they each decided to join her law firm.

All three women are members of the National Network of Estate Planning Attorneys, Arizona Women Lawyers, the Pima County and State Bar Associations, and other professional organizations. Royanna is president of the Joseph and Mary Cacioppo Foundation, and is a member of the National Academy of Elder Law Attorneys. Annalisa is on the board of directors of 88Crime, is a member of Junior League of Tucson, and serves on the Executive Council of the State Bar Family Law Section. Angela serves on the steering committee for Arizona Women Lawyers. The firm members are frequent speakers on estate planning and family law issues, and provide volunteer legal services to the community.

The firm has flourished with the experience, expertise, and personalities that each brings to the firm. The three women have a close relationship, work well together, and share the same commitment to providing clients the highest quality of services, professionalism, and ethical standards. They have each found the right balance between professional and personal lives, with outside interests and activities, community service, travel, friends, and family. This unique family law firm has found success in helping other Tucson families.

From left to right, Angela, Royanna, and Annalisa Moore.

PINNACLE PEAK/TRAIL DUST TOWN

Pinnacle Peak steakhouse, a division of Agro Land & Cattle Co., Inc., is one of the oldest and perhaps the most popular restaurant in the State of Arizona. Under the direction of Daniel M. Bates, President of Agro Land & Cattle Co., Inc., Pinnacle Peak, Agro Land & Cattle Co., Inc. and the Bates Family have a long involvement with 'Western' enterprise.

In the early 1950s, Tucson, Arizona was a sleepy desert community of approximately 45,000 people. It was then, as legend has it, well outside of the Tucson City limits on East Tanque Verde Road, that several 'Old West' buildings were constructed as a set for a Glenn Ford movie. Afterwards, this conglomeration of buildings developed into a western theme commercial complex known as "Trail Dust Town," anchored by the "Pinnacle Peak" steakhouse.

Agro Land & Cattle Co., Inc. was formed by the Bates Family in 1961 in Tucson, Arizona as a livestock company. In 1963, with the purchase of Trail Dust Town and Pinnacle Peak by Agro Land

Trail Dust Town circa early 1960s. Pinnacle Peak is shown on the left with the cow on the roof.

Early view of Trail Dust Town Gazebo.

& Cattle Co., Inc., the ability to market their own cattle gave the Company an integrated system that was developed and continued for decades. Coinciding with Tucson's growth, Pinnacle Peak steakhouse grew in popularity and operations expanded dramatically. With the addition of numerous other restaurants in California and elsewhere, the company soon exceeded its own ability to furnish beef for its restaurant division.

Pinnacle Peak's prosperity paused briefly in 1970 due to a devastating fire. Like a phoenix rising from the ashes, Pinnacle Peak and its Silver Dollar Saloon were relocated to a more advantageous spot on the property and rebuilt, bigger and better than ever. Besides its focal point Pinnacle Peak, Trail Dust Town was then a rustic collec-

tion of shops and home to live theater venues, the "Playbox Theater" and Tucson's "Gaslight Theater."

Then as now, the heart and soul of Trail Dust Town is Pinnacle Peak, Tucson's original cowboy steakhouse where tourists and locals alike experience the traditions of the Old West every year. Often copied but never equaled, The restaurant is the originator of the mesquite-broiled Cowboy Steak™. Since its inception, Pinnacle Peak's immense popularity acted as a magnet, drawing numerous other restaurants to Tanque Verde Road and serving as the catalyst that transformed it into Tucson's "Restaurant Row." Due to popular demand, Pinnacle Peak has undergone several expansions, including a separate banquet facility and an outdoor seating area, increasing seating capacity to accommodate approximately 1,000 diners. Upon entering the restaurant's two-story lobby with its oversized, antique couches and chairs, guests gaze at six-foot-high flames leaping from the massive grills (where the steaks are cooked over huge mesquite logs) and marvel at the thousands of neckties hanging from the rafters. In a Pinnacle Peak 'signature' tradition, there are NO TIES ALLOWED! If a guest is 'caught' wearing a necktie, with great fanfare the tie is summarily cutoff and hung from the rafters (all in good-natured fun). Possessing authentic Old West atmosphere, quality, service and value, it perpetually wins many top honors in Tucson's annual Culinary Awards.

The phenomenal popularity of Pinnacle Peak and the demand

for hosting large corporate and private banquets spawned the creation of Pinnacle Peak's Savoy Opera House. Although it is open to the public weekdays for lunch, the Savoy is Trail Dust Town's single-largest facility for conventions, banquets, theme parties and receptions. This complete recreation of authentic, turn-of-the-century ambiance accommodates groups up to 600. One enters through the intricate wood and beveled-glass French doors imported from London's famed Savoy Hotel (once the 'Royal' Entrance). Elegant Victorian chandeliers, traditional opera boxes, antique back-bars and pressed-tin ceilings set the mood for the elegance of a world long gone, but not forgotten.

Dan Bates, president of Agro Land & Cattle Co., Inc. and a nationally-renowned western sculptor, is primarily responsible for the artistic design, historical authenticity and ongoing improvements to the town. Assembling a team of talented artisans whose love of the Old West is evident, Dan Bates has created what is today, Tucson's premier 'in-town' western town. Besides the Old West architectural authenticity and integrity for which Trail Dust Town is so well known, great emphasis has been made over the past 12 years to add western theme attractions that will appeal to the entire family.

Although some of Trail Dust Town's original rustic character has undergone subtle refinements, one can still enjoy authentic buildings that are reminiscent of an earlier time, including the centerpiece gazebo in an old-fashioned town square lighted by real gas street lamps. Red brick paved streets, however, have long replaced the dirt streets of yesteryear. Visitors still enjoy Trail Dust Town's many distinctive shops where one may find items such as western apparel, southwestern gifts, fine arts, hand-made candies, photographers, antiques and even other full-service restaurants.

Besides maintaining the high degree of historical and artistic accuracy throughout the town, Dan Bates is primarily responsible for the addition of many Western theme family attractions. Trail Dust Town's tradition of theater continues with the "Dragoon Street, Wild, Wild West Stunt Shows" where the entire Dragoon Street serves as center stage for these light-hearted, action-packed theatrical performances. Other popular family attractions include the "C.P. Huntington" narrow gauge railroad and mine tunnel tour, the "Museum of the Horse Soldier", the "Fiesta del Presidio" carousel (the oldest operational carousel in Tucson), panning for gold at the "Ol' Terrible Mine" or playing the western theme games in the "Shootist Arcade." Families also enjoy the newest attraction, the "Rifle Saloon" Shooting Gallery. Many new and spectacular western theme family attractions are being planned for the future.

Today, the operations of Agro Land & Cattle Co., Inc. are based solely within the state of Arizona. The company employs approximately 300 people and it ranks amongst the top 200 corporations within the state. The primary operating divisions of Agro Land & Cattle Co., Inc. include Pinnacle Peak, the Savoy Opera House, Trail Dust Town, the Cobra Ranch, Agro Properties and El Corral restaurant (a Tucson favorite in continuous operation for over 60 years and a consistent, multi-category winner in the annual Tucson Culinary Awards).

Trail Dust Town and Pinnacle Peak have been Tucson landmarks for over 50 years and now rank as Tucson's most popular western theme destination, drawing approximately 500,000 visitors each year. At Agro Land & Cattle Co., Inc., under the able direction of Daniel Bates, President, the heritage of the 'Great American West' is a treasure to be protected and perpetuated for the generations to come.

Pinnacle Peak Steakhouse, present day, Tucson, Arizona.

THE SUNDT COMPANIES, INC.

To many Tucsonans the name Sundt is synonymous with construction. For more than 70 years the Tucson-based company has played a vital role in the city's evolution from a dusty desert outpost to the vibrant metropolis of today.

Mauritz Martinsen Sundt, a Norwegian immigrant, founded the company in New Mexico. The year was 1890, and the West was truly wild. In those days successful business dealings often depended solely upon the integrity of the parties involved. M.M. Sundt quickly became known for his honesty, integrity and ability to complete projects swiftly and within budget.

Mr. Sundt's business prospered, and soon all types of buildings bore the proud mark of his firm.

In 1929 Mr. Sundt's son John came to Tucson to build a Methodist church near the University of Arizona that had been designed by Thoralf, another of his sons. In the tiny town John saw a future filled with promise, and decided to stay.

John Sundt's vision, of course, was correct. The company was to play an important part in Tucson's growth throughout the succeeding seven decades. On the University of Arizona campus, Sundt built six projects during 1936 and 1937 for the Works Project Administration, a Depression-era federal agency. That work was to become the beginning of a long association between Sundt and the state's oldest institution of higher learning. To date Sundt has completed over 50 projects on the University's mid-city campus, the most recent being the Scholarship Suites at Arizona Stadium.

Scattered throughout the city are numerous other Sundt projects, including office buildings, hospitals, retail centers, schools, industrial facilities and churches. Sundt built two of Tucson's landmark buildings—the Unisource Energy Tower downtown, which is the

The Methodist Church near the University of Arizona campus.

city's tallest building—and the luxurious Loews Ventana Canyon Resort on the northeastern edge of town.

As Tucson has grown, so have nearby industries. Sundt has built many major projects for mining companies in Arizona, Nevada, New Mexico, and California, along with doing construction work at power plants in Arizona and New Mexico that supply Tucson's electricity. During the mid-1950s Sundt diversified into heavy/civil construction. Since then many of the roads that crisscross Arizona, New Mexico, and California have been built by the firm, along with numerous bridges, drainage structures, and related projects. Sundt's Heavy Construction Division also builds airport facilities, dams and railroad projects.

Loews Ventana Canyon Resort.

The Scholarship Suites tower over Arizona Stadium, University of Arizona.

As Sundt has continued to expand, so has the diversification of its construction services. The Sundt Housing Division, formed during the 1980s, specializes in the design and construction of military family housing. The Division has completed over 10,000 housing units at military installations throughout the country. Another Sundt specialty is senior living. This Sundt operation provides a variety of services to the retirement market, including feasibility analyses, entitlements, financing, design, construction, furnishings, and operations management. C.R. Fedrick, a wholly-owned Sundt subsidiary headquartered in Novato, California is an underground utilities contractor specializing in the installation of fiber optic cable. It also constructs water resource projects including dams, pipelines, water-transmission and distribution lines, pumping stations, and canals.

Sundt now has offices in Tucson, Phoenix, Dallas, San Diego, Sacramento and Novato, and builds projects for both private and public clients. The company has also taken its construction expertise abroad. To date Sundt has performed work in Saudi Arabia, Chile, Australia, China, the Philippines, Mexico, Russia, and several South Sea Islands.

Now one of the 100 largest construction companies in the United States, Sundt is nationally recognized for its innovative techniques and uncompromising dedication to meeting its clients' goals with quality and dependable construction services. Sundt has been an employee-owned corporation for a quarter-century, and each member of the Sundt team takes special pride in the firm's growth and accomplishments. Numerous national, state and local awards have recognized Sundt's contributions to the construction industry. To date, the company has received 12 Build America Awards from the Associated General Contractors of America. The two most recent awards recognized the company's emergency construction of a flood control structure at the Los Alamos National Laboratory in New Mexico, and reconstruction of a major freeway in Phoenix, Arizona.

Sundt also gives back to the communities where its employees live and work through the Sundt Foundation. The Foundation uses employee contributions, which are matched by the company, to provide grants to nonprofit organizations in each of the cities where Sundt has an established office.

Now in its second century of building the West, Sundt continues the tradition of excellence in construction.

Unisource Energy Tower, a 23-story office building.

TRICO ELECTRIC COOPERATIVE

In 1945, electric lights, refrigerators, stoves, washers, central heating, air conditioning and radios—even heated swimming pools—were as common in Tucson as they were in most American cities and towns. Even as late as the mid-1940s, all the electrical conveniences that urban residents took for granted were not yet available in rural areas of South Central Arizona. Farmers and ranchers had no electricity and no hope of having it supplied by existing utility companies. All across America the story had been the same. For-profit electric companies declined to build electric lines into sparsely populated areas because there was no profit potential.

For this reason, President Franklin D. Roosevelt created the Rural Electric Administration in 1935. Its purpose was loaning money to farmers and ranchers in rural areas to build power lines. Non-profit electric cooperatives were organized to buy and distribute electricity to local members and to maintain the power lines. Today there are over 900 electric cooperatives across America. Their lines reach across approximately 75 percent of the country's land mass and serve about 10 percent of America's population.

In this area, seven ranchers and farmers of the Avra–Altar Valley area recognized rural peoples' need for power, when Trico was chartered in 1945 to provide electric service to rural areas of Pima, Pinal and Santa Cruz counties. The new cooperative was named Trico in honor of the three counties that it serves.

In 1946 to 1947 Trico built a small, temporary generating plant near Marana and constructed its first section of power lines covering 115 miles to serve 77 members in areas north, south and east of Marana. The lines were energized on July 8, 1948. From there the system grew to include Mt. Lemmon, Three Points and Sasabe, Twin Buttes, Madera Canyon in the Santa Rita Mountains and down through Green Valley to the Arivaca area. Today with almost 2,500 miles of energized line, Trico's lines reach north into

With 1,400 members in attendance, Trico's 1964 annual meeting set an attendance record over all previous annual meetings. The event was held at Hi Corbett Field in Tucson. Over the years, thousands of Trico members have attended the cooperative's annual meeting. In addition to board elections and reports on the state of the cooperative, members enjoy a meal and have the chance of winning billing credits, cash prizes and small electrical appliances at the meeting.

Trico's old generating plant, located in Marana on the corner of Trico and Silverbell roads, provided power to the cooperative's consumers from 1948 until the Arizona Electric Power Cooperative generating station went on line in July of 1964. Trico and five other area distribution cooperatives are joint owners of AEPCO.

Pinal County to serve the growing Saddlebrooke community and southeast of Tucson to serve the expanding developments in the Corona and Vail areas.

The Cooperative replaced its temporary generating facility with a new diesel generating plant with five 1250-KVA units. This plant went into operation in early 1948. As the system grew, Trico built substations to improve service to its expanding customer base. One of Trico's oldest substation facilities in Tucson was retired in 1994. Trico operates substations at Marana, Mt. Lemmon, Three Points, Green Valley, Saddlebrooke, Avra Valley and on Valencia Road. Between 1997 and 2001 additional substation facilities have gone on line in Sahuarita, at Saddlebrooke (a second facility) and on Tangerine Road, in response to the rapid growth in the cooperative's service territory.

One of Trico's greatest challenges as a young cooperative was in generating its own elecricity at affordable prices for its consumers. Thus, in 1961, Trico and three other electric cooperatives in the state formed Arizona Electric Power Cooperative (AEPCO) to serve their generation and transmission needs. Eventually, the original owners were joined by two additional area cooperatives. The 520 MW Apache Generating Station, located near Cochise, Arizona, is AEPCO's primary power resource. Trico gets 100 percent of its generated power from AEPCO. AEPCO will soon add 40 MW of generating capacity to meet projected future needs.

Trico's operations were originally headquartered in a converted sanitarium building located on the corner of Roger and Oracle roads. In 1953, an old house on West Miracle Mile was converted into offices. Twenty years and two expansions later the need for a bigger and better facility was recognized. A new headquarters at 5100 West Ina Road was completed in 1974. In 2001 with 27,000 members, Trico is one of the fastest growing cooperatives in the nation. Membership is anticipated to reach 65,000 by 2015. In May 2001, Trico began the process of building a new and much larger headquarters facility at 8600 West Tangerine Road and anticipates a move-in date of April 2002.

Electric cooperatives differ from investor-owned utilities in several important ways. Since Trico belongs to the people it serves, its focus is on benefiting these people. These members also share in the control of the cooperative through attending Trico's annual meeting and electing fellow members to serve on its board of directors. Trico's first

annual meeting was held on August 23, 1946 and was attended by four of the cooperative's five original board members: T.J. Smith, J.E. Farrell, W.H. Lane, Jesse W. Jones and A.R. Aguirre. Over the years, thousands of Trico members have participated in this popular annual event.

Another way that Trico differs from non-cooperative utility companies is through awarding capital credits to its consumers. If Trico makes more money than it needs to cover its expenses in a given year, the surplus is allocated to members' capital credit accounts. Before refunding this money to members, Trico uses it for a period of time as working capital. Over the years Trico has returned approximately $11 million in capital credits to its members.

As a cooperative, Trico also operates a number of member and community service programs. One such program is its Scholarship Foundation. The Foundation began in 1984 and is funded by unclaimed capital credits. The number and amounts of the scholarships has grown over the years. In 2001, 22 scholarships worth over $70,000 were awarded to Trico consumers and their children. Trico also offers funding to

worthy community organizations through its Charitable Trust, sends members' children on the annual Rural Electric Washington Youth Tour, teaches electric safety classes in area schools, involves its members on a special advisory council and much more.

With the prospect of the deregulation of the electric utility industry on the horizon, rural electric cooperatives began to band together under a unifying co-brand in 1997. More than 560 of the nation's electric cooperatives, including Trico, are now Touchstone Energy Cooperatives. The Touchstone Energy brand is relationship-driven. It helps Trico demonstrate its belief in "the power of human connections" to the residences, businesses and communities that it serves. As a Touchstone Energy Cooperative, Trico promises to continue to uphold four values embodied in the heritage of America's electric cooperatives— integrity, accountability, innovation and commitment to community.

Trico's headquarters from 1974 through early 2002 were located at 5100 West Ina Road. In 1982 construction was completed on a separate transformer and meter shop and the building's east wing was added in 1992. After serving the company well for 27 years, the building could no longer accommodate the employees that were needed to serve Trico's growing number of consumers.

TUCSON PLUMBING AND HEATING

The year was 1947. Jack Owens and his wife June, both in their twenties, had just returned from the doctor's office. He had told them that a move to a drier climate would be the only relief their young son could expect from an asthmatic condition. So they said good-bye to family and friends in Huntington, West Virginia, and settled in Tucson, Arizona.

They bought an acre of land— "$25 down, $25 a month!"—and built a home in the 5700 block of East Lee Street. "Times were a little different then," June said. "The thing everyone had in common was trust. We never locked the door. I don't even think we had a key," Jack added.

Jack used his GI Bill benefits from his service in the Army Engineers to attend school two nights a week. With his previous pipefitting experience at Rockwood Sprinkler Company in Cincinnati, he needed only two years to earn a plumbing apprenticeship and, in 1949, he hired on full time with Aweco Plumbing.

Jack's expert work was valued by building contractors, and he and June decided the demand for plumbing installations was great enough to justify going out on their own. In 1952, they incorporated their new business as Tucson Plumbing.

"It was still a matter of trust," Jack said. "There were no contracts. No county inspectors. Our customers trusted us to do good work at a fair price and we didn't disappoint them."

"People depended on one another," June said. "If you got a flat tire, two or three people would stop to help fix it. In the business, we'd loan materials and even workers to our competitors."

They bought a parcel of land near River and Dodge, and put up the first Tucson Plumbing building in 1959. Jack attributed the early success of his company to slow and steady growth. "There was enough work out there for everyone," he said. "We stayed debt free so we could handle the ups and downs of the building industry." He estimated that his company installed the plumbing in one out of every five homes in the Tucson area.

Tucson Plumbing not only served its customers well, but also built a reputation for treating its employees with the same respect and consideration as its customers. They employed a diverse workforce including Hispanics, Native Americans and African Americans. Football players from The University of Arizona took summer jobs there, and generations of families made a living alongside Jack and June.

In 1982, as they were nearing retirement, Jack and June Owens sold the company to their nephew Chris McGinnis, who had worked with them for many years. At the right place and the right time for the Tucson housing boom, Chris has guided the company with the same philosophy of trust, good work, controlled growth and caring for employees for which Tucson Plumbing has been known.

"We continue to install the plumbing in many of Tucson's new homes," Chris McGinnis said, "so it's a logical extension of our business that we have expanded our services to include residential repair, renovations and upgrades. And in keeping with Jack and June's philosophy of both life and business, our slogan remains, 'Tucson's most trusted since 1952.'"

Jack Owens, Tucson Plumbing's founder, with the firm's first pick-up truck.

UNIVERSITY OF ARIZONA

Through their intertwined histories, the University of Arizona has become synonymous with Tucson. Today, the University of Arizona has an estimated statewide economic impact of approximately $2 billion, between the main campus, its related medical programs in Tucson, Phoenix and statewide locations; the world-class UA Science and Technology Park; the UA South campus in Sierra Vista; and other facilities throughout Arizona.

Since its inception in 1885 as the state's land-grant institution, the University of Arizona's mission has been to educate Arizona's citizens, create new knowledge through research and creative activities, and then to share that knowledge. More than 34,000 students study in the UA's 15 colleges and eight schools. The University creates unique cultural and social opportunities for the community through its top ranked performing and fine arts programs, museums and galleries, readings, lectures and films, special events, and intercollegiate athletic competitions. The UA is also recognized as one of the top research institutions in the country, and home to hundreds of millions of dollars of sponsored research projects in medicine, space sciences, biology and engineering, to name just some of its wide range of inquiry.

The University's early interest in astronomy programs, aided by cloudless desert skies, fostered its premier optical sciences program. That program, while maintaining leadership in advanced telescope optics, has expanded to include new technologies such as lasers, medical imaging and fiber optics.

The many companies created as a result of the University's optical research and education have earned Tucson the 21st century nickname of "Optics Valley."

The Arizona Health Sciences Center provides training for the growing health care industry. The Colleges of Medicine, Pharmacy, Nursing and Public Health that constitute AHSC provide medical care and knowledge statewide. Through its 13 comprehensive centers of excellence, such as the Arizona Cancer Center and the Arizona Emergency Medicine Research Center, and its many outreach activities, such as the Telemedicine and Rural Health programs, as well as patient clinics and specialty services, AHSC

Old Main, the first building on the University of Arizona campus, is still serving students after more than 100 years.

An aerial view of the University of Arizona campus looking east towards the Rincon Mountains.

reaches well beyond the Tucson area to benefit all Arizonans.

The impact of the University of Arizona also can be seen statewide through the College of Agriculture and Life Sciences. Founded to provide knowledge and new research to the state's ranching and farming industries, CALS has expanded to biological sciences, while maintaining its historical roles. In addition to conducting cutting-edge research in genetics and biotechnology, CALS also coordinates the statewide county extension offices and 4-H youth agricultural programs.

As a student-centered research institution, the University of Arizona has continued to fulfill its mission to educate and create knowledge. Likewise, in its mission of outreach, the University has become deeply ingrained in the unique tapestry of both Tucson and the state of Arizona, providing services and opportunities vital to the current and future wellbeing of its citizens. The University of Arizona looks forward to continuing these roles and meeting the challenges of the future throughout the 21st century.

BIBLIOGRAPHY

"Abandonment of Tubac." *Arizoniana*, I (Winter 1960): 27.

Altshuler, Constance W., ed. "At Noon in Mesilla," *Journal of Arizona History*, IX (Winter 1968): 219-21.

___, ed. *Latest From Arizona! The Hesperian Letters, 1859-1861.* Tucson: Arizona Pioneers' Historical Society, 1969.

___. "Military Administration in Arizona, 1854-1865," *Journal of Arizona History*, X (Winter 1969): 215-38.

Bartlett, John R. *Personal Narrative of Explorations and Incidents in Texas, New Mexico, California, Sonora and Chihuahua, Connected with the United States and Mexican Boundary Commission, During the Years 1850, '51, '52, and '53.* New York: D. Appleton & Co. 1854.

Baylor, George W. *John Robert Baylor, Confederate Governor of Arizona.* Tucson: Arizona Pioneers' Historical Society, 1966.

Bieber, Ralph P., and Avram B. Bender, eds. "Cooke's Journal of the March of the Mormon Battalion," *Exploring Western Trails*, Vol. VII. Glendale: Arthur H. Clark, 1938.

Bieber, Ralph P., ed. "Through Mexico to California: Letters and Journals of John E. Durivage," *Southern Trails to California*, Vol. V. Glendale: Arthur H. Clark, 1937.

Brandes, Ray. *Frontier Military Posts of Arizona.* Globe, Ariz.: Dale Stuart King, 1960.

Bourke, John G. *On the Border with Crook.* New York: Charles Scribner's Sons, 1891.

Bret Harte, John, ed. *The First Fifty Years of St. Luke's-in-the-Desert.* Tucson: Privately published, 1973.

___, ed. *Frank Lockwood's Pioneer Portraits.* Tucson: University of Arizona Press, 1968.

___. "The San Carlos Indian Reservation, 1872-1886: An Administrative History." Unpublished Ph.D. Dissertation, University of Arizona, 1972.

___. "The Strange Case of Joseph C. Tiffany: Indian Agent in Disgrace." *Journal of Arizona History*, Vol. XVI (Winter 1975): 383-404.

Brinckerhoff, Sidney B., and Odie B. Faulk. *Lancers for the King.* Phoenix: Arizona Historical Foundation, 1965.

Brinckerhoff, Sidney B. "The Last Days of Spanish Arizona." *Arizona and the West*, IX (Spring 1967): 5-20.

Browne, J. Ross. *Adventures in the Apache Country: A Tour through Arizona and Sonora, 1864.* New Ed., Tucson: University of Arizona, 1974.

Caywood, W. Eugene. *A History of Tucson Transportation: The Arrival of the Railroad, Beginnings of Transit in Tucson.* Tucson: Tucson-Pima County Historical Commission, 1980.

Chambers, George W., and C. L. Sonnichsen. *San Agustín: First Cathedral Church in Arizona.* Tucson: Arizona Historical Society in collaboration with Arizona Silhouettes, 1974.

Clarke, A.B. *Travels in Mexico and California . . .* Boston: Wright & Hasly, 1862.

Cooper, James F. *The First Hundred Years: The History of Tucson School District 1, Tucson, Arizona, 1867-1967.* Tucson: Tucson School District 1, 1967.

Commemorative Book, Temple Emanu-El. Tucson: Privately published, 1970.

Cosulich, Bernice. *Tucson.* Tucson: Arizona Silhouettes, 1953.

Dobyns, Henry F., ed. *Hepah, California! The Journal of Cave Johnson Couts during the years 1848-1849.* Tucson: Arizona Pioneers' Historical Society, 1961.

___. *Spanish Colonial Tucson: A Demographic History.* Tucson: University of Arizona Press, 1976.

Drachman, Roy P. *Just Memories.* Tucson: Privately published, 1979.

Federal Census: Territory of New Mexico and Territory of Arizona, Excerpts (1864). Senate Document 13, 89th Congress, 1st Session.

Finch, L. Boyd. "Sherod Hunter and the Confederates in Arizona." *Journal of Arizona History*, X (Fall 1969): 137-206.

Forecast Review and Data Inventories. Tucson: Tucson Area Transportation Planning Agency, 1972.

Gallego, Hilario. "Reminiscences of an Arizona Pioneer." *Arizona Historical Review*, VI (January 1935): 75-81.

Goff, John, "John Titus, Chief Justice of Arizona, 1870-1874." *Arizona and the West*, XIV (Spring 1972): 25-44.

Hall, Dick. "Ointment of Love: Oliver E. Comstock and Tucson's Tent City." *Journal of Arizona History*, XIX (Summer 1978): 111-30.

Hayden, Carl T. *Charles Trumbull Hayden, Pioneer* Tucson: Arizona Historical Society, 1972.

Holterman, Jack. "José de Zuñiga, Commandant of Tucson." *Kiva*, XXII (November 1956): 1-2.

Kessell, John L. *Friars, Soldiers and Reformers*. Tucson: University of Arizona Press, 1976.

Langdon, Thomas C. "Harold Bell Wright, Citizen of Tucson." *Journal of Arizona History*, XVI (Spring 1975): 77-98.

Lamar, Howard R. *The Far Southwest, 1846-1912: A Territorial History*. New Haven: Yale University Press, 1966.

Lockwood, Frank C. *Life in Old Tucson*. Tucson: Tucson Civic Committee, 1943.

___, and Donald W. Page. *Tucson: The Old Pueblo*. Phoenix: Manufacturing Stationers, n.d. (1930).

Luttrell, Estelle. *Newspapers and Periodicals of Arizona*. Tucson: University of Arizona General Bulletin No. 15, 1949.

McCarty, Kieran. *Desert Documentary: The Spanish Years, 1767-1821*. Tucson: Arizona Historical Society, 1976.

___. *Desert Documentary: The Mexican Years, 1821-1863*. In press.

Mansfeld, Jacob. "Literature in the Territory of Arizona in 1870: A Reminiscence," *Arizoniana*, II (Fall 1961): 31-34.

Memorials and Affidavits Showing Outrages Perpetrated by the Apache Indians in the Territory of Arizona During the Years 1869 and 1870. San Francisco: Francis and Valentine, 1871.

Moore, Mary Lu, and Delmar L. Beene, eds. "The Interior Provinces of New Spain: The Report of Hugo O'Conor, January 30, 1776." *Arizona and the West*, XIII (Autumn 1971): 265-82.

Myrick, David F. *Railroads of Arizona, Vol. I: The Southern Roads*. Berkeley: Howell-North Books, 1975.

Officer, James E., et al., (comp.). *Tucson, the Old Pueblo: A Chronology*. Tucson: Tucson-Pima County Historical Commission, 1977.

Pattie, James O. *Pattie's Personal Narrative of a Voyage to the Pacific and in Mexico, June 20, 1824-August 30, 1830*. Ed. by Reuben Gold Thwaites. Early Western Travels Series, Vol. XVIII. Cleveland: Arthur H. Clark, 1905.

Pederson, Gilbert J. " 'The Townsite is now Secure': Tucson Incorporates, 1871." *Journal of Arizona History*, XI (Fall 1971): 151-74.

Reynolds, Elsberry W. *Harold Bell Wright: A Biography, Intimate and Authoritative*. n.p., n.d.

Roberts, B.H. *The Mormon Battalion: Its History and Achievements*. Salt Lake City: Deseret News, 1917.

Sacks. B. *Arizona's Angry Man: United States Marshal Milton B. Duffield*. Tempe: Arizona Historical Foundation, 1970.

___. *Be It Enacted: The Creation of Arizona Territory*. Phoenix: Arizona Historical Foundation, 1964.

Safford, Anson P. K., and Samuel Hughes. "The Story of Mariana Diaz." *Arizona Citizen*, June 21, 1873.

Salmon, Roberto Mario, ed. "No Hope for Victory: Pineda's 1791 Report on the Apache Frontier." *Journal of Arizona History*, XX (Fall 1979): 269-82.

Schellie, Don. *The Tucson Citizen: A Century of Arizona Journalism*. Tucson: Citizen Publishing Co., 1970.

___. *Vast Domain of Blood*. Los Angeles: Westernlore Press, 1968.

Smith, Cornelius C., Jr. *William Sanders Oury, History-Maker of the Southwest*. Tucson: University of Arizona Press, 1967.

Smith, Ralph A. "The Scalp Hunter in the Borderlands, 1835-1850," *Arizona and the West*, VI (Spring 1964): 5-24.

Sonnichsen, C. L. *Tucson, Arizona: Its History, Its People and Its Problems*. In press.

Splitter, Henry Winfred, ed. "Tour in Arizona: Footprints of an Army Officer, by 'Sabre.'" *Journal of the West*, I (July 1962): 74-97.

Stewart, Janet Ann. "The Mansions of Main Street." *Journal of Arizona History*, XX (Summer 1979): 193-222.

The Story of the Tucson Airport Authority. Tucson: Tucson Airport Authority, 1966.

Wallace, Andrew, ed. *Pumpelly's Arizona*. Tucson: The Palo Verde Press, 1965.

Wallace, Jerry, "How the Episcopal Church Came to Arizona." *Journal of Arizona History*, VI (Fall 1965): 101-15.

Warner, J. J. "Reminiscences of Early California from 1831 to 1846." *Annual Publications of the Historical Society of Southern California*, VII, pts. 2-3, 1907-1908.

Wyllys, Rufus K. *Arizona: The History of a Frontier State*. Phoenix: Hobson & Herr, 1950.

ACKNOWLEDGMENTS

The author of any work of history incurs countless debts. He ensnares people to pick their brains; they smilingly oblige, furnishing him insights that add substance, color, and flavor to his narrative. He corners a friend at a cocktail party to ask about a particular incident that perplexes him, and comes away with a clearer understanding of an entire era. Kindly people help him with research, steering him to sources he knew nothing about; they offer him the very advice he needs when he needs it; they smooth his way when it is rough, console him when he is depressed, and generally make a difficult task not only bearable but fun. All the author can do in requital is to acknowledge their many kindnesses with humble thanks.

I am deeply grateful to the Reverend Kieran McCarty, O.F.M., premier historian of Spanish and Mexican Arizona, for permitting me to review his still unpublished documentary history of the Mexican period.

Equally generous was C. L. Sonnichsen, the author of numerous works of regional history, who invited me to read the manuscript of a book he has in preparation on the history of Tucson. I gladly accepted the offer. I am most appreciative of it.

Virtually all the research for this book was done at the library of the Arizona Historical Society and, except where otherwise noted, all historical photographs that illustrate it come from that library's collections. My debt to members of its staff is immense: first and greatest, to my wife Margaret, head librarian; then to Susan Peters, Lori Davisson, Cynthia Owens, Barbara Bush, Heather Hatch, and Joan Metzger. I owe special thanks to Susan Luebberman, photographer for the Society, who did all the photograhic copy work and, along with Stephen Burns, also took the color art that appears in the book; to Thomas H. Peterson, Jr., of the Society, for many helpful suggestions; to Sidney B. Brinckerhoff, Society director, for his constant enthusiasm about the project, his reading the entire manuscript and his guidance to sources in the Spanish and Mexican periods; to Donald Bufkin, for his help in geographical matters; to Jose Cisneros, for permission to use four of his drawings in this book; to Geoffrey Peters, for the use of his research in the period after 1930; and to my sister-in-law, Dianne M. Bret Harte; her mother, Yndia Smalley Moore; Lucille B. Juliani; the late Alene D. Smith; and the late Sybil Juliani Ellinwood Pierce. They all offered both encouragement and enlightenment.

Heartfelt thanks are due to Don L. Spring, former editor-in-chief of Windsor Publications' historical series, who was the soul of kindness and helpfulness; and to Rita Johnson, who edited the manuscript with an easy, yet exacting, skill. It is quite impossible to imagine working with two more pleasant people.

John Bret-Harte

ADDITIONAL ACKNOWLEDGEMENTS

Many of the good people who helped in the preparation of this book 21 years ago have passed on, while others have retired or moved away. In the first category, the deaths of C.L. Sonnichsen, Yndia Smalley Moore and Lucille Budd Juliani have left me feeling most bereft. Among the retired, my wife, Margaret S. Bret-Harte; Susan Peters; Lori Davisson; and Sidney B. Brinckerhoff have left the biggest hole. Sonnichsen's book, *Tucson: The Life and Times of an American City*, was published by the University of Oklahoma Press in 1982, a little less than two years after the first edition of this book appeared. The two works, Sonnichsen's and mine, were aimed at different but overlapping audiences, his to scholars and general readers, mine to amateurs wanting to know more about their city's history. It takes nothing away from this book to say that anyone writing about Tucson in the next half-century must first read and digest Sonnichsen's. It really is that good.

Whatever is commendable in this book is due largely to these many good souls. Both tradition and candor, however, oblige me to say that the responsibility for the errors it doubtless contains is mine alone.

John Bret-Harte
September 2001

INDEX

Aviation Committee of, 101, 103;
Tourist Hotel Committee of, 105
Tucson Citizen, 64, *65*, 74, 80, 88, 106, 110, 121, 127, 131, 134, 148
Tucson City Council, 155
Tucson City Government, 152; courts 152
Tucson City Hall, 148, *148*
Tucson Community Center, 138, 142, *145*
Tucson County Government, 152
Tucson Electric Power Co., 173
Tucson Friends of Music Society, 161
Tucson Gas & Electric Light Power Co.; office of, *77*
Tucson General Hospital, 174
Tucson Golf and Country Club, 105
Tucson Heritage Foundation, 142
Tucson Heritage Society, 156
Tucson High School, 72, 120; band of, *73*
Tucson Historical Committee, 142
Tucson Land and Street Railway Co., 82, 84
Tucson Lumber Co., *63*
Tucson Mall, 154
Tucson Medical Center, 95, 164, 176
Tucson Metropolitan Chamber of Commerce. *See* Tucson Chamber of Commerce
Tucson Opera Company, 162
Tucson organizations, generally, 95;
Alianza Hispano-Americana, 85;
Ancient Order of United Workingmen, 84;
Arizona Friends of Music, 120;
Arizona Historical Society, 80, *140*. *See also*: Society of Arizona Pioneers;
Arizona Poetry Society, 121;
Benevolent Paternal Order of Elks, 86, 137;
Brotherhood of Locomotive Engineers, 84;
Camp Street Mess. *See* Owl's Club;
Club Filarmomco Tucsonense, 114, 116, *117*, 118
Junto Patriotica Mexicana, 85;
Knights of Columbus, 84;
Knights of Pythias, 84;
Knights Templar, members of, *85*
Las Tres Ratas, 114;
Mariner's Juvenile Band, 116, *116*, *118*;
Mariner's Orchestra, 116, *113*, *118*;
Masons, 84, 118;
Odd Fellows, 84;
Old Pueblo Band, 116;
Owl's Club, 85-86, *87*; first building of, *136*; of second building of, 87;
Saturday Morning Musical Club, 114, 116, 118-119, 121;
Society of Arizona Pioneers, 86, *87*;
Tucson Art Center, 121;
Tucson Fine Arts Association, 121;
Tucson Museum of Art, 121, 138, 142;
Tucson Philharmonic Orchestra. *See*: Tucson Symphony Tucson Rimers, 121;
Tucson Symphony, 119-20, 126, 145, 161;
Tucson Women's Club, 118, 121;
Turn Verein, 84
Tucson Organized Charities, 96, 130-131; Emergency Relief Committee of, 97
Tucson, Pima village of, 5-6, 10-12, 15-16, 21
Tucson Plumbing & Heating, 206
Tucson *Post*, 131
Tucson Public Library, 82, 136, *137*
Tucson Realty & Trust Co., 177
"Tucson ring," 48, *49*
Tucson School District 1. *See* Tucson Unified School District
Tucson Sunshine Climate Club, 105, *105*, 126
Tucson Tourist Hotel Co., 105, 107-108
Tucson Unified School District, 68. *See also* individual school names
Tucson Warehouse & Transfer, 178
Tully & Ochoa, 46, 64; attack on wagon train of, by hostile Apaches, *iv*
Tully, Carlos H., 64
Tully, Ochoa & DeLong. *See* Tully & Ochoa
Tully, Pinckney R., 46, *47*, 64, 82

U
Uncle Sam, 158
U.S. Government:
Air Force, 147
Army, 29-78 *passim*, 101-103;
Army Flying Circus, 102;
Bureau of Indian Affairs, 46;
Civilian Conservation Corps., 130;
Department of the Interior, 51;
Federal Arts Project, 130;
Federal Writers Project, 130;
Public Works of Art Project, 130;
Post Office Department, 36-37;
Veterans Administration, 96;
Works Progress Administration, 130
United Hotels Co., 107
University Hospital, 164
University Medical Center, 164
University of Arizona, 64, 72, 74, *75*, *89*, 119-22, *133*, 138, 142, 148, 156, 158, 162, 179, 207
University of Arizona College of Medicine, 164
University of Phoenix, 162, 164
Up With People, 180
Urban: decay, 151; renewal 148, 154, 155, 156, 160; sprawl, 151, 152

V
Valley National Bank, Tucson, 108. *See also*: Consolidated National Bank
Van Hulse, Camil, 119-20
Valasco, Carlos I., 66, 85
Vegetation, 148, 167
Velderrain, Juan B., 15
Verde River, 25
Veterans Administration Hospital, 96, 103, *141*
Villa Carondelet, *See* St. Joseph's Academy
"Vin Fiz Flyer," 101

W
Wainwright, Jonathan, 110
Wakefield, Maria. *See* Fish, Maria W.
Ward, John, 40
Warner, Jonathan, 28
Warner, Solomon, 34, *35*, 41, 64
Warner's Lake, 80
Washington, D.C., 96, 103, 158
Wasson, John, 64, 70
Watts, Sylvester, 84
Wedge, The, 88, *89*
Weekly Arizonian, The, 33, 48, 64
Western American Mortgage Co., 181
Western Savings Building, *141*
Whitwell Hospital, 95
"Why I did not die," by Harold Bell Wright, 97
Willcox, Ariz., 78
Williams, Wheeler W., 46, *48*, *65*, 118
Wittelshoefer, Julius, 68
Wood, J.S., 82
World War I, 101, 110, 116, 164
World War II, 103, 107, 124, 129, 134, 147, 148, 160, 161
Wright, Harold Bell, 97, *97*, 130
Wrightson, Thomas, 33
Wrightson, William, 33

Y
Young, Mahonri, 5
Yuma, Ariz., 42-43, 51, 70, 72

Z
Zeckendorf, Louis, 45-46, *47*, 84
Zeckendorf, William, 45-46, *47*, 64, 88, *88*
Zellweger, John, home of, *140*
Zinns, Edward, iv
Zuniga, Jose de, 16-17

ILLUSTRATION CREDITS

Buehman, Henry and Albert, Memorial Collection, Arizona Historical Society: Pages 19, 61(center), 79 (center), 79 (bottom left), 103, 104 (top), 109, 127 (top), 130
Burns, Robert J. (published in *The Arizona Daily Star*, February, 1938): Page 131
Cisneros, Jose: Pages 4, 6, 9, 22
Dar Conte, Lorraine: Pages ix, 133 (top left, top right, and left), 134 (left), 135 (bottom), 138 (top and bottom), 139 (top and bottom), 142 (top and bottom), 143 (top and left)
Greenway Collection, Arizona Historical Society: Page 111 (top and bottom right)
Huth, P.E., Arizona Historical Society: Pages 139, 142
Kuiper, Paul, Arizona Historical Society: Page 106 (right)
Library of Congress: Pages 27, 39
Luebberman/Burns: Color photos not otherwised specified
Peters, Cal, Arizona Historical Society: Pages 13 (bottom), 22 (left)
Record Publishing Co.: Page 80
Reynolds, A.S., Collection, Arizona Historical Society: Pages 16, 57, 61 (bottom), 63 (right), 79 (bottom), 83 (top left), 83 (center left), 83 (bottom), 87 (top) University of Arizona Special Collections: Pages 41, 48 (top left)
Tiller, Frank: Pages 132 (top, bottom left, and bottom right), 134 (bottom), 135 (top), 143 (right), 146, 147, 150 (right), 151, 153 (top), 155, 158, 159 (bottom), 161, 163 (top and bottom), 165 (right), 166, 167
West Point Museum Collections, U.S. Military Academy: Pages 30-31

All other historical photos are from the general photographic collections of the Arizona Historical Society, and are used by courtesy of that institution. Accession numbers noted.

p. 5 – 5362
p. 13 – Top – 56327, Center – 59715
p. 15 – Top – 5209
p. 16 – Top – 20729
p. 19
p. 22 – Top – 45152
p. 22 – Center
p. 27 – 41551
p. 30–31 – 28824
p. 35 – Top Left – 28103, Top Center – 11030, Top Right – 242, Bottom Left – 1590, Bottom Center – 7453, Bottom Right – 1844
p. 39 – 41550
p. 40 – 1821
p. 41 – 6949
p. 45
p. 46 – 1833
p. 47 – Top Left – 1804, Top Center –

3924, Top Right – 49654, Center Left – 2079, Center Center – 1929, Center Right – 1703, Bottom – 62105
p. 48 – Top Center – 49771, Top Right – 1932, Center Right – 3797
p. 49 – Top – 14223, Bottom – 11220
p. 50 – 41292
p. 52 – Top – 654, Bottom – 18337
p. 53 – 21200
p. 55 – Top – 41568, Bottom – 14848
p. 57 – 25449
p. 58 – 7667
p. 59 – Top Left – 40826, Top Right – 51486
p. 60 – 51474
p. 61 – Top Left – 42811, Top Center – 12606, Center – B144, Bottom – 13375
p. 62 – Left – 47885, Right – 6682
p. 63 – Left – 2872, Right – 25284
p. 65 – Top Left – 47862, Top Right – 26607, Bottom Left – 20600, Bottom Right – 15483
p. 66 – Top Right – 13318, Center – 14346
p. 67 – Top – 12643, Center – 45198,
p. 71 – Top – 95706, Bottom – 4247
p. 72 – 1675
p. 73 – Top – 4255, Center – 60066, Bottom – 41460
p. 75 – Top – 13851, Center Left – 4845, Center Right – , Bottom – 29162
p. 77 – 14344
p. 79 – Top – B124, Center – 7219, Bottom Left –, Bottom Right – 2898
p. 80 – (not AHS)
p. 81 – Top – 2094, Center Left – BN24160, Center Right – 27072, Bottom – 18009
p. 82 – Top Left – 11237, Top Right – 24542
p. 83 – Top Left – 25294, Top Right – 17376, Center Left – 13607, Bottom 51320
p. 84 – B13474A
p. 85 – Top – 44621, Center – 2648
p. 87 – Top – 25946, Center Left – 12635, Center Right – 41445, Bottom
p. 88 – 14101
p. 89 – Top – 25946, Center – 24815
p. 91 – Top Left – 26851, Top Center – 42623, Top Right – 1928, Center – 6702, Bottom Left – 22136, Bottom Right – 13313
p. 93 – 44651
p. 94 – 13338
p. 95 – Top – 870, Center – 11393
p. 96 – Left – 28871, Right – B38145,
p. 97 – Left – 1997, Right – 55075
p. 98 – Top – 14457, Center – 24885
p. 99 – Left – 27186, Right
p. 100 – 44231
p. 101 – 28883
p. 103 – BN39203
p. 104 – Top – BN39,361, Center – 45523, Bottom – 51392

p. 105 – 61430
p. 106 – Left – 61599, Right –10445
p. 108 – Top Left – 24871, Top Right – B111211, Center Left – B32475, Center Right – B32955
p. 109 – BN200545
p. 110 – 58874
p. 111 – Top Left – 51969, Center Right – MS311F.3127, Bottom Left – 652, Bottom Right – MS311F.3128/M
p. 113 – 28276
p. 114 – 29040
p. 115 – 24485
p. 116 –13574
p. 117 – Top – 29039, Bottom Left – 51210, Bottom Right – 2878
p. 118 – 2656
p. 119 – Top – 10387, Center – 59213
p. 120 – 11939
p. 123 – Top – 43676, Center Left – 91481, Center Right –
p. 124
p. 125 – Top – 5274, Bottom – 51850
p. 126 – Top Right – 50956, Center
p. 127 – Top – BN33267, Center – 6769, Bottom – BN35580
p. 128 – Top – 41345, Center – 15537
p. 129 – Top. 41344
p. 130 – Top Left – BN23111, Top Right – BN35113
p. 131 – 11899
p. 135
p. 139 – Top – 44423, Bottom
p. 142 – 43975
p. 146 – 52911
p. 149 – Center, Bottom
p. 150 – Top Left – 13316, Top Right
p. 151 – Center , Bottom
p. 153 – Bottom Left –66362, Bottom Center – 10951, Bottom Right – 65851
p. 157 – Top – 59679
p. 166 – Bottom Left, Bottom Right
p. 167 – Bottom Right
p. 168 – Left, Right
p. 172 – Top – 49874, Center Left, Center Right – 51385
p. 173 – Top – 27139, Center
p. 177 – Top Left – BN29040, Top Right
p. 178 – Top
p. 179 – Center Right